FROM *Calvin* TO *Rousseau*

FROM *Calvin* TO *Rousseau*

Tradition and Modernity in Socio-Political Thought from the Reformation to the French Revolution

BY

HERBERT LÜTHY

TRANSLATED FROM THE FRENCH BY
SALVATOR ATTANASIO

BASIC BOOKS, INC.
Publishers
NEW YORK LONDON

Library of Congress Catalog Card Number: 75–94294
SBN 465–02574–9
Manufactured in the United States of America
Originally published in French as
Le Passé Présent: Combats d'Idées de Calvin à Rousseau
by Éditions du Rocher, Monaco.

DESIGNED BY VINCENT TORRE

PREFACE

"From Calvin to Rousseau" is a round trip, as it were: a preacher come from France who subjugated Geneva and made it over into his image and, several generations later, a renegade from Geneva who was to bring to France the torment of his rebellious spirit, nourished by remote echoes of Calvinism. All that we retain of both, through these three centuries which by somewhat antiquated scholarly classification form already "modern" but not yet "contemporary" history, is a single common denominator: the constant placing into question of any hierarchical order in the name of an affirmation of equality that was initially a theological postulate. Whatever party or social group claimed it in this or that moment in history, or whatever successive definitions it was given later—equality of the children of God, of the subjects of the prince, or of the citizens of the State, or, finally, of the world—this affirmation of equality has nourished and continues to nourish all revolutions against established orders. For there was never any revolution which was not made in the name of the equality of men and which did not, subsequently, deny this principle because of a new need for order and for the government of men, thereby creating the conditions for new revolutions in the future. This history is still ours, but it is more recent than we think. It is the movement which, basically, defines the "modern age"; and it is only by abuse of language that we apply to other epochs the term "revolution" in the sense we give to it here. We are not saying that the revolutions of the West began with Calvin: it is futile to wish to assign a single birth date and author to a ground swell. The contestation of the hierarchies of divine investiture was inherent in the secular emancipation and in Christian humanism. Subversion flexed its muscles in the imbalances of a society which was slowly being "defeudalized." But radical Calvinism was the point of convergence of so many confused ferments, the transition (catastrophic in many respects) from an enlightened elite humanism on the one hand to secret and inarticulated revolts on the other, up until the definitive and clear break. Obviously, this is an all too summary working hypothesis, which will require many shadings. But it is valid to the extent that it enables us to give order to the multiple eddies of these first centuries of modern history which, for us, are the past present today.

In any event, this is the red thread that ties together the scattered pieces of this collection, all of which deal with the social order, the government of men, and the paths of subversion. But, needless to say, these very different texts are not a series of chapters of modern history written at one stroke and arranged in logical order by following this guiding thread which, in truth, appeared only after the event. Originally they were merely scattered reflections, with backtrackings, repetitions, and apparent contradictions, inscribed in the margin of fifteen years of investigation of a wholly different order, through yellowed balance sheets and notaries' jottings, in the rudely shaken human setting of French Calvinism. And, most particularly, in the web of affairs and relationships through which its most violently uprooted group assured its survival: a fragile and ever rewoven spider's web, whose repeatedly broken and reknit threads were impossible to follow without running, on all sides and often unexpectedly, into the framework of the social structure to which, willy-nilly, the thread had to be attached.

Hence these questions as to the constitution of this society came into being peripherally in the course of an investigation into a marginal phenomenon of the constituted society. Notes, essays, and insights which, separated from the body of the particular inquiry whose findings formed the two volumes of *La Banque protestante en France*, have nothing in common but the perspective proper to an inquiry aimed primarily not at the history of French institutions or the French monarchy, but at that of a dissident group on its periphery: a paradoxical approach, indeed, but one which also has its advantages. Perhaps it is by starting out from these blurred frontiers, rather than from its center, that we can perceive the solid interior cohesion not only of the regime, but of the royal political economy so brilliantly analyzed by François Quesnay.

Is it necessary to apologize for what should fundamentally be a fashion of the day, if not of the century? This method of approaching "politics" (in the broad sense) on the basis of economic archives would appear to be in keeping with the demands of historical materialism—preferable at any rate to the current procedure of the exponents of this doctrine who most often are content to decree authoritatively a "class" motivation to political behavior without showing any concern for digging out the facts of biography, civil status, and social contribution that alone would enable them to demonstrate how this or that figure could have been bound up with this or that "class interest." In this respect, the tiny vignette of Genevan diplomacy of the eighteenth century, as it appears to us through the study of a group of shareholders of a privileged large-scale enterprise, could be the proper model for a Marxist study of diplomacy. But we also confess that such a study of "class diplomacy" presupposes a socially transparent regime that simply could not have existed save in tiny city republics like that of Geneva. In our time, perhaps, the relationship of some so-called "banana republic" with its all too powerful neighbor would lend itself to a similar analysis, despite the extreme difference in the political and social contexts. In a more complex State, the relationships between political aims and economic interests and between the manipulators of the political power and the manipulators of the economy are less evident, and the power relations between both are far from those between valet and master.

The most grievous sin that the invading school of doctrinaire historical materialism has committed against history has been that of considering the State exclusively as an instrument in the service of others, and the political regime as a reflection of the relationship of forces between social classes. In so doing, it has cut itself off from the genuine study of institutions, laws, regimes, in short of the political organization of societies; and of the autonomous action, ever weighty and often crushing, of the constituted power on the evolution of societies and economies. For political history, in the full sense of the word, is neither an epiphenomenon nor a category alongside other histories—economic, social, cultural. It governs them and unites them all as integrating parts of the history of the State. There are only different ways of approaching this totality from the tiny part which an historian can know at firsthand and which he strives to relate to the ensemble as he can perceive it, by transmitting the hypotheses suggested by his work for verification to the workers who plow in neighboring fields, historians of the Church, of the peasant world, or of the Farmers-General. In a body as rebellious to collective labor as that of historians, this indeed is the closest equivalent to teamwork.

With the exception of the essays on Quesnay and Rousseau, the following texts, which are fragments rather than essays, have for the most part been slightly retouched for inclusion in this volume. But we have not tried to impose a perfect unity of views upon them, or to eliminate completely the repetition of some facts or arguments in different contexts whose suppression would have required a complete recasting. The first of the three "Variations on a Theme by Max Weber" was first published in *Cahiers Vilfredo Pareto* (1961–1963); the other two include passages extracted from the two volumes of *La Banque protestante en France* (1959–1961). The same applies to Chapters Five, Six, and Eleven, grouped under the title "Lights and Shadows of the Eighteenth Century," which appeared in the *Bulletin de la Société d'histoire et d'archéologie de Genève* (1960–1961). The other texts were published in the revue *Preuves*. We wish to thank the publishers who have graciously authorized their reproduction here.

CONTENTS

Contents

PART I

VARIATIONS ON A THEME BY MAX WEBER: THE PROTESTANT ETHIC AND THE SPIRIT OF CAPITALISM

Introduction

THE VAST inquiry "as a preliminary to history" which Max Weber extended to the civilizations of antiquity and of Asia, as well as to the modern West, forms, as it were, the counterproof to that conducted by Marx. After the attempt to establish that ideas and beliefs were determined by the social economy and its attendant class antagonisms, we have the attempt to establish that economic and social behavior is determined by religious consciousness.[1]

Is it a converse demonstration, a salutary counterweight,

[1] Max Weber, *Die protestantische Ethik und der Geist des Kapitalismus,* Vols. XX and XXI (1904–1905) of the *Archiv für Sozialwissenschaften und Sozialpolitik,* under the original German title. This celebrated essay has been translated into English by Talcott Parsons, *The Protestant Ethic and the Spirit of Capitalism,* with a foreword by R. H. Tawney (New York: Scribner's, 1930). André Biéler, *La Pensée economique et sociale de Calvin* (Geneva, 1959), provides a good bibliography of the lengthy debate aroused by this thesis. To it must be added two recent works which were unknown to me when I prepared the present book: Kurt Samuelsson, *Religion and Economic Action* (Stockholm and London, 1959), and H. R. Trevor-Roper, "Religion, the Reformation, and Social Change," in *Historical Studies,* IV (London, 1963). On the interpretation of the English Puritan revolution, in addition to R. H. Tawney, "The Rise of the Gentry" in *Economic History Review* (1941); H. R. Trevor-Roper, "The Gentry" (*ibid.,* 1953, supplement), and J. H. Hexter, "Storm Over the Gentry" in *Encounter* (May, 1958). For the sociology of French Protestantism under the *ancien régime,* I refer to my own work: *La Banque protestante en France* (Paris: S.E.V.P.E.N., 1959–1961). Several passages in the present essays have been included or adapted from the introduction to Vol. I and the conclusion of Vol. II of this work.

or, rather, a complementary research? Although both take as their point of departure a sane, "evident," apparent correlation—for example, that between "the bourgeois spirit" and the Reformation—neither is finally conclusive. The behavior of men and the course of human history cannot be reduced to a single causality, material or spiritual, from which all the rest assertedly flows. Any practical behavior is equivocal in its relation to faith, and, in secularized societies, to ideology; any absolute concept, religious or surrogate, is equivocal in relation to practice. Hence to subjugate the one to the other is to condemn it to extinction. Perhaps the originality of the Christian West was the recognition of this irreducible yet inseparable duality between the spiritual and the temporal, the experienced contradiction through all its phases and at all its levels, between the Judeo-Christian heritage and the Greco-Roman heritage transmitted to its barbarian societies, between the Church and the State, between the community of believers and the civil society, between divine law and human law, faith and reason, dogma and science, charity and rationality, the millenarianism of accomplished redemption and secular history lumberingly continued, an endless series marked by innumerable metamorphoses. All this no doubt was what constituted the dynamism of a civilization in continual ferment, which never ceased to question and transform itself, as opposed to the Byzantine or Mohammedan civilizations which were nevertheless so close, and those of India and China, all going back much further in time but immobilized in the unity of authority or in wisdom reconciled to itself, so that only the provocation of the West could set them agog with excitement again.

The Reformation, no doubt, marks a privileged episode in this ferment of the West: the affirmation of individual conscience as opposed to spiritual authority itself. And in the logic of this affirmation, if not in its immediate realization, is implied the "lay priesthood," the community without incontestible dogma and without a sacred hierarchy, egalitarian and democratic in its aspiration. But the Reformation, contemporary and bound up with all the upheavals of the "end of the Middle Ages," fitted itself into Western history without breaking its course. It was one of the responses to the challenge of the twofold truth, neither the sole nor the most revolutionary response of its epoch nor the last, and by itself it cannot give an account of the watershed of history that was crossed at that time. The secularization of knowledge, the advent of the critical spirit, the substitution of exact, experimental, and mathematical science for speculative knowledge, the secularization of law and of the government of men—which had been under way for three centuries and was almost an accomplished fact in some States that, partly for this very reason, were not to feel the need to follow the Reformation—the technical and scientific revolution already manifest in the engines of war and navigation which upset the political structure of Europe and its knowledge of the world and simultaneously shattered the world view inseparable from the view of man. Who would venture to affirm that all these elements of an historical epoch, so fantastically accelerated (like our own on this score) can be summed up in the religious schism, or that these elements as a whole count less than such a schism in the advent of the "capitalist," "rational," and "bourgeois" spirit?

This schism within Western civilization, despite its acts of violence and destruction, did not shatter the fundamental unity of the civilization as the schism between Rome and Byzantium had shattered the fragile unity between the

Christendoms of the East and of the West. It added one condition more, a new ferment to so many others, none of which acted in isolated fashion. At no moment, even in the thick of the wars of religion, did Catholic Europe and Protestant Europe separate into two worlds apart, with each following its own inner law, by ceasing to be bound up one with the other. There was violent combat, certainly, but confused in character, in which neither camp was homogeneous, in which the dividing lines were crisscrossed and blurred, in which at no instant was there a lack, either of intermediaries or "third parties," or alliances in reverse, or, finally, of neutrals between the two conceptions, both of which remained in conformity with the genius of the West and with its fundamental polarity. In short, there was no breaking of civilization into two pieces which would have brought an end to any dialogue, and in which each one would have then found its rest in a single affirmation.

The question which Max Weber raised a half century ago has experienced the fate of all profound questions which do not allow for a simple and direct answer. Let us first eliminate the most serious and most gratuitous misunderstanding that has weighed so heavily at times on this debate. It is evidently impossible to explain the character and the achievements of the West—even the "modern" West, whose very essence is pluralism—by a single episode of its recent past, even an episode as pregnant with consequences as the Reformation, or by a single one of its elements, even one as virulent as Calvinism. But is it at least possible to isolate this element and to discern its remote action, not in the sphere of theological controversies where the apparent rigidity of dogmas conceals fundamental ambiguities and agreements, but in the sphere of secular material and intellectual life where neither men themselves, nor their daily acts, nor even their works of art and of the mind always bear a confessional label? What, after all, is this Protestant mentality, or to be more precise, this Calvinism mentality, in which Weber perceived the great ferment of "modern capitalism"? And, first of all, what capitalism?

For those who listen attentively, that which Max Weber designates, according to his methodology on the "ideal type," as "capitalism" or the "capitalist spirit" is the very creative principle of Western civilization in its singularity, as it appeared to a sociologist of civilization at the beginning of our century, and whose characteristic traits—not found in any other form of civilization—Weber studied ever more deeply. He saw this as the principle of rationality pervading all spheres of life, even the creations of art, positive science without taboos, based on the exactness of measurements and experimental verification, scientific technique applied to human labor, an integrated economy founded on the precise calculation of costs and returns, all value being assigned an exact date and a coefficient of growth or decrease figured by the rate of interest or amortization; an historical science which was not the chronicle of incoherent, disconnected events, but an effort at self-comprehension and at pinpointing the continuum of mankind in time and space; a jurisprudence which recognized only the free contract, mutually respected by partners conscious of their interests, as the base of the economy, of society, and of the constitutional State itself; a science of administration seen not as an instrument of power, but as a public service, after having stripped temporal power of all sacred investiture and spiritual authority of all means of temporal constraint. Such was, potentially, if not always in fact, this unique attempt at the willed creation of a rational world within the framework of a discipline based on consent. An attempt, in turn, based on a fragile union of two complementary principles: individual freedom and responsibility on the one hand, and rationality, which spontaneously performed an organizing function, on the other. All these elements were combined in the being endowed with reason, namely, rational man, viewed as egocentric but enlightened, whom textbook vulgarity reduced to "economic man."

It is necessary to pay careful attention to this comprehensive conception, in which properly "capitalist" activity, the pursuit of economic gain, is only the materially indispensable motive force. For such a definition of capitalism is not the most accepted current version of this term coined by Marx to designate the final form of the exploitation of man by man; further, Marx's horrified admiration for this demiurge of a new world, which ceaselessly prepares the way for its own liberating catastrophe, is much closer to Weber's view than any purely economic description—be it vulgar-Marxist or bourgeois-orthodox—of a system of production and distribution of wealth. This misunderstanding, rarely explicit, has also enveloped the debate in a cloud of confusion. Already with Sombart, whose very researches and conclusions have run parallel on many points, "capitalism" again became the unbridled and endless spirit of material accumulation, in contradistinction to the concept of a domestic economy based on the simple satisfaction of needs, a capitalism of merchants, usurers, and monopolists which, at bottom, was common to all epochs of human history. This made Sombart the indefatigable inventor of successive capitalisms through all history and through all civilizations. Early capitalism, High capitalism, Late capitalism, commercial, financial, industrial capitalism, matched by all kinds of mentalities—Catholic, Protestant, Jewish, courtier, bourgeois, or "metic." Since comparative sociology has taught us that this greed is no less evident among primitives, and even more fierce to the extent that primitive peoples confuse signs of wealth with magic power, nothing would stand in the way of an analysis of the capitalism of the caveman.

In such a perspective, the debate over the role of Protestantism in the advent of capitalism became a somewhat sterile discussion, because identical words conceal radically opposed affective concepts. The correlation between the Protestant ethic and the capitalist spirit, posed by Weber in singularly laudatory terms, became little by little an insulting imputation, triumphantly welcomed by some, indignantly rejected by others; indeed, agreement on conclusions could therefore conceal a total misunderstanding as to the heart of the matter. For all, the greed for gain explains too well and too completely the dealings of ruthless and rapacious types in all ages—moneylenders, monopolists and hoarders of foodstuffs, agricultural usurers, intendants of manorial domains, the tax collectors and Farmers-General of Rome, China, India, or France, corsairs, slave hunters or purveyors of war supplies—for it still to be able to account for the singularity of "capitalist civilization." It is evident that the quest for profit by itself does not explain this effort, expended voluntarily and without aim, even if it is its apparent motive force. For the pursuit of individual gain has no meaning unless it culminates in enjoyment and stops there. By rejecting this enjoyment the effort is pursued without pause and without end, like the search for an impossible redemption. It is here that Weber introduces the motive force drawn from the depth of the consciousness which he claimed to perceive in the Puritanism of Calvinist inspiration: the asceticism of work, the horror of enjoyment, the incurable disquiet of the believer who can never be entirely sure of his salvation.

In the last analysis, therefore, the distinctive feature of Calvinism supposedly lay in the rejection of the sedatives, consolations, and certainties which the Church offered the faithful in the face of the metaphysical horror of the Infinite and of death. And it supposedly was this horror which lashed "capitalist man" into his frantic race. The grandeur of this thesis and its kernel of profound truth sufficiently justify its lasting repercussions. But is it true in the precise terms in which it is posed?

If the Weberian concept of "capitalism" could give rise to confusion, his definition of Calvinism has been no less contested. Is it a question of the Calvinism of Calvin, or of that Calvinism already torn apart by the mushrooming sects of the synods and of the formal statements of belief of the seventeenth century—in which the theologians, hastily forging a militant orthodoxy, deliberately and inflexibly wielded the most extreme and terrifying positions of dogma in order to re-establish an iron discipline over the flock in disarray—or, finally, is it a question of this "practical" Puritanism of the eighteenth century in England and in New England, whose robust moral conformism dispensed with any unity of doctrine? Two particularly striking texts have served as landmarks in Max Weber's thesis. The first is the Confession of Westminster of 1647, the instrument of terror created at the height of the Puritan revolution in England, which, with a startling ferocity, formulated the dogma of predestination, according to which from all eternity and without recourse or intelligible reason a part of humanity is saved, the rest damned. A dogma so inhumane that it caused Milton, the militant cantor of this Puritan revolution, to say: "Though I may be sent to Hell for it, such a

God will never command my respect." The other landmark text, apparently running counter to these anxieties of soul, was provided by the maxims of Benjamin Franklin which for a long time figured in American schoolbooks. The very titles "Advice to a Young Tradesman," "Necessary Hints to Those That Would Be Rich," suggest a perfect code of utilitarian moralism and of bourgeois virtues, the guarantors of success. What provision would Weber have made for Jacques Savary, who preceded Franklin by a century and whose "The Perfect Tradesman" enjoyed a considerable international vogue—if, as ill luck would have it, Savary had not been Catholic? If that was Calvinism, Calvin was certainly no Calvinist, and Weber—before Tawney—knew it well. But in his demonstration, these texts mark the stages of a dialectical chain which leads the tormented Calvinist, knowing himself to be saved or damned from all eternity without his being able either to know or to deflect this unfathomable judgment, to seek in activity and in the achievement of success here below the external sign of blessing. Or more simply, plunged into the darkness of an absurd ordeal, he will ply his trade, whatever it may be, with a stiff upper lip and without asking himself about the meaning of this life in the world.

This transfiguration of the terrors of the solitary soul, acquiescent to discipline in a harsh capitalist society, was at the center of Weber's thesis and it constitutes its most well-known, indeed its most fascinating and its most fragile part. Not only does this dialectic of a mental process remain artificial, but it in no way compels assent, being easy to turn around in all directions and valid only in a very particular social and moral context. The dogma of predestination, in its trenchant affirmation, belongs to the seventeenth century, where it marked a moment of violent crisis in Calvinism—and not of Calvinism alone, because it was an exact contemporary of Jansenism and it seemed to correspond as much to the deep metaphysical despair of a catastrophic century as to a pitiless will to scientific rigor in religious exegesis. It is not possible (as has been done by too many commentators whose knowledge of Calvinism seems to have come through the Weberian interpretation) to make this dogma the cornerstone of Calvin's teaching; nor of the religious movement, essentially shifting, open, and pluralist in character, which took its rise from Calvin's teaching; nor, with greater reason, of Protestantism in general, which was always divided over the question of the insoluble mystery of grace. In Calvin's monumental theological work, this doctrine plays only a belated and secondary role; it was formulated with caution, almost incidentally, in a precise context which alone illumines its significance. In full missionary combat, speaking of those who hear the Gospel and do not heed it, Calvin says that God no doubt made them blind and deaf in accordance with His will, a will beyond the fathoming of human reason, which has elected some and rejected others. This is a painful reflection, which always imposed itself upon the Apostles in the presence of deaf ears, and which we find almost verbatim in the Gospels, in the fathers of the Church, and in many Catholic theologians, and which meets up with the mysteries from which all Manichean heresies flow: God alone having created man and the world, from whence come evil and wickedness? Did not Christ die, then, for all, and if so how can the perdition continue as before? Rather than a dogma, Calvinian predestination is a confession of ignorance and frightened bewilderment. Let us not try to fathom the reasons why God, who alone can illumine man, opens the hearts of some and closes those of others; it is beyond our comprehension. But, in Calvin, it is not true that the reformed man does not know whether he is elected or damned, for all he has to do is sincerely and serenely to feel his faith. The fact of hearing and believing Christ's word is a certain sign that he has been touched by grace.[2]

If the Calvinist theologians of the following century, through a more terrifying formulation of the dogma, applied themselves to lessen this proud assurance of the faithful—certain to the point of smugness of their election through the sole fact of their Calvinist faith—nothing proves that they succeeded. Where Calvinist faith remained alive, it always remained the credo of a chosen people; where it waned, the doctrine of predestination was the first thing to be forgotten. There was no need in any case to look for the sign of grace in professional success, indeed nothing runs more counter to Calvinist doctrine. The compensatory mechanism installed therein by Max Weber is a subtle mental construction which could only have functioned in exceptional cases, because the anxieties of the conscience uncertain of its salvation and the moralizing utilitarianism of Franklin were not contemporary. And the

[2] "It is true that the word of the Gospel calls everybody to share in Christ, but many, blinded and hardened by unbelief, disdain this so singular grace. . . . In this dissimilarity it is necessary to ponder the great mystery of God's plan: for the seed of the word of God takes root and fructifies only in those whom the Lord, through His eternal election, predestined for His children and heirs of the celestial kingdom. . . . Now, the reason the Lord uses mercy toward some and exercises the strictness of His judgment toward others, is something that we must leave as known only to Him, and which He has willed to conceal from all beings. . . . Christ is the One to whom the pledge of our election is presented, if we receive Him and embrace Him through faith. If therefore, by possessing Christ through faith, we likewise possess life in Him, we need naught else but to inquire about the eternal plan of God." Calvin, *Catechisme Française* (1537) (Geneva, 1878). These citations are taken from Biéler, *La Pensée économique et sociale de Calvin;* the study on Calvinist doctrine by Pierre Maury, *La Prédestination* (Geneva, 1957) was also consulted.

formulas of the customary piety of Anglo-Saxon Puritanism often cited in support—which piety, for that matter, was less specifically Protestant than has been declared—in which even in account books and partnership contracts success is implored from, or attributed to, God's blessing, prove the Puritan's disquietingly good conscience rather than his supposed disquiet.

Such has been the case with almost all the elements of the Weberian demonstration. None of the correlations he attempted to establish on points of doctrine or ethics between Calvinist teaching and capitalist economy has truly held up under criticism. But his thesis has remained no less alive, indeed it has grown in stature as a monument of inspiration and methodology. After having criticized and often refuted him on particulars, all his critics—or almost all—have finally declared him to be fundamentally right, while setting forth their own interpretations and their own shadings and refinements. Sombart described Calvinists as "Jews, without being aware of it," and according to John U. Nef, the elimination of the monarchical Church with the pomp and splendor of its public worship from the economy gave free rein to a "quantitative civilization." Or, for example, the notion of Protestant individualism, Calvinist democracy, the outstripping of the medieval conception of society—there is no end to the list of the learned or subtle deductions proposed to buttressing the Weberian thesis, as well as to the logomachies and abstract concepts engendering themselves by parthogenesis until the capitalist anthill is made to issue from the Calvinist theocracy. Since they were not agreed on either the content of Calvinism or the definition of capitalism, all ended up by being in agreement on the more or less close affinity between the two by virtue of a kind of comprehensive evidence which it was impossible to define exactly in detail: the societies imbued with the Calvinist spirit were the best prepared for the rigors of the capitalist organization of the economy.

Sixty years after the first publication of Max Weber's thesis, the time has come to re-examine this comprehensive evidence. For it seems true that Protestant societies, more than others, have honored work and censured idleness, or that, by virtue of the same mental bent, they were earlier than the others in granting a legitimation, stripped of enthusiasm for that matter, to the lowly material rules of the economic life which the religious and philosophical systems of former societies had disdained. In other words, the centuries-old tradition of the submission of the common man to divinized seigneurial or sacerdotal powers has weighed less on the course of their development. But if in discussing such a change it is not only a question of a hierarchy of values but of a social order, then it is necessary to set this in the context of the general history of the West, whose chronology poorly confirms the role that has been assigned to the Reformation as a watershed between two epochs. Nothing lends itself to revision like the "comprehensive evidence" according to which each epoch interprets the past so that it teologically, as it were, culminates in its present. And this is the essential reason, much more compelling than that of advancing our knowledge of past events, why history is constantly engaged in rewriting itself.

CHAPTER ONE

Reformation and Counter Reformation: The Faith and the Regime

Max Weber's definitions achieve their true and subtle meaning only within the context of his monumental, highly fragmented, and difficult work. In his search for new routes in the social sciences he was not essentially concerned with history proper or even with social or economic systems: the point of departure of his vast investigation was an interrogation into the fundamental psychic and spiritual motivations of human behavior. Weber did not analyze constituted, complex, imperfect societies that contained a mixture of disparate contributions, such as history has produced them, rough and incoherent phenomena without an intelligible meaning. Rather, his analysis focused on the coherent and noncontradictory idea such societies could form of themselves: it was the "ideal-type" system of essential values on which, hypothetically, these societies unconsciously modelled their behavior structures; in short, their significant utopias, detached as much as possible from any contamination by history. A close reading of his studies of religious sociology and of his analyses of economic and social history proper—which, even if they deal with the agrarian history of the antique world or the castes of India, constantly center on the problem of the uniqueness of modern Western civilization—discloses that what he means by "capitalism" or the "spirit of capitalism" is the sum total of the distinctive characteristics of this Western civilization. Not only its economic system but also its juridical system, its political structure, its sciences and its institutionalized techniques, its music and its architecture impregnated with the mathematical spirit, its moral principles and its life styles are all included. Economic calculation, work discipline, the depersonalization of exchanges and social relationships are only the significant exterior signs which represent *pars pro toto* the totality of this type of civilization. Weber's key word here is "rational": a rationality which pervades all spheres of social behavior, the organization of work and enterprise as well as the positive sciences, law as well as philosophy and art, the State and politics as well as the behavior of the private individual. A rationality which, impelled forward by its own dynamism, was able to shatter or overcome all the forms of resistance offered by the prerational elements of human nature: magic and tradition, instinct and spontaneity. It is with the Reformation that this process of rationalization for the first time advanced to the heartland of human motivations, invading the domain of religious faith where it made a clean sweep of all the old irrational, obscure, magic, symbolic or mystic ingredients, superstitions, holy images, rites, and traditions in order to establish the Christian religion in the harsh and naked light of the Word, on the seemingly unshakeable foundation of Holy Writ, verifiable by the critical mind.

Such is the Weberian knot which ties economic mentality to religious doctrine. He rightly asserts that the quasi-monstrous historical singularity of modern Western civilization is not explainable exclusively in terms of its material foundations. The material and technical conditions from which Europe developed its modern civilization since the end of the Middle Ages existed in an equal or higher state of development in many other great civilizations, those of the Hellenic Orient, Rome, India, China, the empire of the Arab Caliphates. But they did not produce this leap from a stable threshold to a movement thrusting indefinitely forward. Today we know how right Weber was to insist on the primacy of motives of spiritual and cultural order in determining the external forms of societies and economies. He was right in contrast to nearly all his contemporaries, whether liberals or Marxists, who viewed the presence of capital, technical means, and a physical labor force as sufficient preconditions for achieving economic progress, and who believed that civilization of the Western type could be transplanted and grafted onto already existing structures anywhere in the world. Weber was also indubitably right to wrestle anguishedly with the question of the reserves of vitality and of the future for a wholly rationalized and disillusioned civilization that would perforce eliminate or domesticate the reserves "of naïve and enthusiastic energy" springing from prerational sources.

The fact that Weber believed that he could grasp the essence of this civilization in the equivocal concept of capitalism, which normally designates a wholly material and materialistic dynamic, is what reveals precisely the deepest conflict of this thought, wavering between enthusiasm and anxiety, if not horror, in the face of the results attained by this civilization at the time of the triumphs and splendors of Wilhelminian Germany. The same internal conflict is discernible in his attitude toward Protestantism, whose ethical and moral "values" he preserved—namely, the rationalized residue of behavioral norms formerly dictated by faith—while considering its religious roots as dead. For here, too, rationalism, after shattering the paganism of images, rites, and cults by leaning on the sure foundation of Scripture, in the end ineluctably undermined this very foundation. It was this fundamental ambivalence of his attitude toward one and the other that enabled Weber to join the Protestant ethic and the spirit of capitalism, and which, in fact, made it possible for him to establish this paradoxical functional equation. The Protestant ethic, in the last analysis, is this internalized rationalism which constitutes the very spirit of capitalism.

Obviously, this formula is too abridged to give an accurate account of Weber's thought, which is more interrogative than affirmative in character. Weber, after all, was an infinitely complex person, a positivist and skeptic, universally open-minded, and passionately pan-Germanist, imbued with a sense of the world mission of imperial Germany yet haunted by the nightmare of its decadence; he died in 1920, in what was for him a crumbled world. The greatness of his personality and of his work lay in the relentless pursuit, to their ultimate ramifications, of answers to the questions posed by ambivalences and contradictions inherent in his mind and in his time. He never found the answers; but he examined these questions in great depth and with tireless zeal. The reverse of this greatness is the realization that this enormous and tangled work, despite the power of its reflections and of its methodology, has contributed much less to laying the foundation of an historical science of society than to furnishing his followers with an inexhaustible mine of formulas and propositions, giving rise to all kinds of misunderstandings and confusions, not all as innocent as the object of our concern.

This preamble is marginal to our subject. Yet it was useful to fix the exact point of departure of this debate, which in a way will also enable us to conclude it in advance. None of those who took up Weber's thesis understood the concept of capitalism in the infinitely broad connotation which he gave it. The problem was at once pulled down to the lower levels of economic organization, the accumulation of capital, or the sheer lust for gain. But it is precisely from this misunderstanding that his short essay on Protestantism and capitalism—the only one of all Weber's works which achieved international fame—draws its inexhaustible power of suggestion. If Weber, forging a completely personal terminology, had not decided thus to represent the part for the whole, if he had given his essay a title that expressed his thought less strikingly and paradoxically, say "Protestantism and Modern Society," or "The Reformation and the Spirit of Western Civilization," he would simply have formulated—admittedly with novel accents and in a novel form—a thesis that would never have been contested and that would hardly have made such a splash. This thesis would maintain that the Reformation marks one of the decisive points of the spiritual and structural rupture between the medieval and the modern world; that it introduced a revolutionary ferment in Western history, and that it placed its stamp on the whole modern world far beyond the spheres of churches and Protestant communities; that neither Cromwell nor Rousseau nor America's "founding fathers" are conceivable without Calvin; that modern industrial societies—as well as the positive sciences, the constitutional State and, in a word, the free society—developed first and most vigorously in the countries impregnated with Calvinism; and, finally, that an indissoluble bond exists among all these aspects of Western civilization. If such had been the object of the debate, we would be able to wind it up once and for all: the concrete manifestation of this evolution forms the content of four centuries of our history and, as such, furnishes an inexhaustible subject for reflections and research. But we all know that this is so, that this evolution did take place from that prophetic event. And we also know, as Weber knew, that this is not the whole story, that everything does not stem from this event, that the Reformation by itself was not this historical turning point. Rather, it was but one of its elements, contemporaneous with and inseparable from many others which *together* transformed the spiritual and material world: humanism, the Copernican revolution, the change wrought in State structures and in the technical means of warfare, the conquest of the oceans and the discovery of new continents, the sudden advent of world empires and world trade, monetary expansion, the splendor and chaos, exuberance and metaphysical despair of a world which thenceforth would be not only without bounds, but also one without shelter and without measure. Finally, we also know that this was not a sudden outburst of energy starting from scratch, but represented the conjunction and acceleration of powerful movements springing from the medieval world itself. The Crusades were prolonged and transformed through the Spanish-Portuguese *Conquista*, the work of the scholastic universities through humanism, and the ecclesiastical quarrels and the waves of heresy that swept incessantly across the Middle Ages through the Reformation. Conversely, is it necessary to remind ourselves how much of the authentically medieval spirit entered into Luther's revolt against the secularization of the Church of the Borgias and the Medicis?

All this is an old story. The new word "capitalism" was loosed upon the world and debate was limited to this single aspect of the relations between the Reformation doctrine and the economic behavior—not those indirect but indubitable relations that exist between all aspects of a coherent civilization and its history, where everything is interconnected, but an immediate relationship of causality or direct function between a religious doctrine and a tangible form of economic behavior. It was as if one had found the guiding thread of history, which was to lead dialectically from the posting of the theses on the door of the Castle Church in Wittenberg to Wall Street and the assemblylines of Detroit. Needless to say, the shadow of Karl Marx hovered ponderously over the whole debate. For the past hundred years, no historian has been able to ignore the gauntlet thrown down by the Marxian philosophy of history. Weber, who struggled so valiantly for a true sociology of history, was more sensitive to this challenge than anyone else. Hence, it is in the context of a passionately sincere confrontation with historical materialism that we must understand his thesis, which demonstrates the decisive influence of spiritual factors, of mentality, and of religious behavior on the forms of the economy. The enormous repercussions it has produced throughout the world must also be understood in this context. Nobody dreamed of disputing the assertion that there was a relationship between mentality and behavior, even if each investigator formulated it differently: as direct or indirect, dialectical or logical—or wholly devoid of logic. But at this point the debate began to show a resemblance to the famous argument over the chicken and the egg: did the Reformation engender the spirit of capitalism, or did the spirit of capitalism produce the Reformation? Only the second interpretation, which makes Protestantism an "ideological superstructure," suited historical materialism, which in the hands of some "bourgeois" historians has become much more simplistic than it was with Marx. The Reformation thus found its place in a view of historical progression stripped of the vain subtleties, corresponding roughly to the schema of history conceived as a monotonous succession of ruling classes. Thus in "modern" history, judiciously aligned on the thread of Ariadne, that is the rise of the bourgeoisie and the decline of feudalism, the Reformation appears as the first bourgeois revolution. Starting out from this point, Tawney, in his analysis of the Puritan revolution of seventeenth-century England as the second wave of the bourgeois revolution, ingeniously threw a bridge across the suspect void which separated Calvin from the members of the Convention, reaching to that third and greatest, most bourgeois of bourgeois revolutions, the French Revolution.

And lo, the second key word was loosed upon the world, twin brother of the first, as dazzling and elusive as the concept of capitalism: the Bourgeoisie, accompanied by its even more hackneyed antithesis, Feudalism. In an interpretation of history which reduces acting and thinking man to the role of a hardly conscious instrument or protagonist of class interests, the reformers thus became the standard bearers of the rising bourgeoisie, dedicated, as we know, to capitalism. "This bourgeoisie," to cite Marc Bloch's *Apologie pour L'histoire*, "whose accession to power is celebrated in the schoolbooks, according to the periods successively proposed to the meditations of our brats; now the accession takes place under Philip the Fair, now under Louis XIV, unless it is not declared to have taken place in 1789 or 1830. . . . Perhaps after all it wasn't exactly the same bourgeoisie any more than it was the same capitalism. . . ." Or at least, if the bourgeois sympathies or connivances of all the reformers were not demonstrable, "the bourgeoisie" took over their theological quarrel to forge a combat weapon for itself. For an entire generation of historians this construction became a self-evident principle of explication, scarcely discussed, which required neither proofs nor even explicit exposition, and from which one could without further ado systematically deduce the confused march of events and developments, spiritual as well as material. Such "self-evidence" is acknowledged so unquestioningly and so extensively, even in popularizations and in school manuals, that we must start from scratch if we are to disengage the history of the Reformation, and its infinitely ramified consequences, from this preconceived schema. For this schema is simply not true.

Let us return to our point of departure. At the origin of Weber's thesis there is a duly verified sociological fact that does not belong to the history of the Reformation, but to the end of the nineteenth century. Max Weber took as the starting point of his essay a study made under his direction by his pupil Martin Offenbacher on "The Economic Situation of Catholics and Protestants in the Grand Duchy of Baden," whose population in 1895 was composed as follows: Catholics 61.3 per cent, Protestants 37.0 per cent, and Jews 1.5 per cent. This study disclosed that the Protestants held a more than proportional share of the movable capital (or, more exactly, of the taxed income from shares and stocks, which is not altogether the same thing), and of leading positions in the urban economy (Catholics held two thirds of the landed property), and furnished a more than proportional percentage of the students of the secondary schools, of the liberal professions, of the officers and functionaries and, furthermore, of the skilled industrial workers. It was a characteristic investigation of the pioneer age of German sociology, similar to others made at the same time on the "overrepresentation" of Jews in commercial and intellectual professions, or to the one that Max Weber himself had made several years before on the progressive Polonization of the agricultural proletariat in the Prussian provinces east of the Elbe. In this connection, this trait of Weber's personality merits mention here. He was profoundly a man of his time and of its bugbears: his academic presentation, in 1893, of his study of the agricultural proletariat in the frontier areas of the East, which created a sensation, was a deliberate accusation of national betrayal directed against the Prussian landed gentry which was "de-Germanizing" the Germanic East by importing foreign laborers, less demanding than their German counterparts. (At the same date, and for exactly analogous reasons, the great bourgeois Viennese Jew Victor Adler, imbued with a sense of the Germanic cultural mission, converted to socialism and to Austro-German Marxism while denouncing the national betrayal of Austro-German capitalism, which was "de-Germanizing" Bohemia by replacing the German *Kulturvolk* with a Czech proletariat.) Such studies were often beyond reproach in terms of statistical accuracy, but we can no longer read them without a certain queasiness because of their obsession with problems of the presumed superiority or inferiority of confessional or ethnic groups, and of their mutual encroachments, infiltrations, or contaminations, halfway between the *Kulturkampf* and the war of the races.

Such is the problem as posed by the more or less clear, more or less trustworthy figures; namely, the statistics of the 1890's: how explain the differences of activity, of structure, and social position between the different confessional groups? It remained for the historian to explain the phenomenon observed. What step could be more plausible than to ferret out the causes of the economic successes of the Protestant segment of the population in the Protestant doctrine itself? Let us recall first of all that Offenbacher's investigation, albeit centered on the economic position of the different confessional groups—demonstrating, moreover, only marginal variations in them on the basis of absolute figures which at times were extremely trifling, their insignificance camouflaged only by translation into percentages—in no way proved a unilateral bent on the part of Protestants for capitalist undertakings. Rather, Offenbacher proved a greater general mobility which sufficiently explains their concentration in the cities: a more than normal attendance at urban secondary schools, or in the exercise of the liberal professions, or employment in the service of the State (was the military career, where Protestants dominated, more "capitalist" that the priestly career which attracted their Catholic compatriots?). But the findings also implicated that there were more Protestants among industrial wage-earners, more Catholics in the rural economy. In this whole, rather fluid tableau of local conditions susceptible to local explanations, Weber set into bold relief and made the most of the one point which supported the conclusions he had formed in advance, and discarded the rest. Thus from the beginning, the historian falsified the data of the problem, no doubt in complete good faith, but this was to have considerable consequences for the continuation of the debate.

Besides, what did Offenbacher's skeletal figures matter since they merely confirmed a general impression which seemed to strike everyone? With sufficient lists, an investigator would certainly have been able to establish analogous statistics and draw from them identical conclusions for many regions where the confessions lived side by side. All we have to do is think of Switzerland, where developed and underdeveloped regions, if we may use, rather anachronistically, a terminology now current, have co-existed for centuries. A statistician of Max Weber's time would have observed an amazing coincidence between economic progress and Protestantism's area of extension. True, the demarcation of the boundaries of these regions of unequal economic development in general goes back to a time prior to the Reformation, and this example serves to invite reflection on the entanglement of "causes" and "effects" in historic reality. Does not the original error lie in considering the confessional groups as primary entities, that had started out from the same level and differentiated subsequently while the regions and groups of the population were already differentiated—rural or urban, economically advanced or retarded—when they opted either for the Reformation or to remain in the Catholic Church, or had one of these alternatives forced upon them?

The results of the same investigation in a country like France would have been even more striking and also more difficult to interpret. Here a tiny Protestant minority, formerly vanquished and persecuted, managed even under the *ancien régime* to achieve a position disproportionate to its numbers, not only in departments of the industrial economy and of banking, but also in the nation's political and intellectual life. Moreover, it achieved this not only in the modern sectors of the society which we can consider as capitalist, but in the poor agricultural regions of the South which, since the sixteenth century, had been centers of resistance of a Calvinism which had been crushed and where the Protestant peasants nevertheless remained a social and human elite. Likewise, but with many reservations, we could also cite the example of agrarian Ireland, Catholic or clerical, where the tiny Protestant minority remained the active elite long after having lost the privileges assured by English domination. Are these proofs of the driving force of the "Protestant spirit" or simply special cases of a much vaster problem, that of social minorities, which still awaits its sociology? Dissident minorities doubtless have played a specific elitist role as a moral, spiritual, *and* economic leaven operating in the dough of human societies, which appear as an historical constant, whatever their professed religions: *Oportet haereses esse!*

Consider, for example, the Jews in many countries of Europe, the religious minorities in the Near East and India. Their role certainly has nothing to do with the Protestant ethic and yet they exhibit traits that are common to certain Protestant minorities: people set before a challenge in the form of social or legal discrimination have been forced or stimulated to greater effort and discipline, unless they chose to accept their loss of rights or to implore compassionate treatment. Indeed, in connection with the role of minorities, or rather of some minorities or of some qualities of dissent, we must also ask ourselves how many others were stiffened into sterility, without counting those who succumbed to overpowering pressures. This raises a particularly delicate subject, where it is difficult to avoid highly disputable value judgments. Nevertheless, we shall risk the affirmation that the Protestant doctrine, at least in its Calvinistic version, because of its concept of the lay priesthood which found an established clergy dispensable, and even more because it submitted the believer's individual conduct to the whole interior tribunal of his conscience beyond any sanction of an external spiritual authority, no doubt morally and spiritually better armed its faithful for survival in the "enemy country," far from the support and sanction of protective authority. Whereas the Catholic can only with difficulty practice his religion outside the bosom of the organized Church, present through its clergy. We would find strong proof of this in the Catholic minority in England, whose external fate, legal status, and living conditions at different times of persecution or tolerance were nearly the same as those of Protestants in France, without evidence that English Catholics ever played a comparable role as a leaven at work in their country's life. Deprived of their Mother Church, some remained orphans, others became men responsible for themselves. That Protestant doctrine had reinforced these qualities of personal responsibility, voluntary discipline, and spiritual independence to which at times commentators have attached, stupidly, the label of bourgeois virtues, and which we could also call hauteur, arrogance, and stubbornness, was an opinion held even by the most passionate foes of the Reformation. Let us add still another trait which was of considerable importance to both intellectual and economic history: the Protestant minorities, even in their lowest strata, throughout the centuries in some Catholic countries, constituted a literate elite in the midst of illiterate masses, since they were under obligation to read the Bible. They were a people of the Book, as were the Jews.

But we need not stick to these micro-sociological comparisons between confessional groups within a given country, whose findings, based on statistics which are always insufficient and difficult to decipher, will always be contestable. We are immediately struck by the divergence of modes of behavior and of "coefficients of activity" when we make an historical comparison between the whole countries that border one upon the other—such as the Catholic and Protestant halves of the Old Netherlands, Belgium, and Holland. Their development, which took a radically different course from 1600 on, cannot be explained by any difference in former conditions, historical or natural, in favor of Holland. Or, if we roughly compare the two halves of western Europe, north and south, Protestant and Catholic, as they looked between 1870 and 1914. Better still, let us extend our comparison on the larger scale of the New World to the confrontation between Anglo-Saxon America and Latin America, the classic example of the contemporary sociology of development and underdevelopment.

Admittedly, here there was a striking disparity between the Protestant and Catholic worlds, so great that the arguments over particulars—highly licit objections to this or that local inquiry, or to this or that particular interpretation—could carry great weight. It was precisely this comprehensive situation that had to be explained, and Weber's explanation seemed to be the only one which could render an account of it in its entirety. One by one, Weber's critics refuted his explication in detail, but ultimately acknowledged defeat because of their failure to come up with a satisfying alternative. There must have been in the Protestant doctrine a powerful leaven of economic and social development—of capitalist development, therefore, to use Weber's terminology, *Quod erat demonstrandum.*

It is the classic example of a problem posed in such a way so as not to admit any other solution save that which is implicitly suggested by its own formulation, and it is most curious that in the course of this debate no one succeeded in breaking out of this *petitio principi.* Many scholars who took part in the debate were greatly troubled by an irksome chronological rift between the epoch of the Reformation and its presumed economic effects. But none of them seems to have drawn conclusions from the enormous *non sequitur* of the Weberian chain of causes and effects. Neither capitalism nor the modern world nor rational thought began at Wittenberg, or even at Geneva.

The attack of the reformers against the spiritual authority of Rome and the Roman clergy occurred at a moment when Europe was being borne along by a forward propelling movement, constantly accelerated at a dizzying pace in all spheres of being—of knowledge, technique, free thought, emancipation of the individual, economic and commercial expansion, and the conquest of new horizons. In none of these spheres did the Reformation mark a beginning, or even contribute something truly novel. All the facts cited in favor of Weber's thesis concern the eighteenth and nineteenth centuries, which were separated from the Reformation by too many generations, events, and changes of mentality to make it possible for a commentator to establish a decipherable and intelligible relationship to it. Further, these social facts were but extensions of developments which had been germinating since the Middle Ages. Actually, it is precisely in the sphere of the forms of capitalist undertaking and organization that the century of the Reformation marks the beginning of a long process of regression. During the next two centuries Europe never again attained that degree of development and economic structuration, or that vigor of individual initiative, or that flowering of great capitalists in the grand manner, which it had known in the fifteenth and at the beginning of the sixteenth century—the century of the Fuggers—within the framework of a still intact Catholicism. On all these levels, we witness a degenerative hardening process or a distinct retreat, beginning around 1560. Are we to hold the "wars of religion" responsible? After all, they merely prolonged and widened the conflict between France and the Hapsburg Empire, already sketched in the wars of Italy and fully unleashed long before the Reformation in a constellation of powers which the religious quarrel was scarcely to modify but which, for its part, would largely determine adherences or submissions to one or the other confessional camp. In this sphere, an attempt to separate the spiritual from the political and even from the military would be a hopeless task: ultimately, the religious demarcations were imposed by force, as happened in Europe in 1945 with the "secular religions": *Cuius regio eius religio.* But once the storm was over, these demarcations became more or less clear, but always perfectly perceptible dividing lines between regions of further unequal development. On one side we can discern a slow or rapid rise from the lowest level; on the other, prolonged stagnation or decadence from, at times, very high levels. If, on the one hand, the Reformation must render account of a further development which was but a continuation, or a revival, it follows as a logical consequence that the Counter Reformation must be responsible for its cessation.

We say the Counter Reformation and not Catholicism because the new fact that emerged was the Counter Reformation. After all, did not the rich and striking flowering of free cities and merchant republics with their proudly independent bourgeoisies that marked the renaissance of medieval Europe take place within the Catholic world and under the protection of the Church? A Church which was still in full communication with all the vital energies of this Europe that, under its guidance, was slowly overcoming the disastrous regression of the barbarian invasions. Did not the proud Republic of Venice, which, albeit remaining Catholic, put up such a savage resistance to the institutions and spirit of the Counter Reformation, defend the heritage of the medieval city against the tyranny of a Church become "Spanish" and relentlessly bent upon refeudalizing the West? One simplification deserves another: rather than attribute the creation of a new economic spirit to the Reformation, there are excellent reasons for maintaining that through the Reformation it was the spirit of the medieval urban republics which was perpetuated. This was brought about by its emancipation from the tutelage of the Church, which formerly had been the key factor in their flowering but which thereafter, by placing itself at the head of an implacable rearguard action, was smothering and ruining them. The successive waves of Italian, Flemish, Huguenot refugees—to whom must be added that of the Spanish and Portuguese Jews harried by the Inquisition—who took with them to Holland, England, Switzerland, and the northern countries the knowledge, techniques, and activities of the Mediterranean and Flemish world, were not exclusively a religious phenomenon because many emigrations had nothing to do with heresy. Rather, this was one of the consequences of the crushing spiritual *and* material dullness of the courtly and of the clerical kingdoms in the Europe of the Counter Reformation. Within this broad canvas, whose contrasts no doubt have been deliberately heightened, our judgments must be finely shaded and broadened, and here too we must be wary of generalizations, although the Counter Reformation presents a greater unity than multi-faceted and differentiated Protestantism. Nevertheless, any comprehensive reading of European history forcibly suggests the idea that the Counter Reformation, wherever it triumphed in the form of an authoritarian reaction to the spirit of heresy and insubordination, for a long time blocked the development of a material, technical, and intellectual civilization. Hence, as a defensive reaction of a Church profoundly medieval in its feudal structures as well as in its means of exercising spiritual authority, it was a reactionary movement in the precise sense of the term.

Not only was the development toward modern times previously on the march in all of Europe, but it had actually originated in that part of the continent which was to go down precisely under the weight of this reaction in a seeming sleep of death, where the only sign of life was the artistic glorification of the Church triumphant that was to flourish for two centuries. Consider the veritable *translatio imperii* of the sciences of Italy to England in the seventeenth century; or the surprising absence of Catholic Germany, so much richer in traditions, in the slow renewal of German philosophy and literature after the Thirty Years' War; or compare the area within the radius of the Enlightenment, of the *Aufklärung*, with that of humanism, so different in character. Let us also consider the exception which confirms the rule: the exceptional and disconcerting role of France, which preserved her nationalized Church in the service of the State, but which on all points rejected the Counter Reformation—the Council of Trent, the Inquisition, and the clergy's control over intellectual life—and indeed, even under her most Christian kings, remained in the Protestant camp of Europe during the decisive struggles of the seventeenth century. Moreover, her militant anti-clericalism fundamentally was reduced to silence only during the thirty years which followed the revocation of the Edict of Nantes.

The most fantastic error of this lengthy debate on the historical role of Protestantism, which ended in tiresome repetitions and supersubtleties, was simply that it totally forgot its counterpart, the historical role of the Counter Reformation. (After all, that too was a Reformation, which in its way marked the end of Catholicity and definitively consummated the split.) It was as if, in contradistinction to the Reformation, there had been a simple continuity of a medieval society, wrongly viewed, for that matter, as homogeneous and static. After formulating the antithesis, scholars furiously pursued the ramifications of one of its terms and forgot to inquire about the other. The fact of the matter is that a break in an ascendant line poses a much graver problem than its continuation.

Let us set one comprehensive view against another. In the age of the Reformation, all the bases of the modern world —the capital, the riches, the highest degree of development in the arts and trades, navigation and trade to distant parts of the earth, intelligence and power—were almost entirely in the hands of that part of Europe which was Catholic and was to remain so. Italy was the prestigious center of the material and spiritual culture of the West. Spain and Portugal held the monopoly of possessions overseas acquired through conquest and the exploitation of the trade of the two Indies, the widest field of undertakings, and the greatest source of riches in the nascent modern world. Flanders was the industrial, commercial, and artistic center of northern Europe. It was here that the intellectual, material, and technical preconditions for what we call the rise of the capitalist economy were gathered; not in the peripheral and semi-barbarian countries on the border of northern Europe and the Northeast conquered by the Reformation. Only one century later, all this had degenerated or was dying. As a subject for study it had gone out of style. But in contrast to economic historians, whose curves inflect only imperceptibly and tardily, the historians of civilization have always known what a brutal rupture with the past the Counter Reformation was in the countries where it ultimately prevailed; what a deathly shadow it threw over things, with its entourage of the Inquisition and its heresy trials. A shadow from which this half of the continent was to begin to disengage itself only two centuries later under the action of an enlightened and anti-clerical despotism, or even much later in the wake of the invading armies of revolutionary France on whose banners were blazoned the slogans of a liberating secularization. The outright totalitarian reaction, not only to the Reformation but to all the dangers of intellectual freedom which it had revealed, wiped out a ferment in a part of the West which had been at work throughout Europe, and along with it that vital minimum of freedom without which a society cannot produce either intellectual or industrial pioneers, scientific research, or economic growth.

This is an historical perspective which simply cannot be reduced to a question of relationship between individual adherence to a religious doctrine or ethic and individual efficacy in the economic sphere. Nevertheless, even on the basis of this narrowing of the debate, the question should have been posed whether the Reformation—or rather the establishment of the Reformed Churches, despite the intolerances or the degeneration to which some were to succumb—had simply been not the cause but rather the least formidable obstacle to emancipation and the rise of innovating capitalism. Whether, for example, its victory in the northern part of the Netherlands, in the shelter of its system of natural defenses—tantamount to saying the liberation of Holland—did not simply make it possible to preserve and develop in this region the great industrial and commercial heritage which had been smothered in the southern part where Spanish and clerical domination was maintained. For the prosperity and prestige of Amsterdam was but a resumption and prolongation of the prosperity and prestige of Antwerp, which had been crushed. In Amsterdam there was freedom, liberalism in every accepted sense of the term, for many—but there was no Calvinism. Cosmopolitan, religiously indifferent Amsterdam rallied so late to the Dutch and Protestant cause that Calvinist fervor found hardly any adepts except among the common people. Here, too, we must be wary of facile conclusions: the fate of Belgium—the battlefield and exchange currency of European politics, strangled and cut off from the sea by agreement among the powers—certainly cannot be explained only in terms of her Catholicism, because once freedom was restored to Belgium this Catholic land became the first industrialized country of Europe after Protestant England.

It is undoubtedly legitimate to isolate and to study separately a particular line of development in the history of the genesis of the modern West, so complex and yet so much of a piece: namely, capitalist industrial society. And it is equally legitimate to isolate, hypothetically, the era of the Reformation as a point of departure, on the condition that it is considered in its entirety and within the framework of the time, with all its implications and its repercussions, not as an act of doctrine and of faith. The era of the Reformation, if indeed it was an era of revolutionary effervescence, also included its counterstroke, this occurrence of intellectual, political, and social reaction (because clericalism was a social phenomenon and the clergy was a feudal order) known as the Counter Reformation. Failure to respect this condition brings us smack up against the irreducible heterogeneity of phenomena which must be meaningfully related to each other, and we are thus reduced to playing the game of vague or insidious connections, as has too often been the case in the debate now under consideration. The historian or the sociologist cannot, any more than the theologian, allow an investigator to seize a trade or bank register, even one adorned with an opening invocation for God's blessing, and then cry out: "Eureka! Here is how Calvin created capitalism!"

We will not reproach the historian-sociologists who took part in this discussion for having been but mediocre experts in matters of theology. What is quite a serious shortcoming, however, is that apparently they knew the Calvinist teaching and dogma which they discussed only by hearsay, and totally ignored the teaching and dogma of the Counter Reformation. For example, they did not know to what extent the old problem of predestination, posed since Saint Paul and formulated in almost Calvinist terms by Saint Augustine—the theological expression of the insoluble mystery of destiny and of human freedom—similarly troubled Protestant and Catholic theologians. Nevertheless, they heedlessly flung themselves headlong into exceedingly elementary psychoanalyses of Calvinian predestination. Even less forgivable is the negligence or arbitrariness with which such fine minds gathered haphazardly and wrongly interpreted isolated facts, whether or not they were significant or entirely devoid of interest, attributable or not to a religious obedience, in order to uphold their thesis. True, they were convinced in advance and thus searched less for proofs than for striking examples. It is also true that economic and modern social history has only just emerged from its infancy. A good part of the most brilliant propositions that were upheld in this dispute were invalidated simply because their authors had rather foggy notions of canon law and of its hold on positive legislations in economic matters, as well as of the basic banking mechanisms, of exchange, and of modes of payment before the nineteenth century. They seem to have naïvely believed, for example, that the normal activity of seventeenth- and eighteenth-century bankers consisted in lending money at interest! Thus all seemed quite simple: Calvin authorized the interest-yielding loans, *ergo*, we have the rise of credit and capitalism.

There is no need to dwell here on the technical questions of banking history, which would lose us in the terrifying complexity of the monetary economy of the time. We shall simply point out that Protestant bankers—whose key position in European economic life at the end of the eighteenth century has excited the imagination of so many historians

—were in no sense moneylenders, but specialized intermediaries of the payments and exchange market on the international and even interurban plane, and that their activity, technically and materially, differed no whit from that of their Catholic colleagues. The canonical interdiction on lending at interest played no role, because it was never applied to the "business of exchange." If the Dutch, English, and, even more successfully, Huguenot bankers in the seventeenth century took the place of Italians and Germans of the South, this was due less to new banking techniques—which were actually regressing in relation to the fourteenth century—than to a progressive shift of commercial centers toward northwestern Europe. As regards the Huguenots more particularly, it was not the particularity of Calvin's doctrine but their fate as descendants of a vanquished party, the fact that they belonged to a community of refugees scattered all over Europe and America while still preserving strong bonds to France, which "predestined" them to "international correspondence," that is to say, among other things to banking activity which by its very nature was an international correspondence. A dispersed people, a mobile element because it was painfully constrained to mobility, a cosmopolitan minority whose success gave rise to scandal, as with the Jews. And in both cases, the scandal monstrously exaggerated their real success, which in truth was marginal. But, above all, how far we had come from the Reformation, spiritually and chronologically, at the time when Necker discoursed "On the Importance of Religious Opinions" and on those "Genevans" nourished on Voltaire or Rousseau!

Here we have anachronistic witnesses to an untenable thesis. Was the Reformation the ideology of rising capitalism? Let us ask the first schoolboy at hand the names of the great representatives of commercial, banking, and manufacturing capitalism of the time of the Reformation; unhesitatingly, he will name the Medicis and the Fuggers. The Medicis were the banker princes of the Roman Curia and finally popes themselves; and the son of Lorenzo the Magnificent, Leon X, was to excommunicate Luther. And it was Jacob Fugger who took their place as banker to the Curia. He paid for the election of Charles V, who was the strongest pillar of the empire and the papacy in league against the Reformation, and headed a wholly modern large-scale undertaking with many branches, which at one and the same time exploited silver and copper mines and the hopes and fears of the faithful for their eternal salvation. It was Fugger who, originally destined for the priesthood, placed the key bishoprics of Germany, Hungary, and Poland on the auction block or had them occupied by his nephews and associates. And it was Fugger who, as a consummate financier, directed the collection and the transfer of ecclesiastical revenues, *servitia*, annates, dispensations, Crusade contributions, and Peter's pence, and, finally, supplied the treasury with the monies paid by the faithful for the graces stored up by the saints and martyrs by a stream (multiplied to infinity) of drafts on the world beyond the grave. Never, either before or after, have bankers so merited the honor, dubious or otherwise, of giving their name to their whole epoch.

Let us continue our impromptu interrogation of the schoolboy, because it is useful to recall here the most patent and well-known facts. We all know that the precise point of departure of Luther's protest was the traffic in indulgences, which at first had been raised humbly through hierarchical channels, and only later addressed to the public because it received no more attention from the hierarchy than had so many other protests. Luther's revolt against Rome was a revolt against the corruption openly flaunted by the Church, and at the same time an uprising against the great and puissant capitalists of his time, who had found their most solid support and their greenest pastures in the financial dominion of the Holy See. To the extent that it concerned itself with the regnant order in this world, it was also, and explicitly, a revolt against Mammon and the worship of the Golden Calf. In modern terminology, it was the venting of an "anti-capitalist" fury which had been incubating for a long time at all levels of the people. At the Diet of Worms to which Luther was summoned to answer for his seditious acts, his quarrel merged with that which had been kindled by the projects of imperial legislation against the monopolies and the big commercial companies, against monopoly, hoarding, and usury. This remedial legislation had been demanded from all sides and its primary target was the Fugger dynasty. Manifestly, the projects remained abortive under an emperor who owed his election to the fact that Fugger had bought up the prime electors; these projects were proposed to a Diet dominated by these very electors. Luther, in his pamphlet "On Trade and Usury" explained: "Thus is the word of Isaiah justified: your princes have become the companions of thieves." If we reread the inflammatory writings and speeches of the reformer and of his companions, such as Hutten, against the monopolies and the capitalist companies, against the moneychangers who had set up their tables in the Temple, against the usurers who devoured the households of widows, we discern the first revival in Western Christianity of the spirit and accent of the Old Testament prophets for whom the divine commandment to secure justice was not a promise to be fulfilled beyond the grave, but a demand that must be presented and realized in this world.

This rebirth in the Christian consciousness of the Reformation, of the prophetic tradition of the Old Testament, which had been so completely muffled for a thousand years in the Roman Church under its pagan, Christian, Roman, and imperial legacy, was an event of incalculable importance to the history of ideas. It touched on all areas of private and collective life and even affected the deepest structures of language. The powerful resonance which a laic intercourse with the Bible in the vernacular had produced in German and English—and which found vigorous expression in the French language of the sixteenth and seventeenth centuries, before it was eliminated by the authoritarian codification of the language to conform with the clarity, reason, and "good taste" obtaining at the time of Louis XIV—remained essentially alien to the Romance and Slavic languages, into which even the most skillful translator cannot grant Shakespeare or Milton fair access. We know that for the French Huguenots and the English Puritans of the heroic age, the Old Testament was a more thrilling reading experience and a more powerful source of inspiration than the New, except for the terrors portrayed in the Apocalypse. For Agrippa d'Aubigné or for Cromwell, Israel's battles or the anger of the prophets came closer to home than did the Gospel of love and clemency. We see the strange Hebrew names with which they baptized their children, we hear them in their pamphlets growing heady with the exaltations and fulminations of the psalmists and the prophets, we observe how effortlessly they transposed the colorful characters and events of Israel's history to their own time. We see how they hurled the imprecations of the prophets at the heads of foes of their faith, how while calling the wrath of God down upon them, they made of Rome the new Babylon, of the Pope the priest of Baal or the new Nebuchadnezzar, of the

Queen behind the Massacre of Saint Bartholomew a new Jezebel, of Charles I a Roboan. And how, upon being persecuted and exiled, they wept with the Jews of the Babylonian captivity on the banks of the Euphrates, or how, after a victory, like Cromwell after Marston Moor, they intone a victory psalm by Amos. "I hate, I despite your feasts, and I take no delight in your solemn assemblies. . . . Take away from me the noise of your song; to the melody of your harp I will not listen. But let justice roll down like waters, and righteousness like an everflowing stream." This outburst from the prophet Amos sums up the whole original spirit of the Reformation. Nor should these be viewed as pale literary allegories. The social teachings of Zwingli and of Calvin, as well as the revolutionary impetus of the Huguenots, the Gueux,[1] and of the Puritans, were imbued with the spirit of the Old Testament. The common people and shepherds who reasoned and quarrelled face-to-face with God, the judges, prophets, and popular leaders who rose up against unjust princes and against priests of dubious character, found their models in the books of Israel. For them the children of God were bound not only to be merciful, but to bring about the kingdom of justice and the sanctification of this world. There is no need to give a subtle interpretation to Calvinist predestination, or to psychoanalyze Protestant solitude, as has been done with such zeal following Max Weber, in order to understand how the Calvinists and Puritans fancied themselves as a Chosen People, and in order to view them in Sombart's phrase as "Jews, without being aware of it." The feeling sprang up spontaneously from this clearly affirmed identification with the people of God of the Old Testament, arrayed against

[1] A name, meaning beggars, adopted by the revolutionary nobles and merchants in the Netherlands, in 1590.—Trans.

paganism and idols. This feature, more than any distinctive theological doctrine, transmuted Calvinism into a form of Christianity that was wholly different from Roman Christianity. The identification produced a vigorous revival in the modern world of a portion of the prophetic spirit of ancient Judaism, which was not centered upon the world beyond the grave and inwardness, but on concrete concerns such as right and justice in *this* world. Further, it introduced into this spirit a ferment of political will and action which has marked all the struggles that have taken place in the modern world to achieve a constitutional regime and a State based on law.

It is simply not true that this revolution was a specifically bourgeois or urban class movement. All historical evidence refutes this claim, which was constructed after the event by proceeding from the present to the past. It was a strange bourgeoisie indeed, this "Christian nobility of Germanic nationhood" to whom Luther appealed against Rome, as strange as that of the Scottish clans who rallied under the banner of John Knox! We know that a number of free autonomous cities—imperial or Swiss cities, for example—through the voice of their bourgeoisie represented by their magistrates or, as at Lubeck, by simply overthrowing their magistrates—namely, men who had the right to deliberate in a constituted community, which is the only admissible definition of the term "bourgeois" or burgher in this context—embraced the Reformation and took advantage of it in order to shake off the suzerainty of an ecclesiastical prince or to seize the goods and properties of the clergy. Temporal lords of all ranks, individually or collectively, followed suit and even ecclesiastical lords turned the secularization to their personal advantage, from distant Prussia to Ireland. History has given priority to the decisions of these privileged persons who were part of the power structure (the least pure but the most effectual), in preference to the multiple obscure choices of individuals and amorphous masses. Actually, the Reformation movement, in Germany as in France, affected important segments of all classes. And if its intellectual propaganda exerted a great influence among the bourgeois, the functionaries, students, and the cultural classes of the cities—in short, among those who could read—we know that it aroused the peasant masses in a much broader and more elementary way, against whom the lords of both confessions immediately formed a united front, and that it drew its main political strength from the reinforcements provided by the great and petty nobility.

As for France, which, unlike Germany, possessed a capital where the decisive contest took place, we should remember that the Catholic League, in its struggle against the Reformation, was based precisely upon the urban masses of Paris. Once the "party" was defeated, the aristocracy and the members of the legal profession returned to the religion of the prince, either with their "heart" or with their "lips," the lower classes and especially the rural masses, deprived of pastors, public worship, religious instruction, and of all material or moral means of persevering the so-called Reformed Religion, could maintain itself only in some particularly compact pockets of the South, and in the cities, only among a bourgeoisie sufficiently independent materially to resist, or to remove itself from the pressures of power. That this occurred was the result of an historical process, replete with acts of violence and abjuration, and not the proof of an original bourgeois vocation of the Reformation. In Germany, on the other hand, the same process caused the Prussia of petty squires and of equally coarse serfs to become Protestant, and the bourgeois and mercantile Rhineland Catholic.

In England, in the past few years, we have been able to

follow a veritable revisionist process of the social history of the Puritan revolution which Tawney and his disciples had analyzed as a bourgeois revolution culminating in Cromwell's republic. Nothing much has remained of this impressive construction. In this gigantic struggle for individual freedom, and for the independence of the judiciary and the control of Parliament, the mercantile and industrial bourgeoisie of the cities, and of London first of all, did not play a notable role and did not provide a single leader. And even outside the framework of politico-religious history, in data apparently of the most matter-of-fact kind, Tawney's analysis of the "social revolution" of the seventeenth century has turned out to be untenable. Even if we admit his thesis of the "rise of the gentry"—which is in no way proven by the available evidence and figures—in order to subscribe to his conclusions, we would still have to accept the veritable terminological conjuring trick which consists in attributing to the country squires a "bourgeois-capitalist spirit," in contradistinction to the court nobility. Such a procedure enables one to turn any historical event in the desired direction and it is quite characterisic of the *petitio principi* with which this discussion has been studded: the Reformation having been a bourgeois movement or one marked by the bourgeois spirit, all those whom it swept along in its train must needs have been affected by the bourgeois spirit inasmuch as the bourgeois spirit was defined precisely through adherence to the Reformation.

Let us be wary of summary affirmations, which make this or that of the Reformation, labelling it either as a bourgeois, feudal, peasant, proletarian, national, or nationalist movement. No doubt it was all of that and something else besides, namely, a watershed between two epochs. What the Reformation was and wanted to be cannot be constructed *a posteriori*, on the basis of the later fate of the Protestant denominations and sects. The latter were the results of the failure of the Reformation at the outset, as a spiritual movement including all Western Christendom, and as an attempt to re-form and re-establish the One and Indivisible Christian Church in its totality, in keeping with the purity of the Word. On the eve of the Reformation, the intellectual and moral elites, clerical or lay, of all nations and social conditions were agreed on the necessity and urgency of this reform, if not on the details of its actualization. That this Reformation, rejected or sabotaged by the hierarchy, installed in its lavish routine and temporal power, under additional pressure from the political, diplomatic, and military requirements of its power (suspended between this world and the world beyond the grave), should finally have been undertaken against the hierarchy, in disorder and by impatient reformers, and that it should have caused the schism and the fragmentation into local reformations, as the result of which the unity of Western Christendom was definitely shattered in the frightful struggle between the Reformation and the Counter Reformation, is a scandal that partisans from both camps rejected for nearly two centuries. The very passion behind the religious wars and the persecutions carried out by both sides testify to this stubborn refusal to accept the cleavage as an accomplished fact. In this immense drama of the Reformation, willed in terms of Church unity and yet causing its explosion, many disparate tendencies came together and again drifted apart; it is just not permissible to reduce them to a simple antithesis.

If the Reformation is to be grasped in its reality as an historical event, we must first of all see the interaction between the effort at *religious reform,* dictated by religious feeling and understanding, and having in view the doctrine, teaching, and practice of Christian life, demanding a return to evangelical sources, and the effort at *reform of the Church as a temporal institution,* having in view its constitution, its administration, and hierarchy inherited from the Byzantine Empire and so firmly integrated into the feudal world, in which the clergy formed one of the constituent social estates. This was a twofold, indivisible effort, the point of convergence of many internal eddies and former heretical movements, as well as of all the constitutional struggles between papal authority and conciliar authority. On the other hand, we must recognize the decisive initial incidence of the *ecclesiastical-political policies* of the secular authorities, extensions of equally ancient lines of development which, however, were oriented toward other goals. The great confrontation between secular power and clerical power continued from century to century, from the dispute over investitures to the great schism of the fourteenth century, to the capitulations of the Roman Church to the State Churches—Gallican, Anglican, and Spanish—and on up to the modern conflicts between Church and State which constantly rocked Catholic countries until the beginning of the twentieth century.

It is in this last area, the closest to secular realities, that the separate destinies of the different reformations are most visible. The grandiose religious impetus of Lutheranism was for a long time bogged down and crushed in the deepest recesses of its being by its subjection to the ecclesiastical policy of the princes and by the acceptance of their sovereignty over the separated churches. On ecclesiastical, political, and even economic planes, the Reformation in northern Germany, in the Scandinavian countries, and in the

England of Henry VIII had been a campaign of brigandage on the part of the princes and the nobles against the prebends and benefices of the Church. To the extent that its forces allowed, the bourgeois oligarchy of the free cities also took part in this spoliation. In Scandinavia, the pillage even preceded the movement of religious reform, which was launched only after the Church was confiscated by the sovereigns. And in England, only the remote waves of the Scottish and Puritan revolutions made the triumph of the religious reformation possible, by the struggle then waged against the Anglican State Church—which in fact had been established before its break with Rome. Calvinism's importance for history derives precisely from the fact that it allowed the reformist spirit to manifest itself on the religious plane with the greatest possible purity, in complete independence from politico-ecclesiastic considerations and princely usurpations. It was reserved to the Calvinists, thenceforth, to recognize no other master over their community save Christ, instead of simply changing temporal or clerical overlords. Admittedly, it was a purity somewhat stained by the pitiless fury of the struggle which had already reached its peak of virulence. Calvin, the only systematic mind among the reformers, had been the revolutionary among them. He already belonged to the second generation of reformers hardened in the fires of combat, a contemporary enemy and spiritual brother of Ignatius Loyola and of the Counter Reformation already being organized, the spiritual and political leader of reformed minorities that had risen in revolt against the established power in all Europe, from Hungary and Poland to Scotland. It is in Calvin that we best discern the imperious prophetic passion of the Old Testament, the pitiless demand for consonance between deeds and words, between daily life and doctrine, and between politics and faith. He forged a special breed of haughty and harsh men, fanatically persuaded that they were answerable for their lives only to God and to their consciences, free men, in short, responsible only to themselves. Further, he was responsible for the birth of those Calvinist communities, fiercely rebellious to any human authority over consciences, for whom the separation of Church and State always took place as a matter of course when the State did not identify itself with the community —as was the case in ancient Geneva and in the Puritan settlements of New England. An international revolution, in the strongest sense of the term, was launched from Geneva, this Zion of the new people of God. It was not their religions that made these people, who were otherwise active and useful subjects, so intolerable to French absolutism which itself was none too docile to the authority of Rome, but rather what the royal intendants [2] generally called their "incorrigible Republican spirit." Now, this man free and responsible before himself, this man active in the world—the antithesis of Lutheran inwardness—became a leaven in the Western world far beyond the confines of the Calvinist diaspora and far beyond the epoch of the intense original faith, the most dynamic factor in the rise of Western societies, of which what our polemic called "modern capitalism" is but a single fact. Let the label "bourgeois" be applied to these men who, nevertheless, descended from all social classes: has not the same label been applied to the nineteenth century, to the whole of France, and to so-called modern civilization? This is tantamount to saying that we have decided to label the spirit of individual freedom "bourgeois."

[2] Commissioners clothed with the King's full authority, sent out from the royal council to which they returned in due course.—Trans.

We know the dangers and perversions of this freedom, the degeneration of individual responsibility into pharacaism and the frightening emotional sterility that at times marks the Protestantism of Calvinist inspiration, placing personal effort and discipline above charity, which is always suspect. A good part of Protestant self-criticism was expressed in the great discussion raised by Weber. Conceivably, it may even have been the fundamental element of this debate through a half century gnawed by doubt and despair about the future of free societies and of the free individual. At any rate, whatever judgment we pass on the merits or misdeeds of this liberation of man-responsible-to-himself to which the spirit of Calvinism so greatly contributed, whether we consider it a boon or (following the example of the Romantics, who became disenchanted with the ideas of freedom after the French Revolution) as a curse, the fact remains that the true and deep relationship between Calvinism and modern economic society resides precisely here, in this liberation of man from spiritual subjection and from the fear of other men. Indeed, this is the same kind of relationship that exists between the aspirations to rationality of Calvinist religiosity and those of wholly secularized positive science, between the autonomous Calvinist community and modern democracy. All the rest is auxiliary. And we should be less inclined than the critics of capitalism of fifty or a hundred years ago to forget to what point these spiritual and political conditions (which these critics viewed as automatic developments) of a free society were likewise at the base of modern economic dynamism and modern industrial capitalism; these were not the accomplishment of a handful of captains of industry but of whole societies set in motion.

All this is basically old history, more than adequately

known, and this exposition perhaps resembles a Puritan gunpowder sermon rather than a contribution to a discussion of economic and social history. But it is precisely those things that everybody is supposed to know which run the greatest risk of being forgotten. For a half century, historians thought it was too naïve and old-fashioned to take for Gospel truth affirmations as banal as the following: that the reformers were in revolt against the disgraceful state of the Church, that their major concern was to return to the Word of God, or that an aspiration to truth intervened in the choice of men torn between veneration for the Church and the need for renewal. It was the fashion of the day to know more about the motivations and intentions of the agents of history than the latter themselves believed they knew. Did they claim to be fighting for the purity of the Gospel, or for the law, or for freedom as they understood these things? The sociologist, formed in the school of historical materialism, demonstrated that they really represented class interests, regardless of what they themselves said and believed they were doing. Ignatius Loyola was the protagonist of feudalism and Calvin of the bourgeoisie. It is not a question here of returning to a pre-Marxian historiography, or of rehabilitating the honor of complacent idealism and abandoning the exploration of the history of the social and material forces which Marx so doggedly revealed to historians. It is a question rather of overcoming this intolerable mixing up of categories and the primitive schematism of the concept of class. Above all, it is a question of relearning what was known a hundred years ago by the great liberal historians (dismissed as so naïve), and which stares us right in the face: that the great drama of history, in spite of all, is something quite different from a mere conflict of economic interests and groups.

CHAPTER TWO

Puritanism and "Industrial Society"

For those who, in terms of the Weberian conception of an ideal type, see in the Reformation the debut of modern history (on the utopian level if not that of immediate social fact), the phenomenon of religious schism is essentially that of a rupture in the spiritual unity of the medieval West; the dislocation of this unified and integrated world embodied in the Universal Church, embracing all activities and conditions of men—whether of high or low degree, clerical or secular—all of which assumed their meaning in relation to a totality where everyone had a place in a hierarchy "like that of the members of a single body." The whole system of reference changed with the Reformation. Now it was no longer with this organic, all-of-a-Christian world, in which God is present through His Church, that the Protestant could or should be in harmony, but with his own conscience, instructed by sacred Scripture and preaching, but in the last analysis, solitary and lost in darkness if God did not illumine it with His grace. The Reformation liberated and isolated him at one and the same time. Whatever the doctrine on the freedom or un-freedom of the will, predestination, good works, or grace, whatever the organization and function assumed by this or that Protestant Church toward its faithful, the Church could institute a teaching and a discipline but it could not inject itself between the Christian and his God. This fundamental difference is best perceived in the essential gesture of the believer: in order to confess and wash away his sins, to face death—in short, in order to reconcile himself with God—the Catholic turns to the Church, the holy, consoling Mother, mediatrix, and depository of the treasure of graces and of the power of absolution. On the other hand, the Protestant, in matters that decide his salvation, is thrown back upon his own resources into the solitude of his conscience, alone before God. Moral judgment aside, it was as a recluse that the Protestant appeared in the eyes of the Catholic.

The contrast is striking once it is thus reduced to its most simple expression. Nevertheless, we must be wary and not draw from this conclusions on social behavior which can all too easily be turned in any desired direction. Many paths are open, ranging from the extremely narrow to the utterly permissive, with this concept of the conscience as immediate sole arbiter as the point of departure. If Luther was indulgent toward human frailty and placed his hope in the goodness of God, Calvin in those parts of his teaching which left their deepest mark on his disciples desired to know only the terrible God of Israel; not the merciful Father, but the judge whose terrifying and inscrutable justice makes a mockery of human reason. Ferocious is the only word for the discipline that he imposed upon his fighting city, bent under the terror of Judgment and wholly dedicated to the glorification of the Eternal One. It may be tempting to find in the "organic totality" of the Universal Church the transposed image of the idealized medieval society, and to see in the Reformation the advent of the individual responsible exclusively to himself, bound to others through objective relations rather than by personal or communitarian bonds. But even in this sense, the Reformation is only one of the multiple aspects of this "end of the Middle Ages"; it was at the same time the religious translation of this emancipation of the individual which the Renaissance and humanism had pursued along other paths, and also the dread counterblow to these movements, a tragic ambiguity which was shatteringly experienced by a good number of the humanists of the sixteenth century and which has been pondered by many historians and philosophers of civilization. In this respect, the Medicis and the Fuggers, Erasmus, Luther, Christopher Columbus, and Copernicus are not only contemporaries but brothers, members of one family whose unity was to collapse under the thrust of modern times. And among these architects of the rupture between two epochs, the least contemporary mind, the one most imbued with medieval traditions, certainly belonged to Luther.

The affinity between the Reformation and the "capitalist spirit" of modern times becomes precise and meaningful when we turn to the reformers of Zurich and Geneva, the organizers of the bourgeois and urban communities, who were citizens, legislators, and political men rolled into one, while at the same time being religious innovators. Obviously, this affinity derives from the fact that these men were at grips with the most "contemporary" problems of the trading and industrial city: it is the legislator as well as the theologian who speaks in their social teaching and public discipline, and we risk confusion when we attribute to their theological doctrine what really belongs to their civil and political teaching. We are not resuming the debate on the doctrine of predestination, nor on the related concept of "vocation"—on which the German Protestant exegesis and that of Max Weber have so greatly exercised their talents by playing on the common root of "*Ruf*," "*Beruf*," and "*Berufung*" (call, calling, and vocation). It was not in Lutheran Germany that the "capitalist vocation" of Protestantism was demonstrated, and when Calvin and his disciples discussed the trades of men they did not speak of "calling" or "vocation" but of "offices." But when we have discarded all these hypotheses as either too venturesome or too subtle, there remains an element which contains nothing hypothetical—the ethic of work, the "sanctification of work," which is the common feature of the Christian city of Zwingli and of Calvin, and which (especially through pietism) strongly impregnated Lutheran Protestantism also, leaving a lasting impression on the character of Protestant societies even when the original piety had been extinguished in them. It was necessary to wait for the advent of the "affluent society" to see this discipline become corrupted.

True, this "sanctification of work" and the rank assigned by the reformers to the virtue of hard work, viewed not as an exclusive or cardinal virtue but as the requirement of a good and worthy Christian life, have often been exaggerated. It was a question not of faith or dogma but of social discipline, a discipline which was inseparable from piety and which reflected a new social concept. The "totality" of the hierarchical medieval society, supporting at its summit the nobility and the clergy nourished by the labor of the common people, had by the same token denied the totality of the individual, whose faculties were torn, so to speak, among hierarchized social orders, one receiving the occupational function of command, another the ordering of the spiritual life, and a third the drudgery of utilitarian labor. By attributing to every man the vocation of a whole man, directly responsible before God and capable of hearing His voice, the Reformation smashed a social hierarchy much more than a hierarchy of spiritual values. We would be missing the point of the sermons on the dignity of labor and the castigation of idleness if we forgot their real target: the provocative luxury of the worldly prelates of the Church of the poor, and the dead weight of a monastic world which had become parasitic and depraved, far removed from its former role as center of civilization—not only of a spiritual and intellectual civilization, but of a material and technical one as well—in the vanguard of those ambitious projects for clearing and improving lands that had marked the activity of the communities of the first centuries after the barbarian invasions.

The imperative of work, in the beginning, was no different than the monastic rule: *Ora et labora*, and even for the friars of lower rank: *laborare est orare*. Only a life that was divided between prayer and work could be lived in a saintly manner: together these two activities formed the discipline which protected the heart of man from the temptations of pleasure and sin, whereas idleness was the open door to all the wiles of the Evil One. Hence the association of prayer and work in one service to God was not an innovation of the reformers, any more than was, for that matter, their hostility to luxury and to the delights and pleasures of the world. The innovation lay in what Henri Hauser has called the "secularization" or—even better—"the laicization of sanctity." In fact, this ascetic discipline assumes a wholly different character when it is applied not to the members of a religious order who have renounced secular life, marriage, and any personal property, but to secular society itself. The Geneva of Calvin and Beza (as Zurich, Basel, and Saint Gallen had been on a more mediocre scale) was an enormous monastery, which embraced the whole city and imposed its rigorous discipline on all the inhabitants. But it did not pursue its own logic to the end, which would have meant the public ownership of property. Now, the labor of the monastic rule is a means of arriving at sanctity because it is not of an economic order, but an ascetic discipline and spiritual exercise, and has nothing in common with the labor for one's subsistence which is the punishment imposed upon man after the Fall. Calvinism, by transposing these salutary virtues of asceticism to secular life and by attributing them to the remunerated work of the "economic man" exercising his profession for his own subsistence and that of his family, changed the meaning and character of such work. It is this humble economic activity which is justified and almost spiritualized, not because of the resultant gain (indeed, almost in spite of this gain, if it exceeds the needs of an honest life), but because it is an expression of man's obedience to God. Thus work is no longer a penance, the deplorable consequence of the Fall; it is an exercise of piety like a prayer, and it is enjoined upon man not for his punishment, but for his salvation and for the glory of God.

Here we confront a new set of values of a new society. The edifice of the Catholic Church rested on the separation of the functions of "those who pray" from "those who toil." In its hierarchy of values, embodied within its own hierarchy, sanctity, meditation, and charity were placed very much above the utilitarian labor required for the needs of the body but not for the salvation of the soul. Calvin—like all reformers, but surpassing them all through his radicalism—destroyed this hierarchy of functions and virtues in order to gather them all into a single indissoluble unity, the unity of a Christian life which was demanded in total from every individual. The duty of every Christian, at one and the same time, is to pray, to read the Word of God and meditate on it, to earn his subsistence, to provide for the needs of his family, to lead a holy life in austerity and hard work, and, if God grants him this distinction, to fight and accept martyrdom for his faith; in short, to lead a meditative and active life simultaneously, according to his energies and his state of grace. The one mode of life can never dispense with the other, and both are set on the same high plane: "To work is to pray." There is no way to diminish this total demand: "Let those who hear the teaching of the Gospel prove they are Christians through sanctity of life."

It is useless to come back to the economic consequences —which have been elaborately discussed so many times—of this introduction of an ascetic discipline into ordinary life. Enrichment could be the only upshot of this combination of work and austerity—and the upshot of enrichment could only be the corruption of this hardworking and austere piety. Everything has been said on this subject and often too hastily. The reality, perhaps, may have exhibited a less logical character. Calvinism did not nullify itself simply by its economic successes; it developed a morality of success. In view of all the talk of "Calvinism and capitalism," it is striking that there has been so little talk of the role of capital in Calvinist morality. Capital found a place for itself only with difficulty in the traditional Catholic conception, because it was likened to riches. Riches and sanctity are incompatible, and the person who does not have the strength to renounce the goods of this world must at least atone for this through charity. This attitude could not be shared by Calvinism, which had sanctified the labor that enriches. The sanctity of life ordained by Calvin embraced prayer and work, meditation and active life; but what was the place of charity in this virtuous state? Before this question, most of the historians of Calvinism—and even Tawney himself—have covered their faces and talked of deviation, negation, and corruption of the original truth. Yet the reformers themselves speak very clearly in their writings, regulations, and mandates respecting the poor in Zurich as in Geneva. Evangelical charity as it had been understood and practiced by Christians with more or less sincerity for fifteen centuries—and we mean charity, not mutual provident societies, or assistance to victims of undeserved misfortune—had no place in the reformed city. The sanctification of work removed any justification for mendicancy and, by a counterstroke, also for almsgiving. Charity had no place in the city because pauperism had no place there. Whoever lives on alms insults the order instituted by God. He who works will find the wherewithal to nourish himself. He who does not work will not eat. Summed up in all its harshness, such was the fundamental rule of the new morality.

It is difficult to exaggerate the importance of such a concept in shaping societies. It is here that the imperative of activity in the world, the anathema hurled at all forms of idleness and of *vita passiva*, assumes its most rigorous significance. And if the Reformation, through the direct confrontation it posited between man and God, was able to contain the seeds of individualism, free thought, and even toleration, it must also be noted that the social concepts of the reformers—or at least of those in Switzerland and in

Geneva, whose teaching shaped the outlines of French Protestantism and penetrated far into the whole Anglo-Saxon world—were marked by a conformism of terrifying severity. It was not a question of maintaining order. Public authorities have never been charitable toward the poor, even if it is possible to contend that, in the Protestant countries, the new morality had pushed them to punish the poor more methodically. Rather, it was the whole attitude of the Christian community toward pauperism and mendicancy which constituted the great social problem until the nineteenth century; the attitude of heart and conscience itself which hardened against compassion. In Catholic piety, the poor man—whether voluntary or not, although the voluntarily poor more than the other—remained surrounded by a halo. It is the poor man who is the most beloved son of the Father, it is he who is the very image of Christ, born on the pile of straw in the manger not knowing where He was to rest His head; but the rich man will find it difficult to enter the Kingdom of Heaven. Mendicancy had its place in this view of the world as a state of grace, illustrated by the mendicant orders and by the sublime figure of Saint Francis, the "*poverello*" of Assisi. And almsgiving is the pre-eminent good work, for he who gives to the poor gives to God. Here too, the Reformation turned the table of values upside down, wounding as though by design all that apparently constituted the very essence of the Christian sensibility. For the Calvinist, begging was not meritorious but ignominious, and almsgiving or "unconsidered charity" not a good work but a sin, because by encouraging "idleness" it preserved this intolerable social plague instead of wiping it out. The only good work is work itself, which simultaneously suppresses the supplicant and the giver of alms. Very significantly, Zwingli held that it was neither the poor man nor the charitable man but the laborer who "in this world is the closest to the love of God"; and finally, it is the laborer alone who has the right to citizenship in the new Christian society. The house of the Father had many dwelling places; now it has only one—a workshop.

It is this harsh, negative, and inhuman side which is immediately striking. Too much has been said about the extreme severities of the heartless rectitude, a veritable perversion of the Christian spirit, to which this new table of values led, and about the pretexts it provided for the abominable good conscience of the just—whose very well-being attested to their virtue—before the spectacle of misery, viewed as the manifest sign of vice. From generation to generation, in the Puritan and Calvinist sects, the spirit of brotherhood and of human solidarity rose in revolt against an orthodoxy that sided so easily with the smug and the satisfied. But these revolts themselves never affected the central pillar of Calvinist morality, the ethical pre-eminence of labor, glorified equally by the exponents of "capitalist" trends and the exponents of the more radical "anti-capitalist" trends of Calvinism. It was possible to fight against social inequalities and the exploitation of the workers in a society molded by this moral imperative; but it was not possible to return either to a passive, obliging compliance or to the medieval view of humanity. For therein lay the counterpart of this harshness, which was more accessible to reason than to feeling. Poverty is not scandalous to the charitable mind. Almsgiving is compassion's immemorial and resigned gesture before eternal and irremediable misery, accepted as such by the giver as well as by the wretch who stretches out his hand. To reject the immemorial practice of almsgiving, to denounce passive misery as a public scandal and a plague to be stamped out, was to opt for and impose effort, exertion, and endeavor. It was a transformation, not a destruction, of the social sense. Calvinist morality involved the obligation (the significance of which perhaps it did not always truly measure) of coming to grips with the immense problem of pauperism not by charity but by the discipline of work, by social organization, by education at work, by education in general—since mendicancy was for these reformers primarily a character defect, just as work was primarily a school for character building—and, finally, often obtained in laws affecting the poor, by forced labor.

In theory, this ethic can be realized in a Communist society as well as in a society based on private property, and in this sense, we can easily find in this original Calvinist society, this enormous laicized monastery extended to the whole city, analogies with the present day. But this is a *jeu d'esprit*. Historically, Calvinism became embodied in bourgeois societies and raised work to the pre-eminent bourgeois value. If work is a duty, it is also a right which Christian society cannot refuse to the poor of good will. If for a man able to work asking for charity is a badge of dishonor, as well as a form of "blackmail," which he must resist, then he can demand work in the very name of this sacred code. Consequently, for the man of means the pre-eminent good work, no longer now almsgiving, is to place work in the hands of the idle. By virtue of this fact the capitalist receives an eminent function in God's plan of salvation, and can consider himself as the chosen instrument of His will.

If most of the relationships between Calvinism and capitalism pointed out so far have been indirect, involuntary, *a posteriori* economic rationalizations of a wholly ethical teaching, and therefore not to be greatly relied upon, this last relationship is very direct and very evident, flowing without any dialectic whatsoever from the sanctification of work. One of the original achievements of Calvinism was to have given the capitalist the means to glorify God not through donations and pious legacies, or by giving up his goods, but by the very exercise of his economic function. But this function was an obligation, and here we need precise definitions, because the very notion of capitalism is not altogether the same in societies pervaded by the Calvinist spirit and the others. The capitalist who is honored in Calvinist society is not the idle rich man, landholder, or rentier, nor the financier or speculator. He is the "active capitalist," the provider of work, the entrepreneur who puts his capital to work by extending opportunities to laborers, the merchant who opens outlets for trades and crafts. And his merit is measured almost according to the number of hands for which he has provided occupation. To be sure, Calvinist attempts, like that of Baxter, to elaborate a casuistry of the "good" or "bad" capitalist, ran aground even more quickly and lamentably than those of the Catholic doctors to fix the limits of licit or illicit profit. But there was no need of casuistry in order to preserve firmly in the public mind the essential criterion furnished by the Calvinist ethic of work. We must likewise be wary of a systematization which would do violence to the teaching of the Reformation by introducing perspectives that were wholly alien to it. At the basis of the social order ushered in by the Reformation was a radically pessimistic judgment of human nature. Obviously it would be paradoxical to search in Calvin's thought for the least trace of that optimism of the industrial age which was able to glimpse the goal of abolishing poverty by the rational organization of work. His concerns were far removed from dreams of earthly happiness and general well-being. In the eradication of pauperism through work, moral reasoning was in the end confused—precisely because of its efficacy—with economic reasoning. Nevertheless, moral reasoning remained at the base even up to the mistaken ideas of utilitarianism and of "justification through success."

It was certainly a powerful leavening of industrial capitalism which simultaneously provided the pioneers and the captains of industry with their impetus and justification and habituated a whole population to the harsh discipline of work. For this leaven could not be efficacious in a hostile dough. Indeed, without this moral substratum, the effort at industrialization common to all Europe from the seventeenth to the eighteenth century had to come from above, dictated by *raison d'État;* but it could be realized only by operating against the current.

Reading Colbert's correspondence—in which he rages indiscriminately against "idleness," almsgiving, pilgrimages, religious holidays, convents, rentiers, and lawyers—we realize how much the economist in him dreamed of a society of Calvinist customs, of a reversed set of values, and how much he despaired over the widespread and dogged resistance he encountered from the institutions and public spirit of a society at once Catholic, nobiliary, and "archmaniacal." The upshot was a confusion of values which led to calling workhouses, where forced labor was ordained, "*ateliers de charité*," and of which an almost ridiculous example is Colbert's attempt to force on convents the obligation to give work, in the form of wool for knitting stockings, instead of alms, to the poor who knocked on their doors. Colbert's tragedy, in his successes as in his failures, lay in the fact that he was forced to replace the absent "capitalist spirit" by bureaucratic interference with the stratagems of privileges, monopolies, and concessions, by capital outlays provided by the State, and by official regulation. From this point of view, Colbertism appears as a substitute for Calvinism in the sphere of social organization.

In the spiritual sphere, Jansenism offered an even more curious phenomenon: an upper bourgeoisie which, after the failure of the Reformation—and within the Catholic Church itself—re-created from out of nothing a doctrine perilously close to Calvinism in all its original rigor and austerity, a kind of "French Puritanism." The striking survival of the spirit of Port-Royal after the destruction of its propaganda center and the dispersion or surrender of its spokesmen, and above all in the "*bourgeoisie de robe*" and in the parlement [1] of Paris in which it had entrenched itself as in a fortress, attests paradoxically the affinity between the Calvinist ethic and a certain bourgeois spirit, and also the divergent path that was taken in France by this bourgeoisie. For in the Jansenism of these lawyers, rentiers, and officeholders there was no trace of the "capitalist spirit" in the sense in which we have defined it, as opposed to the rentier mentality, and no leaven issued from it with respect to the industrial economy. Colbert's State capitalism and the spirit of thrift and austerity of the Jansenist bourgeoisie did not meet; indeed, they ignored one another. For, obviously, "work-ethic" could not govern a society which placed success through work infinitely lower than that through birth; in which a career in the hierarchy of power had distinctly the upper hand, in dignity as in the enjoyment of material goods, over any productive endeavor; and in which the reign of law did not protect men who were creators of

[1] The royal "parliaments" were high courts of justice, membership in which was sold as private property and had become hereditary in a very closed circle of officeholding families. This venality and the heredity of high offices were characteristic of the French "*bourgeoisie d'ancient régime*."—Trans.

wealth from the arbitrariness of State power. The social ethic can never be separated from the political regime. It is not only for want of spiritual support but also, even more bluntly, for want of justice that many societies, today as well as yesterday, find it so difficult to implant in their midst the industrial society, which in the last analysis is a work-centered society.

CHAPTER THREE

Lending at Interest or The Competence of Theology in Economic Matters

Among the questions raised by the debate on the relationships between the "Protestant ethic" and the "capitalist spirit," those formulated with the greatest theoretical precision unfortunately are often those to which, given the present state of research or the very nature of the interrogation, it is not possible to give a conclusive answer; or else it must be objected that too many pieces are missing from the record in other areas. In the first place, a comparable explanation, with similar criteria, of "Catholic" capitalism and finance, whose existence, albeit a vigorous one, seems to have been forgotten. Finally, the problem may be posed too abstractly to be of use in the interrogation of the evidence furnished by history. How can we hope to weigh the attitudes of the churches toward material life in a precise way, inasmuch as each one, by turns or even simultaneously, assumed the most contradictory attitudes when it was not seeking refuge in equivocations and vague moral exhortations? Or how can we pronounce, with a full knowledge of facts, on the basic motivations and presumed religious dilemmas of businessmen who most often have left behind only invoices and scraps of bookkeeping records? At best, in exceptional instances, it is possible to furnish case studies; but only a context of particular facts, reported and analyzed in detail, can save these from the danger of being used for unwarranted generalizations. The cases in which theology pronounced itself without ambiguity on a clearly posed question of economic technique are rare indeed. Herein, in fact, lies the exceptional interest of the controversy over "lending at interest."

Among the many works published during the celebrations commemorating the birth and death of the reformer of Geneva, one of the most remarkable is the exposition of Calvin's economic and social thought by André Biéler, a theologian who is also an economist. Biéler took great pains to make a systematic search into the enormous and difficult maze of Calvin's works for direct evidence of his attitude toward problems of economic and social life, and to put the original texts before the reader and, equally important, to acquaint him with the theological context of the positions taken by Calvin.[1] Nowhere is what we call Calvin's social doctrine expounded in the form of a body of coherent ar-

[1] André Biéler, *La Pensée économique et sociale de Calvin* (Geneva, 1959).

guments; it must be reconstructed, with all the risks entailed in an undertaking of this kind, from the affirmations scattered in his sermons and his commentaries, which were always presented in the form of exegeses of Scripture and not as lessons in economics—but exegeses made with a view to coping with the difficulties and moral problems of the scattered Calvinist communities and of the besieged city of which he was the guide and councillor. Calvin speaks as a pastor and as a teacher of the Christian religion, and what he says, more or less incidentally, respecting the economic behavior of men is always an exegesis and an explication of the teaching of the Scriptures as they relate to human conduct. This in itself precludes any possibility of indulgence in, or of compromise with, purely material motives. However open Calvin's mind may have been (the only one of the Reformers who was the son of a bourgeois—but a bourgeois who held office) toward the society of his time, neither the body of theological doctrine nor the sermon or catechism lends itself to an analysis of economic facts considered from the economic point of view. The preacher's thought was always stirred by contact with the sacred texts he interpreted which were always the same and which imposed their archaic vocabulary and their eternal view of things upon him, and even if they spoke of the gestures and actions of material life, viewed them only in terms of the soul's salvation, not of their materials utilitarian effect. Therefore, we should be little surprised if finally in examining all these questions we find a Calvin less different from the doctors of the Church than what has been said. What stands out in this wholly theological thought, curiously but logically, is a declaration of the incompetence of the theologian on a most delicate question of economic technique: "usury."

This break with scholastic doctrine, this so-called watershed in economic thought, has often been elucidated—most rightly and justly by Tawney. Nevertheless, it seems to me that the scholars have not perceived its exact significance, which does not lie in the fact that it granted a license to usurious practices, or even in the recognition of a mode of profit which for Calvin remains odious and contrary to nature,[2] but in the fact of its wholly novel intellectual rigor.

As on many other points that did not essentially interest him, Calvin took up a position on lending money at interest because the subject was unavoidable. The question had been posed permanently. The doctors of theology had held

[2] "It is also a very strange and shameful thing, that while all other men obtain the means of their subsistence with great toil, while husbandmen fatigue themselves by their daily occupations, and artisans serve the community by the sweat of their brow, and merchants employ themselves in labors, and also expose themselves to many inconveniences and dangers, that the moneymongers should sit at their ease without doing anything, and receive tribute from the labor of other people"—Calvin, *Commentary on the Book of Psalms*, 1557, in Biéler, *op. cit.*, p. 466. R. H. Tawney, *Religion and the Rise of Capitalism* (London, 1926; New York: Mentor Books, 1947) called attention to the fierce struggle conducted by the Consistory under Calvin and Beza against usury and monopoly, and makes short shrift of the legend of a Calvin indulgent to usurers: "Legends are apt, however, to be as right in substance as they are wrong in detail, and both its critics and its defenders were correct in regarding Calvin's treatment of capital as a watershed. What he did was to change the plane on which the discussion was conducted by treating the ethics of moneylending, not as a matter to be decided by appeal to a special body of doctrine on the subject of usury, but as a particular case of the general problem of the social relations of a Christian community, which had to be solved in the light of existing circumstances." Nevertheless, Tawney is mistaken when he asserts that, for Calvin: "The financier is not a pariah, but a useful member of society"—p. 95. If Calvin admitted that interest could have a legitimate economic function, he formally, totally, and on many occasions expelled from his city any person whose profession was moneylending: "Any man, therefore, who by regular profession gives money for profit, must be entirely cast out of the company and society of men"—*Commentaries on Ezekiel*, written on the eve of Calvin's death; quoted in Biéler, *op. cit.*, p. 468; see also p. 459 and *passim*.

forth on the subject voluminously and Geneva, former city of fairs then in decline, enjoyed—like Lyon, its rival—one of those exceptional regimes which the Catholic Church had always tolerated in order to help markets and merchants. Two centuries before Calvin, the bishop had granted the city the unrestricted freedom to "practice moneylending," and city laws regulated the rate of interest. The question, therefore, was not posed on the practical level but on that of principles. Was it necessary, in the name of the faith and by looking the other way, to maintain the solemn and futile condemnation of something that was customary and overtly admitted in practice? Was theology supposed to feign the strict interdiction of something it did not even try to prevent? Calvin, against his own intentions, grudgingly involved himself in this debate knowing full well that whatever he might say his words would be distorted in every direction. But once he was forced to speak, he did so with an incomparable frankness and freshness, sundering the frightening knot of confusion, exegesis, casuistry, and evasions in which scholastic doctrine had tied this vexatious problem.[3] Rather than examining his conclu-

[3] Calvin made a pronouncement on this problem for the first time in 1545, ten years after his arrival in Geneva, in a private letter to a friend (published in 1575 by Théodore Beza): "I have not yet experienced it, but I have learned by the examples of others how perilous it is to give a response to the question about which you ask for counsel . . . if we permit it in the least degree, many immediately will take unbridled license under this cover. . . ." He publicly expounded his views in the last ten years of his life, in his biblical commentaries of 1554–1564; Biéler, *op. cit.*, pp. 543–547, provides a chronological résumé of them. All the citations that follow are taken from this passage of his book. To understand the particular urgency of the question of loans for production, we must remember the exceptional situation in Geneva at the time of the Reformation. The influx of refugees, stripped of all their belongings, but able to resume a commercial or industrial activity like that which they had left behind, created an intense demand for capital, for productive employments, as well as an enormous need for charitable assistance. Calvin's letter, published posthumously on the

sions, which on most points coincide with traditional morality, we should heed his lucid and direct reasoning:

> The Gospel says: "Give ye to one another without expectation of aught in return." This utterance was misunderstood when it was restricted to moneylenders. But Christ does demand a gratuitous liberality from His disciples, that they take every care to help the poor, from whom we cannot expect any recompense. . . . Thereby Christ's words are equivalent to saying that He commanded the subvention of the poor rather than of the rich. We do not yet see that all moneylending is forbidden.

In fact, the question at issue is not lending at interest, or lending pure and simple, but giving without the idea of repayment or recovery. The Christian is invited to give without reward or hope of reward, if his gift is to please God. This is the rule of charity. But nobody is ignorant of the fact that the merchant or the peasant who brings his products to the market does not do so in order to give them away, but to sell them at a price. This is the rule of exchange of goods, which is that of reciprocity and, as such, of equity. Of the two, one must be chosen: either we admit only the law of charity as a rule of economic life, in which case we close the market; or we admit the market, in which case we must not require that it be ruled by the law of the free gift. The injunction *Mutuum date nihil sperantes* does not refer to economic exchanges. Do Deuteronomy and the prophets forbid moneylending between the brethren of Israel while condoning the practice with foreigners? Here Calvin boldly has recourse to the historical and philological

morrow of the Massacre of Saint Bartholomew, had the almost revolutionary merit of distinguishing these two forms of "assistance"—the confusion between which lay at the base of all scholastic teaching.

criticism of sacred Scripture: what is at issue here is a "political" law, namely, one of circumstance, which cannot be transposed mechanically from one epoch and one people to another.

> It is well known that usury was forbidden to the ancient people. But at the same time we must confess that it was a part of the judicial law which God appointed for the Jews in particular; whence it follows that usuries are not to be condemned today, save wherein they contravene equity and brotherly union. . . .
>
> This Hebrew word, *Neshek,* which David employs, being derived from another word which means to bite, sufficiently shows that usuries are condemned insofar as they involve in them or lead to a license or robbing and plundering our fellow men. . . . Since the wall which formerly separated the Jews from the pagans has been torn down, our condition today is different. This is why we must have mercy for everyone without exception so that we may keep ourselves from plundering and devouring the poor, and we must preserve a similar equity toward all . . .

Does the fact remain, nevertheless, that the rich man who exploits the needy man by lending him money at interest violates the laws of the Old and New Testament, and the morality of pagans and Christians? Calvin makes this condemnation his own with all the merciless severity he can muster. But what of the man who lends to another who is not in need, is indeed even richer than himself? It would be absurd to set against him the law of charity in a transaction in which misery plays no role: "If a rich and affluent man, desirous of purchasing a good small farm, borrows a part of the sum of his neighbor, why could not the lender derive some profit from the income until he has recovered his money? Many similar cases occur every day, in which with respect to equity, moneylending is no worse than a purchase."

Finally, we come to the heavy artillery of the scholastics, Aristotle's celebrated argument as repeated by the fathers and doctors of theology: "Interest is contrary to nature, because money is sterile and does not engender money." Sophistry, says Calvin.

> To be sure, I confess what children see, namely, that if you lock money up in a coffer it will be sterile. . . . I receive a revenue for renting a house: does the money grow because of it? Is not money more fruitful in goods than in any conceivable possession whatsoever? What? When one buys a field, does it remain to be seen whether money engenders money? How do merchants increase their goods? Nobody borrows from us on the condition that he is then to lock up the idle money without making it engender profit . . . this is why the fruit is not money but revenue. Therefore, we must conclude that such subtleties move us at first sight, but if we consider them more closely they vanish by themselves, because they have nothing solid within them.
>
> I conclude now that we must judge usuries not according to some certain and particular sentence of God, but only according to the rule of equity. Now the summary of all this, in short, is that providing we have properly engraved in our hearts this rule of equity which Christ prescribes for us, that each does unto his neighbors as he will have done unto himself, it will not be necessary to enter into lengthy disputes concerning usury.

This rule of "equity" was severe. We shall not hark back to the strict and remarkably effective ordinance which fixed the maximum rate of interest at 5 per cent under Calvin and Beza, nor to the moral imperatives that were strictly enforced: prohibition against requiring interest from needy persons, the primacy of labor over capital, the banishment from the city of anyone who set himself up as a moneylender. Hostility in principle remained intact; the Christian who goes to market cannot be prevented from acting more like a merchant than a Christian. The mind upon reflection resigns itself to this circumstance, but not the conscience. But the rule of equity was a moral rule of reciprocal and social utility. "In the sixth place let us not concern ourselves only with the private convenience of the person with whom we are dealing, but let us also consider what is expedient for the public." As for the ordinance inspired by this maxim, it was merely a judicial measure, particular to a given social body, and not an unalterable law of God: the theologian's greatness lay in making theology irrelevant.

This was an intellectual event long before it became an economic event: nothing indicates that there were immediate consequences for the economy or for economic behavior, good or bad, as a result of this break with a tradition that had long been illusory. Except for imposing greater severity, Calvin did not release usury upon the world. Such an assertion can be ventured only if we voluntarily choose to close our eyes to the most flagrant realities of Europe before the Reformation. It is probable that the practice of lending money at a moderate interest helped Italian refugees and Huguenots to set up their industries and trading offices again in Geneva; it is probable, and of great moment, that the same practice in England furthered the slow elaboration of new techniques of credit, and in particular of discount, which were to give that country such a headstart in the eighteenth century. But a very exhaustive inquiry would have to be conducted on these two points before any pronouncements could be made based on a real knowledge of the facts. On the other hand, what is certain is that the legitimation of interest by Calvin in no way led to a flowering of the "profession of moneylending," which indeed did not flourish in Protestant countries; the figure of the usurer belongs to the imagery of medieval economics which, here and there, was extended up to modern times. A tenacious misunderstanding has confused matters here. Until quite recently the profession of banker, as exercised up to the end of the eighteenth century, has been one of those most poorly understood by historians. Let us simply recall that the "Protestant bankers" under the *ancien régime* did not practice moneylending at interest in a way that was different, or more general, or earlier in time than their Catholic colleagues, under perfectly "canonic" conditions and forms—maritime credit, commercial credit implicit in the commerce of bills of exchange, and, more rarely or later in time, settlement of annuities and credit through acceptance or advance on bonds. The material economic repercussions of the admission of the principle of interest by Calvin have been exaggerated and at times invented out of whole cloth. Inevitably, this has been accompanied by an underestimation of its intellectual significance. Calvin did not destroy the dikes that had been erected against the profit motive, he destroyed one that had been erected against the knowledge of the facts of economic life.

What was no doubt expressed first of all in Calvin's sorrowful recourse to common sense is the primordial demand for veracity and clarity which was one of the motivations of the Reformation: to effect a harmony between word and deed, between the morality preached and the morality practiced, and finally, between man and himself. Calvin saw nothing that had not been seen by others before him;

as one who had pulled the weeds from dogma, he could and dared to say it. Let us note carefully that by so doing he was making neither a moral nor even less an economic judgment; it was strictly a theological pronouncement. Calvin was in no sense concerned with economic theory. But in applying the trenchant and critical reason of his juridicial culture to the textual analysis of sacred Scripture, recognized as the sole source of authority, in order to cleanse it of the accumulations that encrusted it from the work of generations of exegesis, he made a significant contribution on one particular point. He disentangled the scholastic confusion that existed between the evangelical imperative of charity toward the poor and weak, the Hebrew law, which is an historic law, and the Aristotelian doctrine of money, which he dismissed as a human conjecture. By this wholly theological analysis, Calvin incidentally enabled economic reasoning to free itself from the fetters of dogma.

If Calvin had no presentiment of the consequences, he nevertheless felt their gravity: it required immense intellectual courage and almost self-denial on the part of a minister of the Holy Gospel to sunder this knot, which was an amalgam of the evangelical worship of angels, folk sentiment, and tradition now two thousand years old, and which scholasticism in particular had refused to disentangle by maintaining (in the face of all evidence) the principle of the free loan, a hybrid gift-loan. Nevertheless, this same scholasticism was always ready to multiply the exceptions and specific cases in order to make it possible for financiers and merchants to get around the problem in practice. As a result of this confusion, the accumulations of commentaries and exegeses respecting the word "*mutuum*," which had fallen to the level of colloquial Latin, had glossed over the simplicity of brotherly charity and of *periculum sortis* (the risk that the borrowed sum would not be returned) into *damnum emergens* (e.g., a lender might himself be compelled to borrow at a high rate through the failure of the debtor to repay) and into *lucrum cessans* (the gain that which the lender might have deprived himself of by handing money over to another). Consequently, the dogmatic condemnation of "usury," breached from all sides, was degraded into a cloak of hypocrisy flung charitably over all the tortuous and shady practices of true usury.

By its refusal to acknowledge the reality of an economic life, which obeyed material motivations rooted in inevitable self-interest, theology had *a priori* forbidden to itself the less exalting and much more difficult effort of introducing simple honesty into the area of human behavior. And in this area, as in others, the consequence of this persistent confusion between the spiritual and the temporal was the corruption of the spiritual itself. The revolt of the outraged consciences and the aspiration to clarity of which the Reformation was one aspect had been directed precisely against this "Babylonian" confusion; ready in turn, however, to stumble into the same confusion itself. The absurd episode which made a tormented Luther the standard bearer of the revolt had been the most shocking example of a contamination which no longer spared anything as sacred. This bank for deposits and clearings, established by the Roman Church on the treasury of grace stored up by Christ and by the saints, a clearinghouse for the surpluses of sin and the surpluses of sanctity conceived on the model of payments in the market place, placed its dividend and redemption coupons, redeemable in the world beyond the grave, on public sale across the length and breadth of the empire, through the agency of the Fuggers. What at the start had been an involuntary confusion, respectful of tradition, had been compounded into the crassest cynicism.

In the material areas of life no one questioned the fact that the acknowledgment of a positive, normal and licit role for moneylending of a noncharitable and remunerative character was crucial—even though its effects were not to be felt until much later—for the organization and generalization of credit indispensable to the rise of the modern economy. On the other hand, at the conscious level of thought, this acknowledgment of the propriety of interest seems to have been a flimsy progress, if it can be called that at all: a concession made to human greed, the existence of which nobody had ever doubted, least of all the doctors of the Church, but against which they had fought. But was it only a question of abdication before the lust for lucre? Have we sufficiently perceived the enormous role of the calculation of interest, not as a tribute levied upon the labor of others but as a bookkeeping operation in the rationalization of economic life? An economy—even one of a monetary and mercantile character—which ignores or feigns to ignore the calculation of interest in all its forms, interest and discount, accumulation and amortization, is immobile in its mentality, if not in reality, because it denies time. It is static, not dynamic. Money provides it with a general measure of values, most often fragile and unstable, but valid at each given moment; but it is exclusively the circulation of interest applied to these values, by allotting them a fixed date and a variable positive or negative coefficient, which adds to them the measure of time and movement; yesterday's or tomorrow's value is not today's, and the delay is expressed in percentages of capital, the future discounted in actual value. This is not the place to examine something as complex as the rate of interest, which fundamentally is a summary arithmetical expression of very complicated relations of force. What is important here is that, through its normal application, chronometry made its entry into economic accounting. A whole economic mentality, with its qualities—and its deficiencies—of precision and harshness, of perpetual and mechanical movement, rested upon this mode of calculation in which, in fact, time itself is converted into money value, in which the interest runs without pause as by the hour of the clock, forcing man to run with it. This is "capitalist man," a totally different being from the rich of all times—indeed, their polar opposite.

This system of measures, in which all is inscribed in homogeneous value and time coordinates, was not a new invention. The Italian bankers of the fourteenth century, who calculated the interests due to them most carefully and had overtly applied the system with remarkable perfection, and the following centuries in which everything was muddled in the mysterious alchemy of the "art of exchange," sheltered from theological prohibitions, marked a distinct step backward in this respect. It appears that the Reformation, at least on the European continent, in no way contributed to any kind of technical improvement. At the end of the eighteenth century still, the calculation of interest worked out by bankers dealing in drafts and commissions—with their flexible delays of acceptance, periods of grace, and protests for nonpayment—seemed to be a very obscure operation, and to be applied episodically and with a remarkable absence of system. It is said that the interest was "implicit" in the rates of exchange, and this is true. But it was concealed from the eyes of the exchange broker under the "speculative" gain, which itself was only implicit. Interest became clearly discernible only through the institutionalization of the technique of the discount, which was imported from England by reformer-economists such as Turgot, at first against the resistance of the bankers whose habits it disturbed. The "speculative" gain was not figured for an exact given day, but by calculating liberally one dispensed with calculating exactly: fortunes were made by many businessmen who were no more expert in mathematics than a farm hand.

Economic obscurantism favors the rapacious men and shady financiers who often can turn things to their advantage more conveniently and, if you like, more "humanely" in a context of obscurity and confusion. It was on the businessman proper that economic rationality first of all imposed harsher conditions, clearer accounts, and, in principle at least, more honest practices. If in France, as in Italy, no law or any tribunal under the *ancien régime* recognized the legitimacy of interest or "sure gain" stipulated in advance in excess of the principal of the sum loaned; if whole libraries of scholastic and juridical treatises on trade and exchange explained everything save this petty, negligible detail of knowing how a banker or a merchant could ever even subsist in his calling on the basis of complete self-denial, let alone gain the smallest penny, then evidently it was no less well known that interest was present in the contracts and the exchanges, but surreptitiously, tortuously, unavowed and rejected from consciousness. The moneylender could exist without making confession of his trade, and generally he even felt more comfortable in such a situation. But economic rationality would not be introduced on the sly. A system of measure is not created by cheating; it was only by being exorcized once and for all, and by being admitted into society as an economic norm, that interest could serve as an instrument of measure. By lifting the ancient curse on interest, Calvin opened up the way for a new mentality which he neither foresaw nor desired, but which nevertheless was not unrelated to his rigor of mind, or even to the "rule of equity."

The path was opened to a new mentality, not a new technique; it marked the transition from a "qualitative," "sentimental," or "artistic" conception to a "quantitative" or "scientific" conception. Or, expressed more simply, from approximation to precision, from game to calculation, from immobile time to time by the clock, from gathering booty to the methodical accumulation of capital. Whatever definition is chosen, it relates to a sobriety or, if you prefer, to an intellectual and moral aridity in the practice of a profession rather than to any particularity of religious conception. By admitting and confessing that economic activity obeys economic motivations, which are not cursed as such, and by striving to rationalize and moralize these motivations—with the underlying error of supposing them all exorcized, reasonable, and admissible—the "Calvinist" spirit in economic matters as its contemporaries distinguished it among "Genevans" is in fact related to the "spirit of capitalism." But if rationality had its source in a moral exigence, it itself did not contain this exigence. Emancipated in its turn, rationality became a pure instrument of reasoning indifferent to its object, at the service of anyone who availed himself of it. This new mentality, in the last analysis, was but the mentality of an economy of money and exchanges, which calmly recognized itself as such, instead of viewing itself as a depraved natural economy.

Prophets of Israel and moralists of all times, learned men of the Church, councillors, and reformers would not have debated this question of interest so much if it was not a key one, inseparable from the whole view of the social order. If Calvin, alone even among the reformers, could come around to admitting the legitimacy of interest according to the "rule of equity," it was only by rejecting, at the same time, an entire immemorial imagery of poverty and compassion which viewed the relationship between the lender and the borrower only as a relationship between a rich man and a man in need; his decisive objection, levelled like an arrow at the ignorant scholars, is voiced thus: "And how about the man who lends to another who is not in need, indeed is even richer than he?" A common-sense objection indeed, but to the common run of understanding it was seen initially as contrary to all common sense, contrary to all normal behavior, to any natural hierarchical order, an objection of sophists drawn from an exceptional, aberrant case. It was not from this unusual viewpoint, in which in fact theology and morality were irrelevant, that theologians and moralists had envisioned lending. To raise this apparent anomaly into an economic rule was to turn all the data of the problem upside down. This simple paradoxical question contained the discovery of credit not as a work of charity toward a starving man asking for bread, but as a loan of capital to a person who would render it fruitful in his commercial, navigational, or manufacturing undertakings, and who would draw from it even more than the interest he offered; in short, also the discovery of circulating capital as a factor of production. This discovery may appear not to have been difficult in the sixteenth century, in view of the fabulous profits reaped by the wholly new trade that was being plied in faraway places, involving large amounts of borrowed capital whose owners were repaid without difficulty at very high rates of interest. But it was precisely one of these "specific cases" which had always been recognized by scholastic doctrine. The loan to the sponsors of a risky venture, with its very high interest rates expressly stipulated in the event of success, was justified by the *periculum sortis,* since the lender shared in the risks of the enterprise. Trade, to be sure, multiplied similar anomalies, around which the exceptions of the casuist doctors accumulated. But to generalize these mercantile aberrations, to apply to a whole society the law of exception of a suspect project of adventurers living on the margin of society, and, worse still, to admit the stipulation of an interest fixed in advance, or "sure gain," without the justification of an exceptional risk, was equivalent to dethroning the natural order of economy and society.

Intellectual honesty was not the only thing at stake; today as yesterday, natural reflection must do violence to itself in order to acknowledge the mechanical rules of a monetary economy. The principles of economic rationality are abstract principles and are applicable only to a highly abstract image of an "objective" reality organized by reason, as distant from perceptible reality as is the Keplerian universe. The market economy of urban civilization, in which everything is done through calculation and mutual contract and nothing through nature, is abstract and organized. This is not true of a rural economy, subject to the rhythm of the seasons, rains, hailstorms, and droughts. A mobile economy and an immobile economy; a commercial and already industrial economy marked by the rapid circulation of goods and capital, and a primary economy patiently subject to delays and uncertainties of harvests; an economy of free movement and an economy attached to the soil, regardless of the social regime: these are not successive stages of the economy, but two forms of economy which co-exist and which do not operate under the same laws. The circulation of capital, credit, and interest find their place in one and have never found a natural function in the other. Land is not a capital of which the peasant can freely dispose; it is the land, property, or real estate upon which rests the economic and social edifice, that encumbers the land with all its burdens, whose yield is always uncertain; and this land could be assimilated into commercial capital only by violent stratagems. François Quesnay perceived this clearly in his article "Farmers" written for the *Encyclopédie*.

> Agriculture, unlike trade, does not have credit as a resource. A merchant can borrow in order to buy merchandise, or he can buy on credit, because he will recover the profit and the purchase capital in a short time; he can repay the sums that he borrows. On the other hand, the husbandman can obtain only the profit of the payments in advance which he has made . . . the capital remains in order to sustain the same agricultural undertaking; thus he cannot borrow it so as to return it on terms fixed in advance.[4]

To mortgage land almost always signifies contracting an irredeemable debt, the interest on which is a perpetual income and, in reality, a quit rent to the person, who has thus become the virtual proprietor of the land. All the more reason, therefore, why in hierarchical societies based on agriculture, in which all the economic relations and the entire distribution of the social product are determined entirely by relationships of dependence, it should normally occur that the peasant at the bottom of the social scale falls into debt. This only reinforces his dependence and the weight of the burden which crush him. It also occurs, to be sure, that the lord falls into debt, but then the entire system is in a state of crisis. Usury questions the social order itself, and it becomes a matter of great urgency to apply remedies in order to stem the threat of subversion.

A history of the moral and legal attitude of societies toward the problem of interest is perhaps best suited to shed-

[4] François Quesnay, *Oeuvres* (Paris: I.N.E.D., 1958), Vol. II, p. 447.

ding light on the evolution and permanence of economic mentalities.[5] The concept of capital, "*cheptel*," productive of interest seems to have been normal and authentically natural in pastoral societies, those first societies of "capitalist" and conquering nomads, with their literally movable capital in the form of roaming and prolific flocks. And it seems to have been transformed into a scourge in all sessile societies of husbandmen where it introduced itself, or was introduced by conquerors of pastoral origin. It is expressed in the muffled or strident wailing of the crushed peoples of the ancient Orient. The legend of Joseph in Egypt sums up in a gripping vignette the enslavement of the peasants of the Nile region after falling into ruinous debt in times of bad harvests. Even without the help of a charismatic domination, the reign of the "usurer" over the rice farmers of Asia has been so similar to a seigneurial regime that historians and sociologists have often confused the two by speaking, for example, of "Chinese feudalism." Classical Greece with its urban democracies—each of which included its agricultural "suburb" in the political and economic organization of teeming regional markets based on individual and independent enterprises—alone among the ancient civilizations seems to have practiced productive credit and interest without attaching a curse to it, satisfied with correcting its effects periodically by the revolutionary cancellation of farm debts. Through the Roman Empire that long-drawn-out agony which beset the antique world, in which any opportunity for free labor and economic independence had once again been crushed, first under the slave armies and subsequently under the weight of the State, the Christian

[5] The most lucid and consistent exposition that I have found anywhere is the work by Fritz M. Heichelheim, *Wirtschaftsgeschichte des Altertums* (Leyden, 1938–1939). An impressive, synthetic treatment of the subject.

West inherited all of the imprecations of the antique world —from the prophets of Israel to the Stoics and mystics of the Byzantine Empire—against money in general and usury in particular.

The condemnation of usury was only one of the aspects, if dogmatically the most elaborate, of the curse which weighed upon money, money dealers, and all the professionals of the monetary and mercantile economy; upon the merchants who transformed everything into money, as well as upon the money changers and bankers; in short, upon all those who, although they were neither lords nor clerics, through some shady practice managed to create an income for themselves without toiling in the fields, or at least by practicing a craft. "Whoever buys things in order to derive profit from them by transmitting them as they are and without alteration, such a person is a merchant who is driven from the temple of God," says the decree of Gratian.[6] These were men and activities on the margin of Christian society, an edifice anchored in the soil and raising itself degree by degree to the Lords of the Church and of the State, like a tree in which—as though in sacrifice to the will of God—the nourishing sap in the form of tithes, rents, quit rents rose from the root to the branch tops. Moneymen and merchants were viewed as spoilers who diverted this sap from its natural course. If the guild labor of the cities (degenerating since the fourteenth century after a turbulent outbreak) was integrated at last into this society and, with it, so far as possible, the local market, thereby bringing the producers and consumers of the city and sur-

[6] *Qui comparet rem ut illam ipsam integram et immutatam daudo lucretur, ille est mercator qui de templo Dei ejicitur.* Deir. Grat. C. II, called 88; the term "usury" is not applied only to interest, but to any commercial profit exceeding the just price; to deals to be settled in the future on specific account days; to monopolies; etc.

rounding countryside into personal contact, this never applied to international trade. The privileges of the cities where fairs were held involved, more or less explicitly, the "privilege of usury," consular jurisdiction through which merchants asserted their own law distinct from any other, the juridical and moral discrimination always observed between merchants, on the one hand, and all other individuals on the other, placing them outside the common law of Christianity: tiny trading republics on the fringes of medieval society.

The Church, which was in no way *a priori* hostile to trade and whose protection to it made possible the slow rebirth of medieval marketplaces, merely codified in a body of doctrine a "natural" economic policy much more ancient than Christianity. Aristotle's *Politics*, whose chapters on money and exchange inspired the whole economic science of the Scholastics, established a fundamental distinction between "economy"—in the specific sense of the word domestic and natural economy—and "chrematistics," the economy of money and of trade, artificial in character, outside the framework of nature and of human dimensions, which he abhorred. It is in this sense that the Physiocrats were able to call themselves Economists and only Economists, in contradistinction to all those who reasoned in terms of money and trade. These two worlds are so far apart that François Quesnay, the last great Aristotelian of economic science, regularly combined as "self-evident" the concepts of economy, society, and State. He spoke of agricultural monarchies as being the only truly constituted societies, in contrast to the mercantile republics placed either on the margin of these monarchies or within them as nations distinct from the nation, alien and parasitical elements in the body of the economic society, and necessarily having the Republican form of organization even under the Sultan or the King of France. What we have here, in fact, are two archetypical images of society so radically different, so mutually exclusive, and each so "self-evident" to those whose imagination it shaped, that a dialogue seemed altogether impossible between the exponents of the one or the other doctrine, without either one ever glimpsing the deep cause of their perpetual misunderstanding. The economy is the wheatfield or the olive grove, where the fruits ripen under the sun and where God is present as the Giver of all good things, distributing His portion to the cultivator, the lord, and the cleric, according to His justice. Such justice is not that of *Do ut des* because the cultivator himself did not "make" the fruit, he has merely served it as a humble agent in the accomplishment of the miracle of harvests, and he is not the sole proprietor. Chrematism, on the other hand, is the market where anonymous buyers and sellers face each other and communicate with each other only by means of abstract signs; where possessions are merely merchandise passing from hand to hand representative of the sums of money which they have cost or will bring; where nothing grows, if not the profit of the intermediaries; and where God is no longer present, or at most, present only in the tables of laws: a code of commercial morality and honesty, the impersonal "rule of equity."

The market, in fact, constitutes an abstract society which makes no distinction in terms of person or rank; juridically egalitarian because it is anonymous and based exclusively on the *Do ut des*, the rule of all exchange and all contract. It is an unnatural society because it lacks roots, and it is contrary to all order because it is without authority and without a hierarchy. Rational to a rational mind, it is strictly demoniacal to the mind of traditional cast. It would be a tempting game, if somewhat gratuitous, to catalogue the two series of contrary concepts (religious, philosophical, moral, political, and social) which on the one hand link the archetype of natural economy to the order of the Church carnally present in the world and, on the other hand—not without some variants and hesitations, "chrematistics"—to this Calvinist religiosity so disembodied that the very notion of the Church becomes doubtful. Human sluggishness geared to the immobility of the soil and to the slowness of the harvests, the image of an eternal order; on the other hand frenzied disorder of the movements of the marketplace, of "payments" and of the stock exchanges, seemingly indifferent to time and place, and whose motives escape ordinary common sense: it is the transition to the increasingly absolute mobility which is the sign of the Evil One, and the popular, or even learned descriptions of these high places of mercantile economy speak of it most naturally in terms of sorcery.

A distant echo of the Aristotelian philosophy of the Scholastics and of all the Councils, an echo, nearer in time, of physiocracy, Rivarol, in the twilight of the *ancien régime*, summed up a whole spiritual tradition in a striking formula of malediction against chrematistics. The government, he said, must favor its subjects "in indirect ratio to the mobility of their riches." In the first rank, "the husbandman, veritable child of the earth, whose riches are as immobile as it is itself." Rivarol placed the merchant one stage lower, already uprooted, "but who nevertheless cannot do without time, roads, rivers and seas." And on the lowest rank, a veritably pestiferous person, the financier who, "like a magician, can with a stroke of the pen transport his fortune to the end of the world and who, never staking anything but signs, escapes equally from nature and society. The government owes nothing to such a man. This maxim is fundamental." [7] The banker, agent of international commercial regulations, effecting ceaselessly "from marketplace to marketplace" the multilateral clearings and equalizations of assets and liabilities which trade engenders at any moment, by the mere execution of increasingly complex documents, without even having recourse to material transfers of money (whose transport would still require "time, roads, rivers and seas") is in fact the perfect incarnation of the cabal of the economy of rationalized exchanges.

If Calvin was able to break the ancient chain of malediction at a precise and crucial point, it is doubtless because he was the one among the reformers who knew how to conceive an economic society in terms of "chrematistics." It is certainly because he found himself the religious and political leader of an isolated commercial city, without an agricultural hinterland, capable of incorporating into its sovereignty only a few scattered and constantly threatened strips —of the surrounding countryside, and which could subsist materially only through its commercial exchanges. To be sure, Calvin nowhere expounded the economic laws of society, but only the divine laws; he busied himself more with exposing the corruption of human societies than with their living conditions. It is only at the turning point of a biblical commentary, on the occasion, for example, of the condemnation of those who use false weights and measures, that we become aware to what extent exchanges were for him the basis of any society.

> Now the falseness which is committed in weights and measures abolishes all legitimate means of entering into contracts. Moreover, when one can no longer sell, nor buy, the

[7] *Écrits politiques et littéraires* (Paris: V.-H. Debidour, 1956), p. 145.

> company of men is as if dissipated, so that he who deceives in weight or unequal measure hardly differs from a counterfeiter. Now we have said that there would be an extreme confusion, if there were no weights and measures; if it were permitted to corrupt weights and measures, there would almost be no order any more in the world. When we, therefore, see that this is required, that we would not be able to converse together, that we would be like savage beasts, we know that whoever violates that order, offends God so much more grievously.

The very severity with which Calvin condemns abuses and cheatings in matters of trade among men, and enjoins merchants to scrupulous honesty, shows how in his view their function is essential in any society. "Moreover, the industry in which each one exercises his office, the vocation itself, the skillfulness of proper conduct, and other graces, are like goods, because their end and usage is the natural communication that exists among men." [8] The malediction was raised from the moment in which the economy of exchanges changed from a marginal to a component element of the human community; the merchant's trade not only became useful but, contrary to canonic opinion, was capable of pleasing God if it was exercised honestly and scrupulously.

Is it then a question of Catholic "economy" against Calvinist "chrematistics"? The question has never been posed in this way. The dividing line between the various sides in confessional struggles did not go through economic conceptions, which were barely sketched in on the margin of the theological and ecclesiastical debate. No testimony attests that a similar link between the politico-economic view of society and the interpretation of the message of Christ had ever been clearly proclaimed or perceived, nor that it had

[8] Biéler, *op. cit.*, pp. 450–451 and 235.

motivated adherence to the Reformation. The description of the Reformation as a "bourgeois" movement is an historical puzzle which clashes with the most obvious facts. The fact that at Geneva, in a conjunction of exceptional local circumstances, a most rigorous reformer, exclusively concerned with the glorification of God but faced by a commercial city in distress threatened from all sides, should consent—despite himself—to question the dogmatic bases of scholastic "anti-capitalism" is in the last analysis one of those secondary accidents which accompany the great spiritual breaks in history, the meaning of which is illumined only much later in time. Two centuries after, with the decline of Scholasticism as well as Calvinist theology, and the general disdain for dogmatic controversy, it would be vain to seek in one side or the other even a vague awareness of these relations. If some Genevans stand out because of their efficaciousness in business, this makes the reputation of a city, and not that of a belief whose most authentic representatives in France, the Protestants from the Cévennes region, truly exhibited no trace of this "capitalist spirit." And if, on the other hand, a well-established routine attributes the "Republican spirit" to the Protestants, the economic ideology is irrelevant. In this respect, the anti-rationalist apostle of the natural and sentimental life, Rousseau, was in fact the representative of an egalitarian tradition essential to Calvinism in another way than the calculation of interest, and his floating theology could vigorously replace Calvin's, which had been forgotten in the minds of Protestant pastors, to end up throwing everything into utter confusion. To be sure, despite the theological decadence and the oblivion into which the dogma had fallen, there remained a vague affinity between the concepts whose connections were no longer perceived.

We are justified in believing in the persistence of archetypal images of society peculiar to each of the religious families, and it could very well be that businessmen or theoreticians issuing from a Protestant tradition evolved with greater ease and at any rate with less loss of balance in the rationalized world of money, whose devils had been exorcised for them, than could those who were nourished on the traditions of the natural economy. But for those who would like to draw from this the conclusion of an opposition, even if only somewhat indistinct, between concepts and "ideologies," the curious episode of physiocracy offers a striking counterproof.

The two concepts of "natural economy" and "chrematistics" faced each other actively one last time in a pitched battle array with banners flying when Dr. Quesnay opposed all the mercantilist or neo-mercantilist theories with his brilliantly renewed economic body of doctrine, armed with all the "proofs" of natural reasoning; it was the most finished formula of a view of the social world centered upon the soil, capable nevertheless of incorporating all the marginal growth of derived activities. On reflection we realize that physiocracy, while avoiding any reference to scholastic teaching, was for a long time the last and loftiest manifestation of traditional Catholic thought in economic matters, while simultaneously the last coherent ideology of the *ancien régime*. We can also find it symbolical that it was Jacques Necker, a hesitant thinker devoid of genius but armed with his system of mercantile evidence, who publicly set himself up as the spokesman of triumphant neo-mercantilism. The clash between these two irreconcilable views of society is distinctly perceived in certain polemic outbursts between the *contenders*. When Necker speaks of "proprietors"—and for him this term, as for the "Economists," always designates the landed manorial proprietors—

he spontaneously evokes the fierce beasts of the jungle, lions, tigers, or crocodiles, devouring or exploiting to the last drop of blood humble, defenseless animals. For a man who viewed society as constituted by the exchanges and contracts of mercantile economy, which depends solely upon reason and free consent, the whole hierarchy of manorial society, based on bonds of domination, can in fact appertain only to the sphere of violence, being by definition noneconomic and anti-economic. He could, for opportunistic reasons, adjust himself to it as an historical fact and reason within this established order, but he could not "feel" this society as natural and identify with it. Conversely, Abbé Baudeau, in his "Clarifications Requested from M. Necker in the Name of Landed Proprietors and French Husbandmen," after recapitulating all the diatribes of his teacher on movable wealth without a country and its sterility with respect to the nation's welfare, passed on to a frontal attack:

> It is easy, Sir, to convince oneself while reading your work that it is dominated by a capital idea on the reciprocal relations of great classes who constitute well-ordered States. In fact, the nature of social relations is the base of your speculations and ours. In the opinion which you have embraced, it is an opposition, a war, a perpetual plundering which you call social harmony,

and thence that in the agricultural kingdom of the Physiocrats there reigns "peace, an eternal concord and a genuine unity of interest." [9]

Hence, we have an open clash between two views, economic and mercantile, "Catholic" and "Calvinist." But who

[9] *Nouvelles éphémérides économiques,* Vol. VII (1775), p. 98. This is the reply to Necker's treatise on legislation and trade in grains.

among the contemporaries involved understood it thus? There was no theological quarrel between the Genevan banker and the abbé disciple of Quesnay, and no one took up a position on the problem in terms of his religious convictions. Puritan England was the example invoked and extolled by the two sides under different aspects. Sully, the Protestant *gentilhomme*, was the holy patron of the physiocratic chapel. And the most active spokesman, and soon prominent leader of the Physiocrats, Pierre Samuel Dupont, who was not yet "de Nemours," was of Protestant stock. On the other side, the whole Colbertist tradition of the royal administration made itself heard, with Necker as its mouthpiece. And with what lasting echoes in this France, still Catholic despite everything! Fifteen years after its birth, after arousing a brief and confused general infatuation, physiocracy in its turn became a cabal even more obscure than the most obscure treatise of exchanges, and fashionable society made it the butt of its witticisms. Those who had been a part of it could be counted on the fingers of one hand. Quesnay's doctrine did not even have the honor of being refuted; it fell into ridicule and then into oblivion like a bizarre idea that struggled against the grain of an entire epoch. From the Founder's coherent and harmonious system, each one, including his own disciples, took in whatever piece suited him and ignored the whole.

For an audience attentive only to the topical questions of the moment, all that rose to the surface in the polemic of the Physiocrats against Necker was a controversy as paradoxical as it was marginal: the Physiocrats were in favor of freedom of trade in general and of that in grain in particular; Necker was against. For the current debate was between the liberal and the regulatory conception of the mercantile economy, between "Colbertists" and the exponents of a free exchange, corporatists and anti-corporatists; and between the two, the rural economy of the Physiocrats foundered like a remembrance of another age. The *ancien régime* itself no longer understood its own ideology and ultimately died of this lack of comprehension. It was a deplorable misunderstanding of a grandiose thesis, whose potentialities are still not exhausted; but it was also a natural misunderstanding. For, after all, the mercantile economy was not an ideology that it was optional to embrace or reject; it was a fact. Physiocracy envisaged it as secondary, obliquely, so to speak; neither the problems nor the suggested solutions lay less heavily upon this economy. Turgot, and with him physiocracy in power, represented commercial freedom, industrial freedom, the establishment of a discount bank, scarcely raising a few embarrassing murmurs in the Sorbonne before this officialization of "usury" in matters concerning negotiable titles (i.e., letters of exchange, checks, etc.): very subtle indeed is the man who perceives here a return to scholastic doctrine. It was not Calvin who killed scholastic doctrine; it died of ineptitude, like alchemy or astrological magic. Or, more exactly, like the latter it did not die, it merely fell from the rank of science to that of a subconscious residue which nonetheless continues to act in obscure ways on the consciousness of men.

PART II

LIGHTS AND SHADOWS OF THE EIGHTEENTH CENTURY

CHAPTER FOUR

The Religion of the King

Reformation and the rise of nationalisms: this combination of themes, which matches that of "Protestantism and Capitalism," has enjoyed a very lasting and hardly less illustrious vogue. Accordingly, it has left behind abundant traces in the good modern history textbooks. After all, it was just as tempting, and basically more plausible, to reduce the great drama of religious conscience of the West to a confrontation of peoples and powers, rather than to a struggle between social classes. The "national" accents are much more clearly discernible in the controversy raised by the schism than are the "capitalist" or "bourgeois" elements; and the politics, whether in the pontifical State or in its adversaries, immediately became entangled with the debates on dogma and the Church, and has remained so ever since. To the extent that the reformation is considered in the context of a rupture in the spiritual unity of the West, it seems naturally to fall into place in the process of the formation of "national consciousness." Have not scholars—in a spirit that also had its nineteenth-century "fin de siècle" feeling—likened Luther's revolt to a "national" Germanic uprising against subjection to Rome and to Latin civilization: an episode which can logically be inserted into place in a history that stretches from the forest of Teutoburg up to Bismarck's empire: this was the dominant point of view on both banks of the Rhine, among the panegyrists as among the detractors, during the commemoration of the fourth centenary of the German reformer; and the echoes still have not completely died out.

No serious historian, to be sure, would take such gross simplifications into account; nevertheless, these simplifications have a way of creeping almost by themselves into the narrative, through the exact recital of events and the quotations—authentic enough—of battle cries. Inasmuch as the sixteenth century was a crucial century with regard to the formation of European nations—as in many other respects, since through the failure of the last rough draft for the universal empire, it accelerated the crystallization of the classic system of territorial States which would set themselves up as nations, it is evident that the simultaneity of the struggles for and against the Hapsburg supremacy and the concurrent struggle between the Reformation and the Counter Reformation produced the inextricable intertwining of the two movements, which had, however, stemmed from totally different sources. So much so, in fact, that from the middle of the century on, the cause of the Hapsburg dynasty and that of the Holy See, fallen into a dependency upon that dynasty, were completely identified, or almost so. The identification was effected in such a way that not only were the individual reformations realized within the framework of the constituted States "nationalized"—in the Holland of the "Beggars" and above all in Elizabeth's England, where Roman Catholicism assumed the features of a foreign and domestic enemy, the Duke of Alba, the Great Armada, or the "Gunpowder Plot"—but also Catholicisms very "national" and very distinct from that of the Universal Church, grew within mobilized nations: the resistance-Catholicism of Ireland bent under the yoke; the holy war —*Jihad*—of crusading Spain against the Mohammedan, Lutheran, and Masaic "sects"; the frontier-Catholicism of Poland and of Hungary, where the victorious Counter Reformation assumed the dimensions of military processions to the borders of the Turks and of Russian Orthodoxy. In a Europe embarked on the road to nationalization, as in a Europe going toward the "capitalist era," the historian of nationalism or of capitalism can undertake to study all the phenomena dialectically linked to the movement as a whole only from the exclusive viewpoint of whatever process he has decided to consider all-determinant, whether this be the elaboration of the national consciousnesses or the forms of capitalist economy. But from the legitimate procedure which classifying facts according to a chosen criterion is, the slope is a slippery one which leads to the apostasy of history. It is true and obvious that the bellicose policy of the dynastic or national powers readily seized on religious fervor, which it forged into propaganda weapons and which it used to arouse enthusiasm; and that, on the other hand, the theological and ecclesiological controversies often exacerbated these bellicose passions. The unpardonable offense, however, is to blow up the marginal consequence into a principle of explication of essential motivations.

These correlations between religious schism and nationalism are superficial but they have existed and they have acted on many national sensibilities. The singularity of France lies in the fact that she almost completely escapes such correlations. Here as elsewhere, the French case does not lend itself to convenient classifications and cavalier views of European history. The perennial character of France as a monarchy powerfully rooted and organized at the center of her territory, as the seat of a consciousness of unity that must be called national (despite the anachronism of the term), at least since her resurgence at the close of the Hundred Years' War, contradicts the alignments of Western history into "dynastic" and "national" history, into cycles of successive predominances, into ascendancies and declines of nations. This perennial character of the French monarchy as such also totally excludes the religious cleavage, despite the violence of the "wars of religion," as a positive or negative element in forming a consciousness of national unity which essentially had already been acquired and was in no way placed into question again by an internal conflict. The conflict was a civil war, not a national war, jeopardizing the regime, the balance of forces, and the succession to the throne; it was not a question of national loyalty, as such, which both sides claimed to serve with equal force. Actually, the Gallican Church had been national, or rather royal, for more than two centuries. And if it was somewhat embarrassed, during moments of crisis, by the alignment of powers arrayed under the usurped banners of the Reformation and Catholicity, in which France almost always was on the wrong side, it is remarkable how little the country was shaken by it: the throne and the altar could not divorce.

As for Calvinism, the only great movement of the Reformation born within the Latin world, it did not even require naturalization. French by origin and universal by vocation, it offered itself to France as a religious choice first and foremost, but also, by descending to the political plane,

as a serious alternative for national orientation and as a rallying point for all the European forces opposed to Roman and Hapsburg domination. In the tangled context of the European "wars of religion," across national frontiers, Jesuit Fathers and Huguenot emissaries worked with equal fervor. From Scotland to the Ukraine they waged subversive war for one camp and then the other; the "Protestant party" was much more at ease in sanctioning a French national policy than was the Catholic League, which was instinctively drawn toward the "Spanish" cause. The Huguenots allied with England and the Dutch and Swiss Protestants against the empire, and the Catholic kings could feel themselves to be better patriots than the courtiers of Catherine de Medici or of the House of Guise, reduced to employing evasive tactics and always under suspicion of treason. Nowhere up to the advent of the "Politiques" do we find accents so violently national in ring except among the Colignys, the Du Bartas, and the Agrippas of Aubigné, heaping curses on the woman of Florence who "has made France the quarry of Italy." Henri IV, the prince who, contrary to approved custom, converted to the religion of the people, was needed in order to conciliate *de facto* Huguenot policy with the Catholicity of France. He thereby effected the triumph of the *raison d'État* over religious passion. It was a conciliation that would never be without equivocation nor profound malaise, and that, in all the epochs of modern history and among very different writers, has produced a strange retrospective regret over the wrong choice that France was thought to have made in the religious conflict of the sixteenth century. We shall not enter here into this debate, which is anything but simple. Its clearest result in French intellectual tradition was to free, earlier than elsewhere, the notions of "pure politics" and

raison d'État from any religious or even moral considerations.

The victory of the national sense, of the State sense, over the "fanatics" seemed to delegate the religious conflict to a secondary plane and, at the end of the civil war, to open up prospects of peaceful coexistence under the authority of a King recognized by all. But this prospect remained only a mental conjecture. The Edict of Nantes was only a truce, and toleration in fact was merely a partitioning of the sovereignty between the Catholic kingdom and a kind of Protestant republic entrenched in its places of security, which could have ended up in a lasting *modus vivendi* only in a regime of local autonomies. Such a regime, however, was absolutely contrary to all the tendencies of the centralizing monarchy. If political royalism ultimately prevailed over religious dissensions, in order to put an end to the civil war, therefore the "Huguenot party," precisely because of its political aspect and by the mere fact of its existence, was bound to become a thorn in the side to it. For that matter, "ultramontane" Catholicism—also because of its political aspect—continued to be as suspect as heresy, indeed even more so. The triumph of the third "political" party could not lead to a lasting religious peace because complete separation between the spiritual and temporal orders remained outside the mental ken of the men of the seventeenth century; if religion had not been able to subject the State, the State had to subject religion to it, by elevating itself into an absolute. Now the State was the King. In the struggle between the Huguenot party and the Ultramontane League, the laurels of victory were handed to royalism, not in the sign of the cross but of the cock.

Less than one hundred years after the Edict of Nantes, France arrived at the same solution that had prevailed else-

where, and which elsewhere was beginning to be outmoded: *Cuius regio eius religio.* If the path was different, the destination seems the same as in the countries of the Counter Reformation. But this identity is deceptive. Neither the Roman Catholic Church nor the Reformation walked off with the laurels; the victor was the religion of the King. And if the consequences for French Protestantism, crushed and proscribed, were the most visible, French Catholicism, now transformed into a royal cult, as well as the French nation, royalty, and State, themselves for a long time also bore the baleful consequences of this burdensome legacy.

France remained Catholic, yet although she rejected the Reformation, she did not engage in the Counter Reformation. The resolutions of the Council of Trent were not accepted in France, and were declared contrary to the "Liberties of the Gallican Church," that is, to the subordination of the national Church to the King. *Raison d'État,* identified with absolute sovereignty, was the overriding motivation behind the religious policy and the foreign alliances pursued by Richelieu and Louis XIV.

Nearly the whole of the seventeenth century in France can be understood as a reaction, carried to its ultimate consequences, against the havoc and humiliations of the civil wars. Between the Europe of the Reformation and that of the Counter Reformation, rallying under the practically identical slogans of Calvin and Ignatius Loyola, *soli Deo gloria,* France of the Grand Century seemed to be wholly dedicated to the cult of the State, to the glorification of the King alone.

Upon the accession to the throne of Louis XIV, following the none too glorious demise of the *Fronde,* everything that could potentially oppose the unity and the absolute au-

thority of the State was crushed, humiliated, and reduced to impotence. The "State within the State" of the Protestants was dismantled after the Edict of Grace of Alais in 1629, and the toleration which was granted to them was precarious and at the King's mercy. The Catholic clergy, strictly subordinated to the King and riddled with courtiers and favorites to whom the King bountifully distributed ecclesiastical benefices, was docile to the point of servility, celebrating the cult of the King on a par with that of God. The nobility, which to a great part had been ruined, condemned to idleness, and stripped of all proper political or military function, was in turn transformed into a courtier clientele and entourage of domestics dancing attendance upon royal favors. It was as subject as it was useless, or was relegated to the coarse, obscure, and often miserable life of the country squire. Even the bourgeoisie—at least that part of it which still appeared in public affairs, which alone had represented the Third Estate in the last Estates General and continued to represent it in the provincial assemblies, and which, even under absolutism, still knew how to make its voice heard through the parlements—in its turn became a clientele of the State. It was the caste of the proprietors, of royal offices in the judicature, administration, and finance; it itself was a privileged class nourished on public revenues and ennobled, either immediately or after a delay of tenure of office; and it too was exempted from direct taxes. Such was the picture of the nation, therefore, when it gathered around the sovereign after the destruction of all the autonomous and independent structures: a nation divided into three rival clienteles, but all equally attached to the King by the chains of privileges and favors: "The clergy, the nobility, and the judicature," according to the definition of Chancellor Séguier. Among these three Estates which

officially constituted the whole of France, none, the Third Estate no more than the others, represented the productive classes of the kingdom. Even though the bourgeoisie occupying the royal offices had emerged from this class, none of them contributed to defraying the expenses of the State, nor to the creation of wealth which could have helped to defray them. None of them had an existence independent of the privileges conferred by the King—even though the "officer class" in contrast to the two others acquired its privileges through money instead of by birth or royal favor. In short, royalty was surrounded only by payees of the honors and finances of the State, and all the rest of the nation was cast into political nullity, without voice, without consideration, without even the means of expressing an opinion, ground under the "foul burdens" of the taxes which were the ignominious mark of "people of no account."

In this transformation of an "official" nation into a clientele of the King, the domestication of the clergy ultimately no doubt inflicted incalculable harm on the Church of France; the domestication of the nobility precipitated its downfall. But it was the deforming of the bourgeoisie, perhaps, which led to the most grievous consequences for the public mentality and the country's economic activity. The venality that was the hallmark of the public offices, and the fact that they were hereditary, was neither recent nor peculiar to France. Nevertheless, it seems that they had never and nowhere assumed dimensions comparable to this spree in the creation of offices by the absolute monarchy. No doubt, we must be wary about generalizing the figures given by Gaston Roupnel for the city of Dijon where a third of the active population was formed of "*gens d'office*"; the census had never been taken properly. But the estimated figure is eloquent, and the unbridled multitude of dignitaries, magistrates, receivers, inspectors, treasurers, and concillor-secretaries of the King is attested by all contemporary authors. And this without allowing for the fact that every new office, no matter how useless, by setting up its function added complications of an increasingly more subtle and onerous kind to the already creaking wheels of the courts of justice and of the administration, as Colbert said: "The administration of justice, besides absorbing 70,000 men and more [in office], occupies more than a million more through chicanery and reduces them to such misery that they cannot even think of applying themselves to any other profession for the rest of their lives."

Obviously, it is impossible to evaluate how much this deviation of bourgeois activity toward what d'Argenson called "civil feudalism" detracted from the capital, talents, and energies of the country's economy. Perhaps the place taken in trade and industry by the Protestant bourgeoisie is explained in great part by the fact that it was more or less strictly shunted away from the offices, and therefore it was less inclined to submit to the temptation of deserting its social station and profession once it had amassed a modest fortune. This temptation cannot be expressed simply in economic terms. The purchase of an office no doubt was attractive as a capital investment, to judge by the alacrity with which the demand sought to catch up with the supply. It was also a means of protecting the wealth acquired, real estate above all, from the tax collector, thanks to the exemptions which were granted to most offices, if not at the moment of taking over the office, at least after exercising it for a certain period of time. And if these material advantages were often threatened by the financial distress and arbitrary measures of the State, the corps of officials constituted the most powerful pressure group in the kingdom for the defense of its interests and its acquired privileges. But for the commoner, or the son of an enriched commoner, the purchase of an office was above all the means of establishing himself, of gaining entry into the sphere of notability and social consideration, of crossing the barrier that separated the mass of ordinary subjects from the royal entourage of the privileged associated with the prestige of the State, and of obtaining a place for himself and his descendants on the ever rising ladder of honors and dignities. In France, the actual act of foundation of the ancient bourgeois dynasties was almost always the purchase of an office, whereas commercial or industrial success was but their prehistory. The importance of this scramble for the offices of State is such that in the France of the *ancien régime* even the term "bourgeoisie" assumed another meaning than that obtaining in international terminology: the creative class of the modern economy, in its most conscious and politically determinant part, was tranformed into a caste of hereditary holders of the levers of judicial and administrative power.

No less serious was the effect on the administration itself, which was engaged in a vicious circle. While inexorably transforming all the public functions—even including mayoralities, municipal offices, and vocational mastership—into venal offices, and while crushing the country under the weight of an encumbering and onerous magistracy and administration, the State saw this administration escape its control and make itself independent by proprietary rights. Financial convenience and *raison d'État* found themselves in agreement on the question of multiplying offices and inspections of offices, and on that of parcelling out their spheres of responsibility so as to neutralize them by pitting one against the other, at the same time, making this irremovable corps of officer-proprietors as useless as possible by creating alongside it a second direct administration, strictly centralized, of intendants and inspectors appointed and removed at royal will. Between the two administrations, what subsisted of local, regional or corporative autonomies was crushed or reduced to a residue devoid of substance.

Paradoxically, the monarchy built its absolute power by alienating the very apparatus of the State, and its omnipotence was on a par with its powerlessness to exact obedience. If the King from then on escaped all control, his administration in turn escaped the control of the King. The danger was not of a political order: this caste of officials did not represent either the populations which it administered, or a class, or group of interests. All it represented was itself and its own interests. It had no power, nor any mandate, save that which it derived from the King. But since it had purchased this mandate, it could no longer be dislodged. Moreover, it was more skillful than the former privileged orders had been in opposing overt resistance, or effective ill-will, against any innovation which threatened its legitimately acquired situation. And it held in check, up to the definitive destruction of the *ancien régime*, all attempts on the part of the State to effect administrative or financial reform of the State. From then on the only limitation of the absolute monarchy lay in this caste of officials. The King could do anything, except tamper with the privileges on which he had established his absolutism and the clienteles which he had fashioned into pillars of the State.

But this is the reverse side of that absolute royalty which, from 1661 on, was at the height of its breathtaking radiance. Nothing resisted it, everything was at its feet, France herself and nearly all Europe. Glory and power were the proclaimed aims of the kingdom, indeed the only aims worthy of such a King; and glory consisted in the humiliation of others, just as power—as conceived by Louis XIV and by Colbert as well, the only point on which they were in agreement—consisted in the degradation or destruction of others. The medals struck to the glory of the King, and bas-reliefs of his equestrian statues, the frescoes which covered the galleries and ceilings of Versailles showed only peoples and sovereigns with bowed heads before Louis the Great. The economy organized by Colbert was an economy of power and grandeur. As Lavisse observes, Colbert associated the high quality of fabrics to the King's prestige, and in 1669 at the end of a list of manufactories which had been established in the kingdom, he wrote, in a spasm of admiration, "Grandeur and magnificence!"

There was not an area of national life which was not subordinated to this cult of the glorious King. It was Colbert also who had the final say on the organization of the intellectual and artistic life, which was strictly regulated and administered like a royal manufactory of sciences, arts, and letters. Architecture and painting testify to the royal road upon which France had embarked; the Baroque style, common to all Europe of the Counter Reformation, so grandiosely expressive of religious exaltation, found no access to France, where the official "Grand Manner"—the royal style of cold, imposing, rigorous classicism—held a monopoly. Literature, wholly gathered around the court, radiated grandeur and prestige; it was left to posterity to separate the masterpieces of classicism from the majestic rubbish of commissioned panegyrics—Racine's literary career achieved its peak not with *Phèdre* or with *Athalie* but upon his appointment to the office of historiographer of the

King. But once the generation which had breathed the passionate and stormy air of the *Fronde,* whose talent had been channelled and disciplined to grandeur, as if constrained thereto by the exigencies of classicism, passed from the scene, once the King and the court became pious devotees, a stifling conformism weighed upon all minds. The literature of the Grand Century and of the Grand Manner died before 1690, and the eighteenth century divided itself between criticism and airy trifles, between the undermining of its very foundations and sheer frivolousness.

The most striking and lasting monument to this royal civilization was the French language itself, which also became an institution of the State administered by the Academy and regulated by the jurists of proper usage, subjected to the discipline of a language of the court, of diplomacy, and of conversation of an ordered society. Thereafter, everything that was thought, uttered, or written in this language was adjusted to the rules of this clarity. Its criteria were elegance and good taste rather than truth and a reasonable common sense that identified itself so well with universal reason that even the boldest thinking could no longer escape it. So violent was the amputation which transformed the exuberant and expressive language of the sixteenth century into a flawless intellectual instrument, brilliant in its precision and clearness, that for almost two centuries all lyricism, all mysticism, all metaphysics, and almost all philosophy—save for the somewhat schematic reason of the Age of Enlightenment which, significantly, considered itself the only possible philosophy, pure and simple—were banished from the French kingdom. Everywhere, perfect order succeeded disorder. At the summit of this majestic structure the apotheosis of the King was accomplished, hailed as Apollo and the Sun. He removed himself from the sight of mortals in order to sit enthroned apart from humanity in that heaven of machines and stage backdrops—an outrage against nature and history, an inordinate allegory of his own glory—which was Versailles, the finely wrought image of an artificial society from which all contradiction and all human accident were apparently banished.

In the context of this glorification of the King as shown in Versailles, a King imparting his law to the elements, to peoples, and to individual consciences, the Edict of Fontainebleau, revoking what remained of the Edict of Nantes, appears almost a routine ordinance. Explanation matters little here: no material or political necessity, no utility even, commanded the revocation. Indeed, the Protestant State belonged to the past; the Protestant Church taught a fervent royalism, and during the troubles of the *Fronde*, the Protestants had been among the most loyal subjects of the King. The persecution followed from the internal logic of this kingdom, which had nowhere encountered a will that dared to oppose its own. Toleration, so alien still to the spirit of this century, was even more contrary to the very idea of the absolute State incarnate in Louis XIV, first member of the clergy of France and guardian of orthodoxy at the same time as he was temporal sovereign. National conformity in the matter of religion was a question of public order at least as much as a question of faith. Throughout the whole length of his reign, Louis XIV, lacking in religious education and knowledge, yet arrogated to himself the right to rule over the consciences of his subjects as over their persons and goods. And he felt himself obliged to make a police matter of any theological dispute, even of the most subtle questions of dogma. Jansenism, quietism, Cartesianism were as much the concern of his government as finance, wars, or the fine arts; and this constant and muddle-headed interference by the royal power in religious affairs finally helped to undermine the authority of the Church as much as that of the State.

In this perspective, the stubbornness exhibited by French Protestants, after their complete political submission, in choosing to remain outside the religion of the prince and of the Church of the State, was an intolerable act of insubordination. Without the destruction of this "cult inimical to sovereignty," as La Bruyère called it, the monarchical order in the full sense of the word was not complete. Without wanting to diminish the religious motivations of the King and his devout entourage, we must nevertheless recall that in the very moment of the revocation—from 1682 to 1693—the Church of France, arrayed behind its King against the Pope, was virtually in a state of schism. At the same time, furthermore, the Most Christian King, who was waging war against the miscreants of his kingdom, had leagued himself with the Turks then mounting their assault against Vienna. In contrast to what happened after the Massacre of Saint Bartholomew, the revocation of the Edict of Nantes was not greeted in Rome with *Te Deums*.

Although it was a manifestation of Catholic fervor, it was even more a further demonstration of the pontifical authority which the King of France claimed to exercise over his subjects. The campaign of repression that was to be directed against French Protestantism at the end of a century which had exhausted religious fanaticisms, contained an original element in that it did not stem from the Church nor from the State viewed as "the secular arm of the Church." Rather, the State acted in the name of its own absolute authority.

It is in this historical context that the revocation assumes its whole meaning. It took place at the zenith and turning point of this great reign. Louis XIV was neither a visionary nor a man of violence. Except for the Pharaonic sense of grandeur and prestige with which he officiated at the cult of his own majesty and the fact that he made the deployment of military forces an indispensable feature of his royal display, his ambitions were rather mediocre. It is difficult to discern in them any farsighted view or grand design. But during the whole first half of his long personal reign, which lasted fifty-four years, nowhere did he run into any opposition to his will, either in himself, or in the courtier society that surrounded him, or even beyond the country's frontiers. The King, like God, could do everything: he could make sovereigns and peoples bend the knee, invade and lay waste neighboring countries, defy the Pope in his own city of Rome, decree the faith and violate consciences, transform a desolate plain into an enchanted garden, order the diversion of rivers to provide water for the fountains of Versailles. The country was so rich and order so well established that nothing hampered this compulsive need to create magnificence. The invasion of the Low Countries, the "Chambers of Reunion," [1] the capture of Strasbourg, the devastation of Flanders, of the Palatinate, of the Rhine principalities, of the valleys of Aosta, the bombardment of Genoa, the provocation of ambassadors: after a quarter of a century of these aggressions, feats of strength, annexations, acts of vandalism in peace time, and of humiliations even more wounding than the violence inflicted upon all her neighbors; after having broken all treaties, violated all pledges, and duped all allies, the France of Louis XIV succeeded in making herself hated by almost all

[1] Special courts composed of the King's own judges, who decided what outlying districts of towns were ceded to France as a result of peace treaties.—Trans.

Europe. From 1686 on began the descent into that interminable war that continued from the League of Augsburg up to the end of the reign, in which France almost alone faced all her neighbors leagued against her.

In this lengthy series of actions which led to the kingdom's great ordeal, the dragonnades, persecutions, and exodus of the Huguenots were but an episode which, while adding little to the credit of the "Too Christian King" (who for that matter was so little a Christian), certainly contributed to exasperating the Protestant countries and to precipitating the most serious failure of Louis XIV's policy, the fall of the last Catholic Stuart of England. If, on the other hand, there is no doubt that this Huguenot exodus weakened France, and if the testimonies of the time, even the most official, do not diverge from each other except on the extent of the damage, it is still hardly possible to evaluate its role in the host of evils that overwhelmed the country and the State itself in the second half of the reign. In its most felicitous period, the policy of magnificence had already stretched to the limit the resources of a country which had not yet completely recovered from a century of troubles. And its recovery was impeded not only by a stifling administration and by the constant misappropriation and misuse of capital for honors and offices of the State, but also by a very unpropitious general conjuncture of monetary contraction—a "drought of money" as was said at the time—and of a drop in prices. These were international phenomena, but they were greatly accentuated in France by the State's fiscal, commercial, and monetary practices. But apart from several years of peace and good administration at the beginning of the reign, at no time were the State's resources ever to be equal to its requirements. Colbert himself, before his death in 1683, had seen his work in great part ruined, his great colonial trading companies dying for lack of capital and initiative, but also because of the State monopoly and above all the costly wars. With its roads and manufactories, fiscal and administrative reform sacrificed to armies and sumptuary outlays, the most magnificent State in the world was reduced to financial expediency of the worst kind. Several years after Colbert's death, there was a return to currency manipulations, which "chased money out of the kingdom," combined with the systematic recourse to those "extraordinary" finances which, under various guises, consisted in devouring the capital of future resources that in turn became increasingly mortgaged. This is not the place to discuss the economic and financial picture of the last thirty years of the "Age of Louis XIV" whose features, for that matter, are sufficiently known. Historians, contemporaries, and those who came later have gladly painted it in black colors; after the magnificent displays of the beginning of the regime, the picture is one of invasion, famine, bankruptcy, sorrows, and disasters, scarcely set off by the majestic imperturbability of the old King—inflexible in his dignity in the face of adversity. The fact that there is something too systematic about this contrast between the two "epochs" of the reign is not by any means due to an exaggeration of the reversals and misfortunes—a detailed economic history only adds features that confirm the general glory—but of the very brilliant appearance of those glorious years. The great ordeal of the wars of the League of Augsburg and the Spain Succession had merely bared to view the contradictions that were hidden behind this unity, and the disorder behind the classic order of absolute monarchy.

The administrative and social edifice of the monarchy as definitively constituted under Louis XIV was strong enough to preserve itself for a whole century after its zenith, and some of its most characteristic structures survived all the later revolutions. But in this strongly constructed whole, in which everything held together because it hung on the central power, it was the keystone itself that was most vulnerable. The absolute monarchy was almost unshakeable, not so much because of its own strength and its means of executing its will, but because everything which counted in the realm—clergy, nobility, the officeholding and rentier bourgeoisie—depended upon it. The King, certainly, had less need of all these onerous and encumbering servants than they had to serve him. Royalty had reduced them to obedience by reducing them to a state of uselessness, while still preserving their privileges. But it was disarmed before these privileges, which it had made the basis of its own power and which constrained its action and burdened its finances. The very conditions of its apparent omnipotence established the monarchy's profound impotence, the tangible sign of which from zenith to fall was the incurable financial wound from which it bled and which, despite optimistic maxims, was to prove fatal.

The monarchy was absolute to the extent that it could do without any cooperation except that of the financiers who, from one treasury crisis to another, procured for it the wherewithal for the subsistence of the State, the court, the courtiers, and the armies. This was the poorly guarded door of this State, which, moreover, had under its authority all public and private activities, high or low, but which did not hesitate to hand over the "Court Bank" to a Huguenot apostate, who simultaneously organized the payment of the armies campaigning across Europe, in Flanders, Bavaria, and Italy, and permitted the escape from France of the capital of the Protestant fugitives, while waiting to entrust the direction of finances to a brilliant Scottish adventurer, a sort of financial faith healer (John Law), liquidator of the bankruptcy of a reign too grand for its own good. And finally, after the long respite of stabilization under Louis XV, a State that handed itself over to the credit of a big Genevan banker (Jacques Necker). There was neither fatality nor conspiracy in all this, and the decline did not become precipitous again until a half century after the death of Louis XIV. But as a point of departure, it was the historical conjunction of the Huguenot exodus and of the beginnings of the financial disasters of the State—a conjunction that was certainly not a result of cause and effect, but that was not purely accidental either—which at one and the same time determined the establishment of a "Huguenot International" born of the dispersion, and the conditions in which this international was able to become indispensable to the royalty which had hounded it out of France.

CHAPTER FIVE

Outlines of the "Age of Louis XV"

Ever since it has been treated by historians, the history of the eighteenth century in France has been written somewhat in the manner of a preface, or epilogue: decline and fall of the *ancien régime*, preface to the Revolution. Or it is described as a light interlude between two acts of a tragedy, but one which is always set on this same slope that stretches from the zenith of the monarchic State to its decay and fall, from the splendor of the Sun King to the scaffold of Louis Capet. But it is only in the history of ideas that this slope *a posteriori* appears as straight and irreversible, because it is the very history of an erosion of established authority, dogmas, conventions, and verities. The century's lines of force are to be read in the movement of the mind, not in its strangely disconnected "events"; and it is only as the Age of Enlightenment that this century assumes its proper individuality. Rightly, this has remained the privileged century of the history of ideas. The progress of the critical and scientific spirit, of disrespect for the established order of things, and of free thought . . . the propagation of liberal ideas and liberal ideologies, which had come from the outside but which had been assimilated and transformed in the Parisian crucible, transmitted through the cosmopolitan salons and by organizations themselves inspired by models on the other side of the Channel—reading and discussion clubs, "societies of thought," masonic lodges of Anglican or Jacobite obedience, in which confessional and doctrinal distinctions were progressively blurred and blotted out in a vague, conciliatory Deism . . . everything effortlessly arranged itself on this increasingly steep slope leading from authority to freedom. That this age of Louis XV, in which the spirit of toleration and even of religious indifference won over all the "enlightened" classes, the highest levels of the State Church as much as the liberal aristocracy and bourgeoisie, should also have seen the codification and most systematic perfection of legal intolerance by the declaration of May, 1724, and the last waves of persecution of the Huguenot heresy and emigration swooping the South of France fully in the middle of the century, is disconcerting only at first sight. If the contours of this age are defined not by an established order and a dominant state of mind but by the conflict between an old order and a new spirit, then all the contradictions shape up as elements of the conflict. Nevertheless, a certain effort of imagination is required to conceive the dragonnades of 1752 and the great heresy trials in 1762 as events contemporary with the reigns of Mme de Pompadour and of the *Encyclopédie*, because these things did not transpire in the same world. The careers of the Protestant bankers and merchants in the large cities of the realm could be pursued economically and socially, without incident or vexation, in the middle of a happy, tolerant, and cosmopolitan society, without ever encountering an echo of the tribulations of the Church of the Desert. Indeed, these "*religionnaires*," as the Huguenots were called, were able to live in the juridical regime of intolerance without even being aware of it. It was not until a decade after Necker's appointment by the King to the office of Controller-General that a legal and civic status was finally granted to non-Catholics by the Edict of 1787.

This is only one aspect among a hundred of the apparent inconsistencies of the "age of Louis XV," in which it seems that completely anachronistic states of mind and of law co-existed even in the royal councils. And this is how the temptation to take a Manichean view of two principles locked in mortal struggle—which historians, according to their personal preferences, were to label Light and Darkness, Faith and Unbelief, Authority and Freedom, Order and Disorder, *Ancien Régime* and Revolution-on-the-march—ensued. For it is only the conflict and the fermentation of minds which made of so disparate a century something more than a simple chonological stretch of time: a logical and intelligible process, starting out from an established state of things to end up with its complete subversion. To be sure, the French Revolution was also, more simply, a "revolution in France," a local manifestation of a transformation which, in different forms, shattered all Western societies. Even if we limit our field of vision to France, the eighteenth century was something quite different from this one-way movement plunging headlong toward the Revolution. The fact remains, no less, that this whole epoch of French history unfolded between two systems of "total" order, entirely coherent and comprehensible in terms of a sole principle of unity: the absolute administrative monarchy and the government of the revolutionary assembly, each of which at its moment of omnipotence imposed its law on the entire material, moral, and intellectual life of the nation. Everything that falls within these two poles appears simply only as a sequence of transitory states that assume significance only in relation to the point of departure or to the point of arrival of the whole movement and are thus allotted a plus or minus sign, according to the system of reference: preservation or decline of the *ancien régime*, preparation or retardment of the Revolution. This highly dramatic view is so forceful, however, that it is difficult even for the least romanticized history to escape it.

Nevertheless, on this imaginary slope, the larger part of the reign of Louis XV formed a sort of stairhead on which history seemed to have come to a halt and on which the *ancien régime* seemed to have consolidated itself by coming to terms with the literary and philosophical tourneys without damage to itself. Far from launching an assault, the critical mind entered the lists before the royal tribune in which the whole court watched and applauded the spectacles. The historian who enjoys tourneys dwells upon them in order to savor the slightly faded pleasures of this interlude, this "delicious moment" between two absolutisms. The historians of the regime, of the Revolution, or of the economic and social movement in general, were in a hurry to pass on to the following act, in which the literary joust became a tumult and to which the final crisis began.

Until recently, the result of the "dramatic" view of the eighteenth century was a polarization of historical investigations. Studies and monographs on the two extremes of the century piled up in quantity and quality, particularly in the area of economic and social history: the great crisis that marked the end of the reign of Louis XIV and its prolongations in the Regency on the one hand, and the Revolution and its preliminary phases on the other. This was helped along by the tendency toward specialization, with its fatal dissection in 1789 of *ancien régime* from "contemporary France." Historians divided this century up among themselves, so to speak; not precisely at that prophetic date but approximately at the center—with the Seven Years' War, the deficit, the parliamentary *Fronde* and the intellectual *Fronde*, the Revolution-on-the-march—without ever really meeting up with each other. Everything seems to have been said about the *ancien régime*, with the bankruptcy and the mad adventure of the Regency, which seems to have wasted all opportunities for reform and to have broken the moral spring of the monarchy, despite the long reprieve it was still granted, because it was unable to take advantage of it either for reforming its administration of affairs or for retrieving its usurped authority. A somewhat superficial view contends that Louis XVI took up the deficit left as a legacy by Louis XIV. A kind of vacant, swampy land stretches between these two reigns. It is an area lacking a principle of unity and hardly propitious to concerted analyses, in which history seems to fragment itself.

In fact the "age of Louis XV" has been, and remains, the favorite terrain of other historical genres, not to mention the history of manners. On the one hand, it is the anecdotal and worldly history of a dazzling and refined society, enlightened to a fault, utterly cosmopolitan and extremely bored, rich and idle enough to have no other problems save that of cultivating the art of living and making brilliant, witty conversation. This is the history of a civilization which flowered in an incomparable literary, intellectual, and artistic setting, rich in the productions of mind and taste, charming, frivolous, or corrosive, but always elegant, in spite of the fact that it exhibits little staying power, being tailored to the measure of drawing-room and boudoir conversations. Finally, it is here that we find the inexhaustible legend of the century, the gay life of libertinage, King, court, and fashionable society. On the other hand, it is the history, or rather the political and diplomatic chronicle, of a ministerial policy whose fabric was seemingly woven of confused strands, of senseless wars that ended in "stupid" or disastrous peace treaties; of unstable dynastic combinations based on misunderstandings and suddenly reversed alliances, the permanent stakes of which became visible only on the other side of the Channel. They were visible, in fact, in the struggle for maritime and colonial supremacy waged without let-up by England with all her most violent and tortuous means, in an almost uninterrupted covert or overt war from 1740 to 1753 on the seas and in the two Indies. This ceaseless struggle was imposed by the active public opinion of a trading and industrial nation which prevailed over the schemes of ministers and coteries, and in which we can discern the nascent contours of that combination of egoism and moral rectitude which was to set its stamp on English Puritanism.

Viewed from France, this great conflict remained at once marginal and incoherent: the war to the knife conducted, or suffered, by the privateers and sailors of the Atlantic coast blockaded even in their own ports by the English navy was not that of the cabinet of Versailles, which was more concerned with interchangeable continental combinations and with marches and countermarches between Hanover, Bohemia, and the Danube; nor was it that of the circles of enlightened opinion in Paris, whose exponents were admirers of English institutions and of the "Philosopher King" of Prussia. The distant, poorly known, costly undertakings of the builders of the French empire in the Indies, which offered no prospects of immediate profit, had not even been sponsored by the India Company. The *Fronde* of the parlements, directed against any attack on fiscal privileges, which was the only apparent link between politics, economics, and institutions, between the concerns of the govenment and those of the public, was kindled as early as the outset of the Seven Years' War. . . . All this exhibits the features of a complete incoherence to the hapless historian.

In the past two decades, economic and social historians have devoted their energies to clearing up this wasteland. Following the path marked out by the great works of Ernest Labrousse, a generation of historians undertook the task of translating the evolution of prices, salaries, incomes, exchanges, and production into curves and diagrams. As a result, the "age of Louis XV" has begun to take on a more distinct character, which, on the material level, certainly does not suggest a state of decline and decadence. The findings of this vast research project, which is still in progress, entirely confirm—allowing for more or less expected shadings and clarifications depending on the role given to the different social classes—the impression of prosperity and "splendor" of the age of Louis XV which the image of this dazzling civilization seemed to support.

From the 1730's on, all areas show a period of expansion, the most marked rise in population on the continent after centuries of stagnation, a rise in agricultural prices, and, even clearer, of ground rent, which doubled in the course of the century. There was a sharp rise in the consumption of luxury goods, colonial merchandise, sumptuous fabrics, artistic furniture, mirrors, clocks, porcelain, perfume, paintings, and costly books. Trade prospered, with that of the sugar- and coffee-producing "isles" in the lead. There was a relatively slow but continuous progress of industry and of nonmanual techniques in still distinctly delimited areas, most often in dependence on the great export trade which had to meet English competition and which, to a larger measure than the domestic market, offered outlets for "mass-produced" commodities, whereas the general popular consumption in France proper remained confined to absolutely essential commodities, and the luxury consumption of the rich and affluent classes, with some exceptions (such as the Royal Manufactory of Mirrors, which entered its golden age), was more favorable to small handicraft industry.

This prosperity, which no doubt had its lacunae, nevertheless presented a remarkable equilibrium and harmony. It marked industrial and technical progress, for a long time under administrative tutelage. But it was no "industrial revolution"; that is, it was not a massive "capitalist concentration," nor an overthrow of the social structures, which were doggedly conservative and remained as if anchored in the soil—and this was true even through the French Revolution. If the peasant mass, imprisoned its customs in the tangled servitudes of its status, doubly crushed under the full weight of the tax levy and the official policy (futile to boot) of bread at cheap prices, did not share in this prosperity—aside from the absence of great famines since the beginning of the century—at least it was preserved from the spoliations and the "proletarianization" suffered by the peasantry at that time equally in England and in eastern Europe, to the advantage of large-scale capitalist or seigneurial exploitation. During the greater part of the reign of

Louis XV, this general combination of circumstances seemed to be perfectly independent of the conjuncture of political circumstances. The financial disorders, the fiscal quarrel, the defeats on sea and land, the stagnation and almost complete collapse of maritime trade under the English blockade, all this did not gravely hamper the prosperity of the regime. A certain exhaustion, which had set in at the end of the Seven Years' War, was followed by a rapid and brilliant recovery after the signing of the peace which, disastrous as it appeared, left intact the bases of great colonial trade—and above all of the flourishing "triangular trade" which furnished the islanders with slaves and from whence it brought back foodstuffs raised in the colonies. We could fancy ourselves in a regime of liberal capitalism in full swing. The economic conjuncture followed its curve, just as the evolution of minds followed its curve, both equally indifferent to the political and administrative activity, itself incoherent, of a monarchy that was nevertheless absolute.[1]

[1] But it is precisely to the extent that the crisis of the eighteenth century was a crisis of regime more than an economic crisis (and herein we think lies the essential fact) that we cannot be content merely with anonymous curves and statistics. The blank space which the middle of the eighteenth century forms in our historical consciousness will disappear only when we have learned something—with names and figures and otherwise than through court anecdotes—about the struggles revolving around the key positions of the royal economy. The history of the administration of the Royal Treasury, from the reign of the brothers Pâris to that of the "Austrian Clan" of Laborde-Micault-Nettine (and Calonne), of that of the "King's grains," of the Farmers-General, of the Company of the Indies all still remain to be written or rewritten. Most of the large financial and colonial companies of the middle of the century, which—in contrast to those of 1770–1790—are still in the hands of officials and financiers, have not yet attracted any historian's interest. Even the history of the successive companies of the Indies and that of the *Caisse d'Escompte* (discount bank) which was closely linked to them must be entirely rewritten from this point of view. Economic history cannot—any more than the rest—set aside the *query cui bono?*

Such a weakness, not to say absence, of interaction between the political, economic, and social sectors is all the more paradoxical inasmuch as the administrative absolutism in no way ceased to act as the organizer and regulator of the country's economic, social, and spiritual life. On the economic plane, the great mass of customary activities remained locked up in its established frame—the land-statute and the manorial regime for agriculture, the corporative organization and administration ordinances for the artisanry and the retail trade. Nothing in principle could escape these consecrated frames without the support, or at least the formal assent, of the administration. There was no manufactory without "privilege" (by definition, an exemption granted to this or that person or company, and which was as good as a contribution of capital) which did not require exclusiveness in order to exist. Nor could any ship be fitted out, or any foreign trade expedition set out, without the permission of the Admiralty which watched over the privileges proper to each port and over those of the established companies. This administrative tutelage was a matter of course for everything relating to right of domain, mines and surface mining, forests, waters, and transportation. When domestic trade went beyond the limit of local trade, especially for commodities produced for mass consumption, it was strictly overseen by the administration, which was responsible for the provisioning of cities and markets and also for the protection of local products. As for essential foodstuffs, the prevailing prices, purchase, transport, and sale were all entirely subject to its authority. And in times of supply crisis, which were frequent, the administration itself took over the direction of such trade, which thereafter was conducted only by order or by agreement "on the King's behalf." As we know, this tutelary administration was criticized and accused of favoring and enriching its protégés, and at times also of speculation and self-enrichment. But greater proof is required to buttress the assertion that its principles were attacked by enterprising capitalists, eager "to throw away their crutches" and to fly with their own wings at their own risk and peril. Obviously, every form of protectionism, which by definition is a distribution of privileges, creates malcontents who would like to bend its activity to their interests. But the complaints of interested parties must not be confused with a general condemnation of the system. Even the influence of trading circles for which Gournay was, as it were, the representative, was far from being exerted only one way. Although it was "liberal" in general, it was often protectionist in particular, each city and corporation having its privileges and monopolies to defend. Whatever has been said of it, economic freedom has never been the ideology of special interests.

We are far better informed on the evolution of ideas on the subject of administrative regulation than on its actual functioning, except in rare sectors which have been the object of thorough studies, like that by André Rémond on John Holker, the inspector of manufactories. A question of economic, political, and social importance such as the trade in grains and the policy of provisions, which aroused the most violent polemics and fiercest accusations, still awaits a general study that would allow us to penetrate not only into the variations in prices but into the obscure bookkeeping of the "King's grains" in which so many of the country's fortunes were made. But the liberal impulse, even doctrinally "liberalist," seems certainly to have come from the royal administration itself, rather than from any special interest group. From the middle of the century on, a brilliant team of important functionaries, who were more or less economists or philosophers, hostile to restrictions, privileges, and regulations, struck out against the fetters hampering the economy. They were forced to retreat at times before the opposition of special interests and of popular opinion which their policies provoked. But they returned doggedly to the attack. While waiting for Turgot, the decade 1750–1760 witnessed the battle over free trade in grains, the lifting of the law against printed fabrics, and the freedom of labor in the countryside, although in all these cases toleration generally preceded the freedom proclaimed, or else the proclamation was not always implemented in fact. It saw too the almost systematic refusal to grant new privileges of corporative statutes, and the spectacular suppression of exclusive privileges, including some that required considerable courage to deal with—those enjoyed by the Royal Manufactory at Abbeville, in 1768, for example, and by the Company of the Indies in 1769. Far from being behind its time, the royal administration seemed to be way ahead of it, if we judge by the reactions provoked by its attempts at reform. Its action was blocked at each step only by the formidable problem presented by an inextricable tangle of acquired rights, prerogatives, and habits. Was it a question of "Liberalism versus Colbertism"? Here, more than elsewhere, we must be wary of labels. In the hodge-podge of customs, servitudes, and particular statutes which encumbered the jurisprudence of the eighteenth century there was no established group—and that includes the "poor peasants" who held to their communal rights, such as the right to gather brushwood and that of access to free grazing land—which did not have privileges which it defended, if only out of blindness and fear of changing the established routine. Thus, in the face of this battery of acquired rights, all that eventually remained in terms of a will to restructure the organization of the economy in the royal administration—whether that will be neo-Colbertist, "liberal," or physiocratic inspiration—had to become revolutionary or risk the penalty of being hopelessly bogged down. In the middle of the eighteenth century, all "progressive" tendencies, beyond their doctrinal quarrels, placed their hopes in an "enlightened despotism"—the only revolutionary force which they could perceive on the horizon—to make a clean sweep of special privileges. This myth of the "necessary" Revolution-from-above, which would save (or which would have saved) the monarchy, and the *ancien régime* finally rid of its abuses, certainly inspired several of the higher functionaries. And in a tenacious state of regret it has survived the *ancien régime* itself, by inspiring a whole school of historical writing. But it does not make the portrait of the age any more coherent. Was the "age of Louis XV" nothing else but such a contradictory tide, these currents flowing in different directions, this absence of direction, and this diffuse prosperity, marked by the absence of any clear and distinct will at the center?

History cut up into "centuries" or "reigns" is much decried nowadays, and rightly so. Nevetheless, it might perhaps be useful to elaborate on a "Louis XV perspective" for the study of this lengthy stairhead of the eighteenth century, which was not only a transition, the decadence of one regime and the preparation of another, but which had a structure peculiar to itself. The reign of Louis XV was the *ancien régime* stabilized, or restored, if you like—after a regency which had also been an institutional crisis and even the sketch of a dynastic crisis—arrived at its full flowering, at its classic form, simultaneously uncontested and itself respectful of legality, absolute but not at all despotic. Now the interaction between the economy and the regime was not reduced to interventions pursued by the government and the administration in economic activities; indeed there is a touch of guile in rendering the economic and financial administration a chapter isolated from its context. If the royal power was not controlled by a political constitution, it was limited on all sides in its possibilities of action, as in its resources, by law; or, rather, by individual laws, which taken together formed a constitution. But this constitution, precisely, was economic and social, not political. This is why the monarchical *ancien régime* was not a mode of government but a regime in the full sense of the word, that is, an order of society, economic and social as well as political, all of whose component parts were interconnected. It was not only a system for the distribution and allocation of functions respecting command, administration, public order, and justice, and a system for the distribution of public offices, but also—and above all—a system for the distribution and allocation of revenues. Indeed, the *ancien régime* ended up by being nothing else but that. Might not then the apparent incoherence of its age of splendor derive from the fact that too often it has been studied by historians on the basis of criteria that are alien, or at least peripheral, to it? At the risk of remaining within a mere aphorism, let us try, in a few summary remarks, to sketch the regime's principal mechanisms and to pinpoint its center of gravity.

We cannot here enter into a profound analysis, which would have to begin with a discussion of juridical terms which "classes" and "subclasses" and their social situations have customarily designated, nearly all of which are equivocal or contradictory. To use a simplification that is obviously somewhat crude, the monarchy constituted itself as an absolute monarchy by stripping the "feudal systems"—a term as convenient as it is unwarranted for designating the separation of power between independent potencies, princes, temporal and spiritual lords, municipal oligarchies, constituted bodies of all kinds—of their autonomous authority. At the same time, however, it guaranteed to them, as the price of their submission, the possession of their special privileges other than political. From the time of the accession of Louis XIV, the royal power definitively domesticated all rival powers which limited or controlled it by transforming them into clienteles. A whole social order, based not on private property but on the more or less hierarchical parcelling out of public power, thus found itself cut off from its origin and transposed from a hierarchy of authorities into a simple hierarchy of revenues and tenures. The "feudal system"—with its entire, religiously maintained, archaic apparatus of heraldry, judiciary forms, investitures, and obeisances—for a long time had ceased to be a diffuse mode of government in order to become merely a mode of tenure, which no threat "to take back a fief" or refusal of obeisance could trouble any longer. There was but one authority, the royal power, the sovereign legislator and administrator, which accounted to no one for its actions, and was limited only by the right of property, the sole title by which its will could be opposed. This was the only doctrine on which the courts of justice could solidly base themselves in their resistance to the King's arbitrary power. But in this case the notion of property assumed a singular extension, mingling with private property all the acquired positions and all the special appropriations of rights and public revenues. Seigneurial rights, special legal proceedings, policing rights, administrative, judiciary, and military functions, all were incorporated into the right of direct or "eminent" property, and in the absence of any other justification, possession was tantamount to legal title.

The persistent effort of the magistracy of the eighteenth

century, a zealous and vigilant guardian of acquired rights and, besides, the first interested party in the matter, was to assimilate privilege and private property, as completely as possible, into a homogeneous bloc of acquired tenures. It was the effort of magistrates, bourgeois-minded despite ennoblement and the acquisition of lordships, which furthermore bore the seed of the negation of all the unassimilable survivals and residues of "feudal" society, but whose immediate effect was to immobilize the whole state of economic and social affairs and to paralyze all "organizational" action of the royal power. In sum, the monarchy was liberated from all political control only by renouncing *per contra* all authority to effect innovations. Having suppressed, at all levels, any organized representation of the different orders and social groups which could have agreed to or even proposed revisions of their acquired rights recognized as necessary, the royal power found itself facing only the judicial power. This, by definition, could be motivated only by the desire to preserve the established order of things and was therefore opposed to all innovation.

The nation, which ceased to exist politically, had disappeared behind a heteroclite code of rights and possessions which nobody could modify in its absence. The result, only seemingly paradoxical, of this reduction of all political rights to the sole right of personal property was to fuse, into a solid, indistinct mass of property to be defended, the rights and claims, of such diverse origin, of the "three orders," or at least of their great hierarchies, which participated in the regime: the upper nobility, the upper clergy, the upper magistrates and "high finance" in the old sense of the word—who were all proprietors of both seigneurial holdings (lands) and of public offices or dignities, and all participants in this private appropriation of the entire machinery of the social, economic, and judiciary organization of the kingdom which blocked and frustrated the royal power from all sides.

In this sense, the vertical distinction between the three Estates, emptied of its content by the disappearance of any political representation, had much less reality than the "horizontal" distinction, which at the summit of each of these three orders isolated the *parties prenantes* of the *ancien régime* and distinguished them from the lower layers, from the petty rural nobility, the lower clergy, and the common run of the bourgeoisie. The unifying principle of this high-level society of the *ancien régime* was the very specific composition of its possession, linked in every case to the established monarchical order. The distinction between the upper nobility—and the upper clergy, which had become its increasingly exclusive appanage—on the one hand and the upper judicial and administrative bourgeoisie on the other, lay only in the difference of origin, real or presumed, of its titles of tenure. Without going into the mysteries of the decrepit feudal right as it shaped up in the eighteenth century and on which the arcane science of the courts of justice fed so ravenously, we simply contend that neither the nobility nor, evidently, the clergy were economic "classes" but "orders." Their codes of honor practically forbade them to engage in any lucrative economic activity, and the lords who showed an interest in the development and improvement of their landholdings were exceptions, even outside the nobility of the court. Indeed, their wealth was not of economic origin (above all, not desired to be) but represented the endowment of a "service of the King," of a command authority, or of a seigneurial or spiritual power of authority, conferred in principle by the King at some time in the past. Although the mass of direct seigneurial domains had been assimilated into landed property pure and simple, and although even the revenues from "eminent domains," which bore the indelible trace of their "feudal" origin and constituted in fact a special fiscal system alongside that of the King—seigneurial dues of all kinds, the *cens*, the *dîme*, the *corvée*, rights relating to the administration of justice and police functions—as well as the exceptions from royal taxes were, after a fashion, incorporated into this landed property and were sold or purchased with the land, this did not mean that the nobility became, or could become, a class of landed proprietors. Too many rights remained attached to the status of nobility and they were far from being purely honorific, such as personal fiscal privileges, or exclusive access to the important offices of the court and the army. Nor must we forget that entry to the "corridors of power" and to the court—which again became much more nobiliary under Louis XV than it had even been under Louis XIV, who had governed with "commis," agents employed by and dependent on the King, from the ranks of the petty and recent nobility—made persons of quality the intercessors and solicitors, often obligatory, for all matters handled by the King's "council" or by his entourage: obtainment of letters patent, commissions and reimbursements for supplies or public works, litigations brought before the council. Naturally, these people saw to it that the price of this protection was included in the putting up of money, in the distribution of benefices, or in the general costs of innumerable and very "plebeian" enterprises—which offered the nobility a very special way of taking part in economic activities without losing caste.

Finally, for all the great families of the courtier nobility, the King's pensions, gratuities, and liberalities formed an indispensable complement to their resources, which, moreover, did not all pass through the Royal Treasury. The King could confer revenues stemming from this or that part of the country's economic activity, such as "grand masterships of domains" which in fact were alienated systems of tax collection; above all, he had the power to make appointments to the great ecclesiastical benefices. These benefices were practically the only ones which, thanks to the fortunate effects of celibacy, had escaped hereditary appropriation and whose net income, after deductions for the expenses of the cult and of religious establishments, the maintenance of curates, officiating priests, and religious, ended up by forming an annual supplement of some hundreds of millions to the nobiliary income. Just as it had done with the great offices of the court and of the army, the court nobility ultimately established its monopoly over the lucrative benefices of the Royal Church so that at the end of the *ancien régime* there was not a single bishop descended from bourgeois stock. But in this diversity of form we always find that these revenues have the same components, the same for the nobility, the King, and the Church: ground rent derived from direct domain and rights of a fiscal order levied by the authority of a temporal or spiritual lordship.

The upper bourgeoisie of the *ancient régime* arrived at the same situation, but along different routes. To be sure, it had sprung from plebeian trades and, with the exception of several very old families of royal "commis," all its possessions, public offices, and lordships, including noble titles, were acquired, "for a financial consideration." Plebeianism always clung to the nobility of money or *noblesse de robe* in the eyes of the nobility of blood. But this official, judicial, or financial bourgeoisie gradually detached itself from its economic origins and became as alien as the real nobility to productive activities. The private appropriation of State functions and revenues, however, was completely carried out only in the judicature, whose offices thenceforth were transmitted, by sale or succession, practically without any intervention on the part of the King. After a brief return to ancient practices under Orry, the tenure of offices likewise ceased to be troubled by any massive creation of new ones. Another more or less hereditary oligarchy, less sheltered from administrative reshufflings and discussions of leases, was ensconced in the financial administration itself: for farmed-out taxes, financial officers who were proprietors of their offices; for direct taxes, farmers who had become practically irremovable since the re-establishment of the Farmers-General. The share deducted directly from the King's resources by the "financiers" before such taxes were poured into the treasury was usually evaluated at 30–35 million per year in the reign of Louis XV. Since the investments in lands and annuities were added to the capital invested in offices, the other components of the revenue of the State bourgeoisie did not differ at all from those of the nobiliar revenue. Thus as secondary oligarchies, respected far less than the nobility, "justice" and "finance" assumed a rank alongside the nobility among the payees of the *ancien régime* in this very particular society in which tenure of "feudal" origin and tenure of royal offices tended to merge into private property, with the whole medley of rights of a public order they brought along with them.

This rather artificial amalgamation was composed of more or less solid parts. "Feudal" property was accorded greater recognition and had been consecrated long before "officer" property, which remained an object of astonishment and even of scandal. If the prerogatives of the nobility of blood and of the clergy seem to have been indissolubly linked to the monarchical order itself, those of the bourgeois officialdom and of the *noblesse de robe* seem, instead, to have been linked to the disorders of royalty. Nothing could prevent the King from buying back or suppressing the offices, if he had the means. Hence, the vigilance of the bourgeoisie in the parlements, which were vitally interested in preventing any fissure appearing in the solid block of acquired rights. The jurists of the eighteenth century always set monarchy, even of the absolutist variety, which was respectful of rights, tenures, and special privileges over against "despotism," which "confuses all subjects without distinction"—a revolutionary and egalitarian despotism of which some reformers dreamed at this time. And the jurists appealed to the "fundamental laws of the monarchy" without finding any other definition for them save this respect for the acquired position. All the remonstrances of the parlements were summed up in these principles set down by the Parlement of Paris—in contrast to Turgot in the matter of forced labor (*la corvée*), the preeminent feudal right:

> The first rule of justice is to preserve to each one what belongs to him. This is a fundamental rule . . . which does not consist only in maintaining the rights of property, but further in preserving those which are attached to the person and which are born of the prerogatives of birth and social estate. . . .

The absolute monarchy, therefore, certainly had a constitution, but it was a constitution of revenues which singularly limited the royal power in the disposition of the resources of the realm. As the "first proprietor of the realm," the royal power shared with all other proprietors the ground rent and the eminent rights which weighed upon the product of the soil, and the bulk of which could not be increased arbitrarily without cutting into capital. "For," as Dr. Quesnay rightly observed, "the advances of a kingdom's agriculture"—namely, agricultural capital, soil, men, livestock, and equipment—"should be regarded as fixed property requiring most careful preservation in order to assure the production of taxes, revenue, and subsistence for all classes of citizens" (*Maximes générales*, Maxime I, which became Maxime V in the publication of *Physiocratie*). The royal financial system tried in vain to strike only at the nonprivileged classes; it was in vain that the direct tax (based on assessment, not on quotas) was distributed, systematically, in an inverse ratio to the taxpayer's ability or means to pay. The fact remained no less that the royal resources, essentially, were based on the same agricultural "fixed property" which simultaneously also served as a foundation for ground rent, quit rent, the *dîme*, and taxes. All the constituent parts of the *ancien régime* were co-proprietors, as it were, of the realm. All shared a revenue which was of the same nature and drawn from the same source as that of the King, if not directly deducted from his own. And he apparently could not increase his share without infringing on theirs, that is, by acts of "despotism" which would violate the "fundamental laws of the realm." The long quarrel over finances, which was to be a bitter one from 1765 on and which was really a constitutional quarrel, in effect was fought out entirely within this society of co-proprietors of the "agricultural kingdom"—nobility, clergy, magistracy—on the backs of the "husbandmen" in whom nothing hinted at a coming revolt. The struggle remained outside the other classes, which Quesnay called "sterile" and which in fact were so with respect to the tax because the royal fiscal apparatus (not to be the last in this case) was in no way equipped to impose or even detect personal or "monetary" fortunes not manifested in landed property.

Thus, we have come very close to that simple representation of the society of the *ancien régime* which sufficed for the Physiocrats to attempt an analysis of its economic functioning.[2] At the top, in a great indistinct unity, stood

[2] *François Quesnay et la Physiocratie,* ed. Louis Salleron (Paris: National d'Études Démographiques, 1958), Vol. II. Quesnay, obsessed by the idea of a ruined agricultural France, badly judged the combination of circumstances of his time, but he correctly judged the functioning of the society which he analyzed. The economics of his *Tableau* rests upon the clear distinction between "the proprietors of lands"—the lords, the King, and the tithe-owning clergy—on the one hand, and the cultivators of all conditions on the other. His disciples, beginning with Baudeau and Dupont, alarmed no doubt by the conclusions of such an analysis, in general preferred to confuse the two groups by disguising the lords and princes of the Church as honorary cultivators. By this single unique trickery they rendered the *Tableau* and the doctrine absurd. Necker wrote a pertinent remark in the margin of "*Éclaircissements demandés à M.N. . . . nom des propriétaires*" by Abbé Baudeau: "People always have the art of confusing the landowners and the cultivators; nothing cures these Messers the Economists of this method." (Copy annotated by Necker in the Bibliothèque Publique et Universitaire of Geneva.) By this conjuring away of the fundamental distinction between those who furnish and those who collect the "net product," they likewise reduced to hollow and stupendous verbiage the main point of their doctrine, Quesnay's great boldness: his theory of taxation that flows from his very definition of the net product as the "only disposable part of the national revenue" above the subsistence of the people. Let us not forget that the *Tableau*, destined for the King, was conceived in 1758, at the very beginnings of the monarchy's financial disasters. An attentive reading suffices to show that it was conceived specifically to demonstrate "scientifically" that since the tax could be levied only on the "net product," which is the revenue of sovereignty itself, it could and should not be levied only on those who share this revenue—on those, therefore, who refused to pay taxes—and that it is absurd, baleful, and ruinous to want to tax the peasants and workers, from whom they have already levied what is taxable. As absurd, Quesnay was to say, as to want to tax oxen and horses in order to spare the proprietors. This was the frankest and most irrefutable argument against the fiscal privileges of the landed proprietors which ruined the monarchy: "Their ignorant greed has never permitted them to perceive

the "class of proprietors," which was the regime itself in its constituted orders—the King, the nobility, the clergy, the office-owning, *rentier*, and seigneurial bourgeoisie; it was a class whose revenue was constituted by net produce of agriculture and whose expenditures regulated all economic movement. At the bottom, on the one hand, was the "productive class" of farmers, on the other the "sterile," or the "kept" (*stipendiées*) "classes," inasmuch as they did not produce for their own food and were not proprietors, but gained their subsistence through their goods and services. Quesnay's "Economic Table" presented the brilliant idea of following, as a single coherent process, the production and circulation of wealth in the social body: the very conception of this wealth as being exclusively derived from the land, that is, from agriculture, was far from absurd in a constituted society which participated in the *ancien régime.*

---

that taxes ought to be taken only from the revenue from lands. . . . The nobility and the clergy have demanded exemptions and immunities without limit, claiming the latter are bound up with their properties and their social estate. Sovereigns have also thought it expedient to grant total exemptions to their officials, and to all those who are invested with offices and employment in all the different departments of the administration. . . . The landed proprietors, who had not foreseen such consequences and who, at the same time as they were destroying their revenues, neither understood nor even perceived the cause of the diminution of their wealth, applauded these indirect taxes through which they believed to avoid the tax. Actually these should have been levied directly on the revenue of their properties, where they would have occasioned no decline in the annual reproduction . . . whereas . . . the indirect taxes [because of their] progressive and inevitable deterioration destroyed their own revenue, those of the Sovereign, and the wealth of the nation . . ." (*Second problème économique*, pp. 977–992). Herein lies the deep meaning of the appeal to "despotism" as the only force capable of destroying the privileges. Quesnay himself uses careful language on this burning point, preferring to convince and demonstrate without polemics (see the "result," *loc. cit.*, p. 992!); as for his disciples, for the most part they deserved Voltaire's cruel mockery.

Even theses which appear aberrant or ridiculous in the perspective of a trading and industrial society reacquire their whole sense once we place ourselves within the framework of the regime. It was perfectly true that the "revenue of the proprietors, of the Sovereign and of the tithe owners," around which the whole *Tableau* revolves, was nothing else but the "net product" of agriculture levied from a "class of cultivators" reduced to the level of mere physical subsistence. And the prosperity of the society of the *ancien régime* under the reign of Louis XV lay in the rise of the income from land, which was more rapid than that of agricultural prices, and much more rapid than that of salaries. All other wealth was but a derivation therefrom; it was very evidently exact for financiers, officials, and rentiers, whose revenue was deducted from that of the King, and for that matter always mixed with land revenues and direct seigneurial dues. But if we examine it closely, is this not also true of fortunes made in trade and industry, which seem to contradict the physiocratic analysis?

To be sure, Quesnay did not push his analysis very far in this direction and his schema does not respond to the whole picture of things: international trade and demographic, agricultural, commercial, and industrial expansion are too interdependent to be traced back to a single source. But it is beyond doubt that the "net product" of agriculture—that which it produces above the subsistence of the producers—remains the determinant factor of economic movement, and that the bulk of this "net product" passed through the hands of "proprietors" before entering into circulation. After all, let us not forget that great popular consumption of manufactured or imported products had not yet come into being. At the rural and popular level, the artisan and small-trade sector still constituted only thin complements of a very starveling rural economy, whose structure scarcely differed from what it had been for centuries, and in which exchanges were reduced to the needs of physical subsistence and the acquisition of rudimentary tools. It certainly was not here that the large, flourishing trade and the nascent industry were to find their outlets. Trade and manufacturing were entirely tributary to the "net product," levied and expended by the "class of proprietors"; and their prosperity depended exclusively upon the growing conspicuous consumption of this high society of the *ancien régime*. The trade with the Indies and with the islands brought exclusively products and foodstuffs earmarked for luxury consumption; "capitalist" industry did not yet exist except, on the one hand, for luxury needs—mirrors from Saint-Gobain, porcelain from Sèvres, Gobelins and fine cloth from Abbeville—and, on the other hand, for exportation which served to finance the importing of luxury items. Cheap-quality fabrics and "*pacotilles*"[3] were produced for the slave trade, not for the internal market. The only exception to this rule were the fabrications and supplies for the armies, that luxury of kings.

Quesnay's great concern was in seeing this "net product" levied on agriculture being squandered in sumptuary or sterile expenditures at the court and in the city, without being returned to agriculture in the form of investments or "useful advances." In fact, it was the "class of proprietors" which alone disposed of the "net product" and which, by the employment it made of its revenues, determined the whole economic movement. Now, by a monstrous aberration, it diverted the net product into "sterile expenditures" and "luxury for purposes of ornamentation" (*luxe de*

[3] Goods taken on board by seamen or passengers for private sale.—Trans.

décoration), thereby creating the purely "monetary" wealth of trade and factories which formed an unhealthy excrescence on the physiocratic economic circuit. Industrial and commercial capitalism thrived only from the consumption of the "proprietors," who ruined themselves and agriculture by diverting from it the revenues derived therefrom. It was, according to Quesnay, a parasitic vegetation which fed on the decomposition of the "agricultural kingdom," an alien element in the harmonious circulation of wealth which Quesnay looked upon with the keenest mistrust: for, "even if this trade were profitable to the merchants who would gain over their citizens in the sale of goods that it would bring . . . the growth of the fortune of these merchants would produce an injurious retrenchment in the circulation of revenues." "The merchants share in the nation's riches, but the nations do not share in the riches of the merchants. The merchant is an alien in his own country" and "monetary fortunes are a clandestine form of wealth which knows neither King nor country." [4]

[4] Quesnay's fierce anti-Colbertism had nothing in common with the nostalgic anti-industrialism of the Romantics, and it was also as far removed as possible from any sentimental infatuation with the peasantry and rustic customs. England was the example that Quesnay, like so many economists of the eighteenth century, proposed to France. Opposed to the artificial creation of privileged manufactories in a hothouse, supported by the State by crushing agriculture, he was not at all opposed to the free development of industry. His apparent contradictions fell into place around a sufficiently coherent view of a balanced development of exchanges between agriculture and industry; but he granted priority to the former, which alone can simultaneously procure a large market and an abundant labor force for industrial activities. Strongly antipathetic is the small-scale anti-economic cultivation practiced by poor farmers and sharecroppers, which fixed an unproductive and starveling surplus agricultural population in the countryside, hostile to servitudes which congealed agriculture in its traditional frames, he extolled large-scale "capitalist" cultivation in the English manner, which would replace human labor as much as possible "through the medium of animals, machines, rivers, etc.," and would thus free

We shall hear this particular ring of the bell often on the eve of the Revolution. It was at this point that Quesnay's economic circuit, which was so perfectly representative of the society of the *ancien régime* as it saw itself, based entirely on income from land, did not close up; there was a constant flight of the "net product" toward the "monetary fortunes" which did not enter into the established framework of this society and did not follow its laws. Sombart, by his demonstration that "capitalism" was born of the need for luxury and ostentation of aristocratic societies, merely resumed the thought of the "Economists" of the physiocratic school at the point at which it had stopped. But a pre-established harmony between the prosperity of the "proprietors" and that derived from trade seemed to reign at the middle of the eighteenth century. The manorial and *rentier* society of the *ancien régime* was firmly on its feet, more ostentatious and dazzling than it had ever been; it commanded and fed the circulation of wealth, and the formation of personal wealth in the hands of its trading servants, who brought its foodstuffs, fabrics, and objets d'art from the four corners of the earth to ornament its tables, its interiors, and its toilettes; yet it still appears as a marginal and subordinate phenomenon. This prestigious "age" of Louis XV was the unshared reign of a high society which consumed the social product and which economically was nothing but consumer-oriented. Its interest in the arts and manufactories; its hostility to corporative and trade monopolies, which served it poorly and adjusted

laborers "for other services and other works." (*Economic Maxim*). Industrialization must begin through agriculture, or in modern terms, through the primary sector. Thereby, Quesnay joins up with and completes the liberal school. His *Maxims* contain the outline of a theory of industrial development for an agricultural country which neither history, nor the modern experiments of "underdeveloped countries," has refuted.

poorly to changing tastes and fashions; in short, its liberalism, was primarily that of a consumer who wants freedom of choice. Was not the "liberation" of printed fabrics imposed by the ladies who, in a society exclusively concerned with furnishing and ornamenting its life, quite naturally gave everything its tone? Quesnay's *Tableau économique* was much closer to the economic as well as the psychological reality of this class than that found in the portrayals of many modern sociologists. Such men have eyes only for the things that usher in the nineteenth century; to them the court, nobility, princes of the Church, and the officer oligarchy do not seem to have an economic existence, whereas in fact the whole economic movement was at their service. The gradual displacement of wealth and influence was still far from that breaking point which was to rock the society's center of gravity.

Seen in this perspective, the worldly and anecdotal history of the "age of Mme de Pompadour" joins up with economic and social history in its most concrete reality, and moralists have written both simultaneously. The whole public, intellectual, artistic, moral, and social life gravitated around this society constituted of privileged orders to whom the "fundamental laws" of the monarchy, while stripping them of any responsibility in the administration of the country, assured the disposition of the social product. This society fulfilled with great taste, imagination, and distinction the only social function that was left to it; namely, that of spending—while living in a lordly, noble style—the "net product" of the agricultural kingdom.

> It is necessary that the proprietors of landed property, who received these revenues, should spend theirs annually so that this kind of wealth may be distributed among the whole nation. Without this distribution, the State would not be

> able to subsist; if the proprietors retained these revenues, it would be necessary to deprive them thereof. Thus this kind of wealth belongs as much to the State as to the proprietors themselves, the latter having the enjoyment of them only so that they may spend them. The proprietors are useful to the State only through their consumption; their revenues exempt them from labor; they produce nothing; if their revenues were not distributed to the remunerative occupations, the State would be depopulated through the avarice of these unjust and perfidious proprietors. Laws would arise against these men—useless to society and withholders of the country's wealth." [5]

If the royal society showed disdain for Dr. Quesnay's precepts as to the intelligent way to spend, and foolishly ignored or ridiculed his theory of taxation, the King's share in his own revenues, it conformed wholly (indeed, to excess) to the commandment to spend without restraint and to avoid "sterile savings which would cut off from circulation and distribution a portion of their revenues." It was the way of life of this "class of proprietors" which created the life style of the epoch, raising to the peak of refinement the art of living in polite society, the art of decoration, of keeping a good table, and of gallantry. And it even afforded itself, with a rare elegance, the luxury of wit, even a wit which was subversive. It was a mode of life which was inaugurated with the inflation of fortunes so easily made during the Regency, supported by the rapid growth of the "net product" during the golden age of Louis XV, and prolonged by wild indebtedness during the last decades of the *ancien régime*, when the bankruptcies and public borrowing of the great noble and princely houses provided the financial news. Finally, it [i.e., the elegant wasteful life]

[5] Quesnay, "Impots" in *Oeuvres, op. cit.*, p. 582.

was defended to the point of blindness, by the violent opposition to any modification in the apportionment of revenues, either in favor of the King or of the "agricultural class," put up by that nobiliary and parliamentary reaction which was to be the prelude to the Revolution. But until the last act the drama of the *ancien régime* was played within the circle of payees, the only ones associated with the regime. Outside their magic circle, the royal power remained absolute; in other words, it could find neither resistance nor support. Nothing which happened on its periphery really counted for the life of this society of the *ancien régime*, as long, at least, as it was not showing a complete deficit. During the first half of the reign of Louis XV, in a period of agricultural prosperity and of peace scarcely troubled from the outside, the regime's economic foundation, broader and more assured than it ever had been in the age of Louis XIV, seemed to be sufficient for its splendor.

Despite its schematism, Quesnay's *Tableau économique* contained an almost complete analysis of this "society of proprietors" which was at the center of the *ancien régime*, and it also gave an account of its apparent incoherence, or rather of its two apparently contradictory "states of mind." For it had the immense merit of shedding light on the distinctive feature of the *ancien régime* which economic history can ignore only under the penalty of being condemned to a fragmentary or marginal view of the epoch: namely, the existence, at the very center of the regime and the economy, of a society sufficiently large, composite, and above all very powerful, which by deducting without counterpart the "net" social product to its advantage was economically only a consumer society, and which determined the circulation of wealth of the "agricultural kingdom." The society of the *ancien régime*—possessed, as it were, an internal economy from which it drew its resources, and an external economy (which was not reduced to external trade but included it almost entirely) from which it drew its luxury items. And those two economies communicated only by way of the high society of State, Church, and court. Once we pass from one to the other, the perspectives, conceptions, and values change: this perhaps may to some extent explain the strange fate of the physiocratic "doctrine" which imposed itself upon some with the force of obviousness and struck others as absurd and ridiculous. Two economies living side by side, under different laws, in the service of the same dominant society which itself had two faces. Just as it was liberal and open to all novelties as a consumer, so it was hostile to reform in its own sphere, and authoritarian in the collection of its revenues—almost by definition, since it actually involved the collection "rights" and not the remuneration for money which had been invested or profit on any kind of activity. The "internal economy" in this sense was first of all the rural economy itself, subjected to a tangle of servitudes and dues, with its very clear and frank separation between the villeins who tilled the earth and gathered its fruits (farmers, sharecroppers, taxable peasant-proprietors who were also subject to the *corvée*, agricultural workers, and often a little of all this at one and the same time) and the notables, associated with the regime, who shared among themselves the deductible net product. But there were also the complementary activities of an essentially agricultural, almost autarchic economy; the circulation of raw produce, whose transport, markets, and prices were strictly regulated; the small trade; and the traditional working classes, subject to the ancient forms of corporative organization and to the regulations of the royal or even seigneurial police. The economic foundation of the regime was organized in a closed circuit, and all the relations within were regulated by acquired rights which formed an integral part of the public order. Here authority reigned over things as it did over minds, and nothing suggested that there could be a violent shattering of the established order.

This schema, to be sure, is only a schema. And the separation was by no means watertight. Thus, by a kind of contamination, the corporative organization had for a long time been broken into by the rural industries which supplied the great export trade, in Brittany, Normandy, Picardy, and in the Languedoc. The viniculture, which likewise furnished a luxury product also for export, in part escaped the servitudes of the rural economy. But these exceptions confirmed the rule. It was always on the margin of the interior circuit analyzed by the *Tableau économique*, in the trade in foodstuffs and exotic products, in the production of luxury items and in the circulation of "monetary fortunes" which resulted from them, that commercial and banking capitalism blossomed. Here the liberal tendencies of the age were manifested, but without invading or, as yet, gravely limiting the core of the society of the *ancien régime*. In this sense, as in many others, the mid-eighteenth century seems to mark a point of equilibrium such as history has known only rarely. No doubt it was transitory, as are all social equilibriums; but it must have appeared to its beneficiaries as the assurance of an unlimited future in the constant progress of enlightenment, law and order, refinement, and the amenities of life. We would be wrongly interpreting what, after the event, appears as the frivolousness of the century of Louis XV, if we tried to see in it some sort of vertigo at the edge of the abyss, rather than an expression of almost cloudless optimism. It was because it was so sure of its unshakeable foundations that the absolute monarchy did not even attempt to make that "Revolution-from-above" which the philosophers hoped for while there was still time.

CHAPTER SIX

François Quesnay and the Economic Society

A bizarre confusion of lines, figures, and formulas, seen as either enticement or hobgoblin, flanks the approach to any study of Quesnay. The *Tableau économique*, the first figurative model of the economic process, the zigzag, the famous secret formula of the Physiocratic School that became the butt of cruel and malicious jokes, was likewise the first popularization of political economy, if we may be so bold as to use this expression for a plan drawn up for the King in person to initiate him into the first principles of the royal economy. When François Quesnay, ordinarily the physician of the marquise de Pompadour, presented this curious scribbling in 1758 to Louis XV, ever in search of distractions, so that the monarch could print it by his own hand in his tiny toy print shop which was decorated in gold, mahogany, and tulipwood, he was applying the principle of pedagogy which recommends that teaching be combined with amusement, a principle as indispensable to courtiers as to tutors.

According to legend, Louis XV is supposed to have set up in type almost half of the *Tableau*, for which he was also supposed to have conceived a great admiration. Then this bored great lord turned his attention to amusements of a less abstract nature. But a small band of disciples of the new science, which soon earned the sobriquet "the sect," gathered as an organized group in Dr. Quesnay's tiny apartment in the *entresol* of the château at Versailles: Mirabeau père, Lemercier de la Rivière, Du Pont de Nemours, G.-F. Le Trosne, the abbé Nicolas Baudeau, Turgot. Soon this secret meeting place became an intensely active literary and worldly propaganda center, the impact of which was felt over the whole of France, then throughout Europe, reaching as far as Poland, Sweden, and Russia. It led to the establishment everywhere of "economic societies" which corresponded with each other in order to spread the "doctrine." In the twilight of the *ancien régime*, the terms "economy" and "economist" designated the doctrines of Quesnay and his disciples, in contradistinction to the "commercial" doctrines deriving from mercantilism.

Quesnay's glory and that of his school was as shortlived as it had been great, lasting no more than fifteen years. The *Tableau économique* and the physiocratic view of social and economic structures dominated the thought of reformers in France, and well beyond her borders, during the last fifteen years of the reign of Louis XV. Then the doctrine sank into oblivion, almost overnight. During this brief period of fame, the *Tableau* cut a figure as a revelation which enabled its initiates to grasp in one sovereign glance the profound nature of the whole economic process with all its ramifications. On the morrow of its decline from glory it had become a piece of arcane twaddle, silly and absurd, a ridiculous nursery tale. It is rare in history to be able to put one's finger on the moral and spiritual end of a social order, but here the actual point of breakdown is strikingly evident. The *ancien régime* had already signed its act of abdication in 1776, when the direction of the kingdom's economy and financial policies was passed from the hands of the Physiocrat Turgot to those of the Genevan banker Necker, even though the regime was to drag on its existence for another fifteen years. It was not only the *Tableau économique* which had become an object of wonder and then of contempt; this fate befell the whole organization and structure of monarchical France.

Every French schoolboy has read *L'Homme aux quarantes écus*, the satire in which Voltaire pitilessly ridiculed the physiocratic theory of taxation according to which the land is the sole source of wealth and therefore the only taxable entity. Voltaire here recounts the story of a poverty-stricken small peasant proprietor crushed by bad harvests, stripped of his last *sou*, and thrown into prison by the Farmers-General, while an affluent merchant whose personal wealth is exempt from taxation, in conformity with the doctrine, regales the poor wretch with a string of philosophical reflections on the blessings of the land. This brilliant and facile persiflage has survived Quesnay's doctrine itself, and the literary public knows about physiocracy only by way of this caricature.

It was only around the middle of the nineteenth century that Quesnay and his theory were wrested from oblivion by the new discipline of the history of economic doctrines, which created an honorable niche for him in the pantheon of the pioneers of economic thought. The common opinion of historians of economic doctrines and of economists, generally expressed with infinite respect, can be summarized as follows: the *Tableau* was brilliant in conception, but wrong. Or, if you prefer, wrong admittedly but brilliantly so. It was brilliant as the first attempt at a comprehensive view of the economic process, wrong in all the assertions it made on this process, and on its operative factors and laws. Indeed, most often economists have dispensed with reading Quesnay himself, who as an author is often obscure and ponderous, in order to hold to the more polished and inoffensive version of his maxims elaborated by the followers for the sake of drawing rooms and ladies of wit. Despite the meritorious editions and commentaries of Eugène Daire and August Oncken, it was only in 1958, on the second centennial of the *Tableau économique*, that the National Institute of Demographic Studies published a complete text of Quesnay's economic writings—none too voluminous, incidentally—which finally enables us to extract his authentic doctrine from the tangle of misunderstandings and distortions that have grown up around it.

Quesnay was a peasant lost and out of his element in the artificial gardens of Versailles. Born in 1694, the same year as Voltaire, in Méré, a little village in the Ile-de-France, of a family of obscure husbandmen, he was self-taught, learning how to read and write from the village gardener, a man of some philosophical bent. His mother, who was widowed when François was thirteen, allowed him to go to Paris to earn his livelihood as an engraver of anatomical drawings while pursuing studies as a "practitioner" in surgery, a manual and despised auxiliary branch of medicine. He enjoyed a career as a rural surgeon and gradually acquired a bourgeois clientele, then a court clientele, being called to assist at deliveries which in the upper reaches of the society of the time often required secrecy and discretion. In addition to his skills as a surgeon and his rather rough and easy-going manner, it was precisely because of his virtues of discretion that many ladies of quality sent for Dr. Quesnay as their confidential physician, indeed almost as their father confessor, until the day when Mme de Pompadour summoned him to assist her with the burdensome task of distracting the King from his eternal ennui. Quesnay was loyal to the end to this protectress of the encyclopedists and economists, without ever worrying about whether he was in the good or bad graces of the King or of his entourage.

We shall not discuss Quesnay's medical treatises here, none of which has left its mark in history, nor his prodigious production of polemical writings in the great quarrel revolving around the precedence of the order of surgeons over that of physicians. But the title of his best-known medical work, *L'Essai physique sur l'économie animale*, is there to remind us of the exceedingly broad character of the term "economy," which embraces all the functions of a living organism.

The first reading, the first storehouse of knowledge for the young villager François Quesnay had been the old popular book, already famous, written by the physicians Charles Estienne and Jean Liébaut, *L'Agriculture ou la maison rustique*. It was a perfect example of that ancient household literature in which "domestic economy" extends to everything of interest to the concerned father of a family. It ranged from the proper administration of a happy household—from domestic morals and the education of the children—to husbandry and the making of tools, to medical advice respecting man and beast, to medicinal herbs and kitchen recipes. "Political" or "royal economy" was to be nothing else but household science extended to the kingdom. This peasant's son got the ambitious notion of becoming a surgeon after reading *La maison rustique*. But, no doubt, it was through this same book that he formed his first ideas of an economic order. Scholars have often tried to establish analogies between Quesnay's economic doctrine and his views on medicine, and especially between his *Tableau* and the system of the circulation of the blood. But the relation between them is deeper than a mere analogy. Physiocracy, that is, "the rule of nature," or the "natural order" as it was called, in reaction to administrative Colbertism, was the last powerful manifestation of the "organic" and "total" medieval view of society. A society that was nothing but the enlarged image of the House of the Father, where God has provided for all the needs of the body and the soul by the laws that He has given to nature. All that men have to do, and kings first of all, is to conform to them. But they cannot violate these same laws without drawing infinite evils upon themselves. In a very deep sense it was the last Catholic doctrine that was altogether coherent on the subject of economics. By virtue of his process of thought, Quesnay was the disciple of Malebranche and of the latter's occasionalist philosophy. According to this philosophy, ideas are not rationalizations achieved through the abstraction of our sense experiences, but pre-exist in us like the image of divine reason obscurely present in creation, and for which the experience of the senses is only the "occasional reason" that enables us to find evidence for the ideas in ourselves.

Quesnay's first nonmedical writing did not deal with political economy, but with philosophy: he made his contribution to the *Encyclopédie* in 1756 with the article "*Evi-*

dence." His whole doctrine was to be constructed from such *evidence*, which he defined as "A certitude which is so clear and manifest that the mind cannot deny it." Those who grasped the doctrine in its central point found that all its details fell into place with perfect clarity; whereas those who had not grasped the first postulate saw it only as a tangle of obscurities and unproved affirmations. Whence ensued the inability of the Physiocrats to discuss the least particular proposition without referring to the "Whole" and without beginning again at every turn the complete exposition of the "Doctrine," which gave their school the character of an esoteric sect accessible only to the initiated.

The *Tableau économique*, in its brilliant apparent simplicity, became an inextricable labyrinth once commentators applied themselves to the task of deciphering its details; and the exegeses of its paths have filled libraries. Hence it will suffice to sum up its idea and formal aspect here. The *Tableau* claims to represent a complete cycle of the process of the production and the circulation of wealth, which according to Quesnay—quite naturally—begins with the annual harvest. The whole dynamic of the national economy of his time followed the same annual rhythm as the sowing and harvest seasons: the annual falling due of payments and of rents, seigneurial dues, etc., but also the annual arrival of fleets carrying silver bullion at Cádiz, the annual departure and return of expeditions for the East Indies, the annual return of international, regional, and local fairs, whose decreasing cycle marvelously corresponded to the zigzag line of the *Tableau.* The entire process starts out on the left from the sector of primary production, whose components remit their surplus product, their "net product," to a tax collector placed at the summit of society, which we shall provisionally call the sovereign power. It is only through the spending of the "net product" by this power group which appropriates the national revenue that the process of economic exchanges is set in motion. The zigzag aims to show how the "net product" expended at the summit in the purchase of the products of the different social classes returns directly, or by way of the detour of the industrial and artisan classes who spend their income in the purchase of foodstuffs and raw materials, to the primary production sector. Thus, its components can reconstitute their productive investments annually: the "renewal of annual advances" or a kind of "working capital" as we would say today, although the term does not exactly fit the circumstances.

It is obvious that any relative modification of the figures from which Quesnay starts out involves a modification of the other relations of magnitude and of their final product. If the primary production is burdened with rents and dues beyond its surplus "net product," or if the expenditure of the national product is badly managed, the primary production sector cannot reconstitute its capital. And this "agricultural disinvestment," to use a modern term, fatally involves a diminution of the product of the next annual cycle: it represents the waste and squandering of the nation's productive capital. Quesnay and Mirabeau employed this schema to demonstrate mathematically the ravages of a bad financial and fiscal policy, and to denounce the pernicious character of "Colbertism." By "Colbertism" they meant the artificial creation of industries to meet the sumptuary needs of luxury and prestige, artificially nurtured, subsidized, and privileged, at the expense of agriculture which alone was burdened with the weight of taxes and of seigneurial dues and crushed by the official ordinances weighing upon agricultural prices. In financial and political policy, Quesnay's fundamental principle asserts the primacy of agriculture: public investments should be directed toward agriculture as a matter of priority in order to increase its yield, and free trade and free exportation of cereals should permit the search for outlets at advantageous prices. As for industry and trade, they will defend themselves on their own in free competition, once a rich agricultural population, enjoying a high purchasing power, assures them a large market.

This polemic is the part of Quesnay's work which most markedly bears the stamp of the disputes of his age. But it is replete with striking insights into the particular nature of the "primary sector" which have basically retained their novelty to this day. For example, the observation that a low cost of living is the sign of a poor country, "such as in our provinces where produce is sold at a very low price, and where abundance co-exists with poverty"; that "agriculture, unlike trade, does not have a resource in credit" because the soil is not capital capable of liquidation since, although it can easily fall into debt, it cannot reimburse itself; that trading and industrial "republics" grow rich by rigorous savings, whereas "agricultural monarchies . . . increase their revenue through consumption" inasmuch as for them it can be said "as is the sale, so is the consumption." These are partial truths flowing from a fundamental thesis formulated in the *General Maxims of the Economic Government of an Agricultural Kingdom*, namely, the assertion that land is the pre-eminent fixed capital of the national economy, "which must be preserved with great care in order to ensure the production of taxes, revenue, and subsistence for all classes of citizens," and which cannot be subjected to the same rules of the economy of exchanges as can industrial and commercial capital.

As a method of visual initiation, the *Tableau* was a brilliant invention. But as for deducing, explaining, and proving the theses implicit in its conception, it was worthless. By wishing to be simultaneously—and contradictorily—a genetic model (in which everything is read in terms of agricultural production as the source of all wealth) and an analytic model of the functioning of a wholly constituted economic society (in which movement originates in the spending of the "net" social product), Quesnay presupposed what he wanted to prove at every point in his analysis. For his further demonstrations he had recourse to another graphic schema, the "Formula of the *Tableau*" which replaced the zigzag by a single series of exchanges of definite contingents. But here all the data are arbitrary, and there is no longer either a process or an annual cycle. Indeed, the Physiocrats always counselled their disciples not to persist in understanding this magic *Tableau*, but to make use of it as a simple visual support for reflection.

But the *Tableau* has not exhausted its virtues as such as optical support, nor as an intellectual brainteaser. It is precisely because it incites to contradiction while also fascinating us that it performs its pedagogical mission in provocatively placing before us the three fundamental theses of physiocracy: the theory of net product, the division of society into three classes, and the central role of the social group which determines the use that is to be made of the net product.

Let us be wary of beginning the discussion of the *Tableau* from its most controversial aspect, which has almost caused the conception as a whole to be forgotten: the division of working society into two classes, of which only one —that engaged in primary production—is called productive, whereas the other, including trade, industry, and the performance of services, is called sterile. By focusing on this pseudo problem of determining whether agriculture is truly the sole producer of economic values, the disciples and adversaries of physiocracy enthusiastically became bogged down in the most preposterous misunderstandings, and the discussion on this bizarre assertion ineluctably ended up with the conclusion that this old peasant Quesnay, despite his brilliant side, was a naïve rustic. In all of this, the way in which Quesnay posed the problem, and above all his conception of the social product, have remained incomprehensible because, in fact, they had become alien to the entire economic thought of the nineteenth century.

When Quesnay speaks of the "net product or revenue for the nation," he clearly specifies that this must not be confused "with the gain of merchants and entrepreneurs," which "must be placed on the rank of expenses for the nation" as well as farm products consumed on the spot by the farmers themselves. It is not a question of knowing whether this or that economic activity produces a benefit for him who produces it. What is at stake is that the social economy as a whole should produce a net surplus value above all the salaries, capital, and particular profits consumed in the economic process—a pure surplus above the expenses of subsistence and of reproduction and of the gains retained by the partners. It is the "net product" conceived as a freely disposable, excessive social product that the economic society remits to the noneconomic society. We shall return later to the question of what historical form this noneconomic society assumes in Quesnay's analysis, and precisely where he pinpoints the birth of this net product in the process he describes. The first decisive point is that Quesnay from the start assigns to economy, as such, an objective which goes beyond it. Consequently, this social "superstructure"—which appears in Adam Smith, in Jean-Baptiste Say, in Karl Marx, and in almost all the theorists of the nineteenth century only as a parasitic accessory of the economy—is for Quesnay the end and justification of the whole process. The whole mechanism analyzed by the *Tableau* is there only to support this "superstructure." The fact that this distinctive feature of the whole doctrine, which is glaringly apparent at first sight, has been cavalierly ignored by the dozens of learned dissertations of physiocracy shows strikingly how systematic thought is incapable of grasping a system other than its own.

This way of posing the problem is not familiar to us. We have not learned to consider political economy in terms of such a criterion. Its principle, perhaps, is more accessible to our historical sense than to our utilitarian economic reasoning. In fact, the history of any civilization and of any organized society, from the material point of view, is indeed the history of this social product not consumed by the productive classes. This product is deducted by the force of the authority to which they are subject, or by violence, so that it may be stored up in the courts of lords and princes, in the temples and treasuries of the clergy, and made available for ends other than those of physical subsistence: for the luxury and the art of living of a class of lords, for palaces, edifices for public worship and representation, and works of art, as well as for the deployment of the domineering power of the State. It was only the material disposal of a social produce, "the revenue of sovereignty," which made possible the establishment of an organized political order. The latter—unless it be a form of ephemeral brigandage doomed to perish of its own peculations—tended to favor in turn the growth of the "net product" on which it fed. It required the compartmentalization of the humane sciences, effected in the last century, to conceive of the idea of an economic process intelligible independently of the State, culture, and the juridical order, and of the idea of all the latter being independent of the economy.

In the history of civilizations we discern the meaning of this disposable social product, above the needs of subsistence and reproduction, which covers the noneconomic expenses of society in the way of luxury, prestige, or cultic religious practices. It is this surplus which bears the plus sign in Quesnay's *Tableau;* whereas in the economic theories of the nineteenth century, which recognized only an economic aim for economy, it was either wholly ignored or labelled with the minus sign as a nonproductive public expense. This explains why to a modern economist Quesnay's whole accounting system is topsy-turvy in its construction.

It seems to us that it is even more difficult to admit the physiocratic thesis, according to which the net product derives exclusively from primary production, whereas all other activity, commercial or industrial, is tributary to this surplus of the primary sector and merely shares in its consumption, being therefore sterile on the plane of social product level. I say primary production and not, as is customary, agriculture. In the "productive sector" of his *Tableau,* Quesnay expressly grouped together all the branches of the primary production of his age, including "forests, mines, fishing, etc."

At the outset, no doubt, we find ourselves confronting a myth of nature: only the good earth gives more than it receives, a grain of seed giving many grains, a tree bearing fruits, a flock reproducing itself. One manufactured article does not engender another, a table does not procreate other tables, a gold piece does not produce offspring. But the doctrinaire stubbornness with which Quesnay developed and hardened this initially hesitant thesis—in the *Tableau* the terms "productive" or "sterile" still were applied only to the different orders of public expenses, in a sense close to common acceptance—derives from his bellicose ardor against Colbertism. It was here that minds came to a separation of the ways: whoever admitted this peremptory assertion could count himself among the economists; whoever rejected it and recognized a productivity proper to trade and industry remained a mercantilist. In the final analysis, it was the formidable rise of trade and industry in the last third of the eighteenth century which suddenly made the whole physiocratic theory look absurd. Thenceforth it was considered as the simple doctrinaire reflection of a primitive agrarian stage of the economy which had been superseded. And this is how it figures today in the museum of economic doctrines.

It was Quesnay's disciples, in particular, who caused his teaching to fall into disrepute and ridicule. They degraded it by endowing it with the contours of a nostalgic feudal and romantic reaction to the rising industrial society. In the first place, Quesnay's doctrine had never been a naïve eulogy of rural life; it had nothing in common with the *bergeries de la Reine* of Versailles nor with a Rousseauist glorification of rustic and simple happiness. This legend is refuted in every line of his writings. On the contrary, Quesnay was an enthusiastic and radical propagandist of large-scale, rationalized, high-yield, and highly equipped farming, indeed, of industrialized farming, employing the least number of persons through the utilization of the farming techniques known to his time, "by means of animals, machines, rivers, etc." His model was contemporary England, the country of agricultural depopulation, where large landed estates administered by "capitalist" farmers, throwing their production on the market while at the same time driving the small peasantry toward the towns, created the conditions for rapid industrialization. For Quesnay, rural overpopulation, the distinctive sign of backward countries, was the cancer of the national economy, "the humble classes occupied in the countrysides, without profit for the State, with a bad cultivation from which they wrest a wretched subsistence" and which served mainly "to keep the population of a poor nation unfruitfully." Only an agriculture employing few persons and large amounts of capital furnishes this surplus production that enables the development of an urban economy and assures the "humbler classes" of the countryside jobs of a more useful character in the cities.

At this point in his reasoning it has been a game for satirists and pedants since Voltaire to accuse Quesnay of contradicting himself. But ultimately the quarrel revolved around words and terminology. Quesnay never claimed that nature was productive without the participation of man, or that machines could not increase this productivity of nature. He merely affirmed, with passionate stubbornness, that all labor and all the technical inventions could not produce a surplus over the single reproduction of invested force and material except by cooperating with the immanent productive force of nature. If he qualified as "sterile" all other forms of activity, it was due to the awkwardness of an amateur who had to forge his own terminology from scratch finding nothing usable in the mercantilist literature of his epoch, but who stubbornly persisted in his challenge so that he would have to surrender nothing in his thesis to the Colbertists: his assertion being that all enrichment and all differentiation in society must proceed from primary production and that any other industry can only add a secondary, complementary activity thereto; only the surplus of primary production furnishes the bases of the division of labor, specialization, and exchanges.

Expressed thus, it was a question of manifest historical fact, and if Quesnay had discovered the term "primary production," which he so laboriously strove to express with circumlocutions, he could have contented himself with the tautological assertion that primary production is certainly primary production—first, original, and fundamental—of which all the others are but extensions displacing, combining, and transforming the material that is furnished to them: through the coincidence of the signifying and the signified, any evidence in effect becomes tautology. This evidence has been rediscovered today; we find its modern expression in Colin Clark or in Fourastié, in the division of the economy into primary, secondary, and tertiary sectors, tillage of the soil and extraction of raw materials, processing industries, trade and services, each of these sectors obeying very different rhythms of technical progress and of the growth of productivity.

By the very fact of this disparity of progress, admittedly, the relations and orders of magnitude have changed entirely since two centuries ago. If in Quesnay's time the agricultural sector dominated, the following century in Western countries witnessed the astonishing advance of the secondary industrial sector. As for the tertiary sector, in which modern economists very democratically range all that is neither agricultural nor industrial—the charcoal seller and the chief of state, the priest, the porter, the waiter, the publicity agent, the musician, the hairdresser, the judge, the scholar, the striptease artist, the lawyer, and the man of letters—in short, the whole composite group defined by subtraction which satisfies those social needs not covered by agriculture and manufactured products, and which in modern societies tends to become the most numerous, evidently is no longer what it was in physiocratic society. Quesnay would have been flabbergasted to see the hierarchic summit of his *Tableau* and the rejects of his "sterile class" combined higgledy-piggledy in the same category. But this is a question of regime and not of economic terminology, and we can still prefer Quesnay's classification without fundamentally altering the analysis of the structural evolution.

What has dated in Quesnay is not the view of the fundamental articulations of economic society, but his material enumeration of the branches of primary production. Since the end of the eighteenth century, the very essence of the industrial revolution has been to place the "immanent forces of nature" in the service of an increasing number of activities which had up to then been in the hands of artisans. The enormous growth of material productivity over the past two centuries has progressed step by step with the utilization of motor forces and of the energy reserves of nature impounded by machines. Today a new Quesnay would find a place, perhaps, in the chapter entitled "Primary Production" for the production of hydraulic and thermal energy, for a great part of the chemical industry. And tomorrow, for the utilization of nuclear energy, and the whole industrial sector fed by these sources of energy, would be subsumed under the rubric "Productive Activities," leaving in the "sterile" class only the liberal, administrative, artistic professions and others, refractory to technical progress. All this would change nothing of his fundamental thesis (considered the most ridiculous physiocratic superstition), which asserts that human labor can create wealth only by allying itself with the immanent productive forces of the earth. What emerges from the economic process of the *Tableau* as the net social product placed at society's disposal is that which entered into this process as the productive force of nature, this "pure gift of the earth" which is added to man's labor and which is the bounteous (i.e., it comes as a gift, is not paid for) share, a common possession of society. Thus, the economic society produces a surplus which does not belong to the economy because it has incorporated a part which did not belong to it, formerly called the share of God. And because at the beginning of the process there is this "gift" or "advance" of nature, because society, like the individual, from its birth "spends" or consumes before producing, and because "everywhere expenditures precede the reproduction of expenditures," the whole economy of the *Tableau* can start out from the spending of the social revenue. Quesnay's economic science then becomes the science of proper spending.

To be sure, since Adam Smith serious economic science has ignored this sort of alchemy; it knew nothing of a collaboration or of a donation of nature and does not count them among the factors of production. At best, the encumbering problem of ground rent still recalls, like an erratic lump, a remote past subjugated to the soil. For the two great economic schools, liberal and socialist, work is the only factor productive of values. Capital—"produced means of production," according to Marx—is itself hoarded work, and these two incarnations of work, labor and capital, contend for the social product. This is where the boundary is drawn between two views of the world. The theory of value is the metaphysics of all economic doctrine, the realm of *a priori* definitions; and the economic metaphysics of the power of labor, creator of surplus value, is no less obscure than that of the creative force of nature of the Physiocrats. It merely displaces, without making it disappear, the irritating *non sequitur* which is produced in any economic system when, at the point in the social circuit of exchanges where all gain is balanced by an equivalent loss, there suddenly appears a surplus value, a value produced above the value consumed.

The gesture which, in a cobbler's workshop, sets into motion only a hammer or awl, consumes the same amount of force which, applied to a lever at a powerhouse, releases gigantic energies. If the labor power consumed alone enters into the product, then Marx's thesis—according to which the worker is defrauded of his right to the total product of his labor so that in our day, for example, the worker of the powerhouse is defrauded of the revenue of the millions of kilowatt hours he has produced, once the cost of the installation is paid off—is at least as plausible as the contrary arguments of the "capitalist apologia." Their philosophical postulate is fundamentally the same: for Adam Smith as for the economic science of the nineteenth century, liberal as well as Marxist, nature was offered gratuitously, *res nullius*, a windfall (for him who knew how to grab hold of a choice morsel) which entered economic accountancy only as an inexhaustible mine, and only the costs of exploitation, which figured on the balance sheet. We are no longer so sure, perhaps, that this philosophy, the most insipid that the world has known, has been the last word of wisdom.

As for the specific problems of primary production which occupied Quesnay, the later economic science could calmly neglect them because Europe, following England, wanted to be the factory of the world. And for its primary production it rested upon those countries overseas which were "backward" or "in a state of nature" and which themselves were considered as *res nullius* offered gratuitously to him who could take, and as inexhaustible mines of raw materials. Today, it again finds these problems of a backward agriculture more than for a revolution, at times in Europe itself, but above all in the so-called "underdeveloped countries," precisely the countries of primary production which have arrived at this stage of veiled crisis that Quesnay had perceived in the France of Louis XV. The anatomical *Tableau* which he drew up from this, his theory of organic growth and differentiation, his polemic against the artificial grafting of industries catering to conspicuous consumption onto a stagnant and starveling rural economy, his fundamental intuition that industrialization must begin by way of the countryside, or—expressed in modern terms—the intuition that an industrial revolution can be successful only if it is based on an agricultural revolution: all this contains even more material for reflection for the experts and technicians of "economic development" than is offered by the whole corpus of "classic" liberal or Marxist literature.

It is not a question of returning as penitents to the wisdom of the old master, to his touching zigzag and his outdated terminology. His economic model clearly bears the stamp of his time, and it is only in this setting of the age of Louis XV that its originality is apparent. This noneconomic society, namely, one not occupied materially with earning its livelihood, which formed the all too high summit of the *Tableau*, which made disposal of the national net product, of the "revenue for the proprietors of the land, the Sovereign, and the tithe owners," and which by the way it spent it determined the totality of the economic circuit, was the royal constituted society of the *ancien régime* itself: the court, the nobility, the "proprietors" in the seigneurial sense, the "tithe-owning" clergy, and that numerous "bourgeoisie de robe" which had incorporated itself into the society by buying royal offices in the administration of justice and finance.

Here we pass from the economy per se to the political regime which, still more than a hierarchy of command, was a hierarchy of payees from the national revenue levied from the society of commoners. Quesnay does not leave a shadow of doubt as to the nature of this revenue, which was essentially seigneurial and which dispensed with any economic justification. Without the slightest equivocation, he defined the social and economic function of this society, which was to spend the social net product and, if possible, to spend it properly. "The proprietors are useful to the State only through their consumption; their revenues exempt them from labor; they produce nothing." This was really their sole function: the absolutist revolution of Louis XIV had guaranteed its seigneurial rights to the nobility, and in addition it had assured it the enormous revenues of the Church, as prebends for its younger sons; but it had stripped it of all public function, feudal, political, or administrative. But the *ancien régime* acquitted itself of the single function that remained to it, that of spending the national income, in an exemplary fashion and even with an excess of zeal, unto its own ruin. The whole brilliant, refined, and frivolous civilization of the eighteenth century, intellectual as well as material, cannot even be conceived outside this very large consumer society. It was indeed the exclusive consumer, of the national income; its occupation and burden were the art of living, of furnishing and ornamenting an almost artificial life; and it pushed refinement not only to generous patronage of literature and the arts but to the point where it treated itself to the mortal elegance of the subversive spirit.

The *Tableau* truly contains the key to the *ancien régime* at the zenith of the age of Louis XV. If historians had paid attention to it, cultural history and economic history would not have diverged from each other to the absurd point where the best economic and social histories examine under the microscope the development of trade, industry, and "capitalist" structures in the eighteenth century, while ignoring (or almost) the existence of the King, the court, the nobility, the princes of the Church, the innumerable lawyers and owners of offices, and the swarming clientele of litterateurs, games-masters, favorites, and salon mistresses, as if all this society, because it was wholly consumer-oriented, had played no economic role. The truth, conforming with the *Tableau*, is that it determined the whole economic evolution, including the rise of the very forces which were to smash it. At a time when "the people" had a purchasing power which was practically nil and when, save for certain vitally necessary foodstuffs, there were by definition no mass consumption and no products designed for a nonexistent mass market, industrial specialization and large trade were almost exclusively pledged to the high consumption of luxury products, and the great manufactories were the creations of Colbertism—the *Manufacture Royal des Glaces*, the Gobelins, the porcelains, the fine linen of Abbeville—and the naval arsenals and shipyards, the armaments of war, luxury of kings. Outside of some starveling village trades assuring the maintenance of a rudimentary equipment, rural and industrial economy were unaware of each other. The flow of exchanges was established exclusively through this high society, which was wholly consumer-oriented and which diverted its seigneurial and fiscal revenues toward luxury industries and the luxury trade, bringing luxury objects and foodstuffs from the fabulous Indies. As an historical description of this economic circuit, Quesnay's *Tableau* is as exact as a formula can be. With it, we can even put our finger on the distortions of the circuit and on those "unhealthy excrescenses" which ended up inevitably by derailing it.

Dr. Quesnay did not call into question this regime which he knew so well, in all its splendor and its private misery by virtue of his office. He tried to demonstrate to the King that the regime could not with impunity hold in contempt its own vital laws and the sources of its wealth. Quesnay's lesson in political economy—and this is why it is so outdated in detail but so modern in its principle—aimed to be a lesson in economic policy. His fiscal theory, the most bitterly contested, ridiculed, and misunderstood part of his doctrine, was the crowning piece and the conclusion of an ineluctable logic. The "net product," which this whole privileged society at the summit of his *Tableau* consumed, was simply the disposable social product, the surplus taken from the commoners' economic society above its needs of subsistence and reproduction, and which "belongs as much to the State as to the proprietors" who "have only the enjoyment of it." It was exclusively on this net product that the public expenditures could be charged and taxes deducted, and this privileged society had to be blind and mad to have tried a second time, after having collected to its profit all the disposable social revenue, to shift the tax onto the rural and industrial classes who retained only the minimum wherewithal to keep them going. As Quesnay put it, it was like "levying a tax on the horses who work the soil." Such a fiscal system "would not be a tax, but a spoliation which reduces the people to forced saving on consumption, which halts labor, which extinguishes reproduction, and ends up by ruining the people and the Sovereign."

Thus Quesnay opened a frontal attack on the fiscal privileges of the nobility, clergy, and upper bourgeois officialdom, which ultimately led the *ancien régime* from financial breakdown to political bankruptcy, at the very moment when, in the first fatal years of the Seven Years' War, the lengthy fiscal quarrel flared up between the monarchy and its privileged members retrenched behind their parlements. The attack was conducted in a wholly didactic way, with a moderateness of terms which barely muffled the vehement tone of the reasoning. The conclusion that fiscal privileges had to be abolished emerges clearly from the *Tableau*, which seems to have been drawn up only in order to make this demonstration.

We see with what bad faith Voltaire, the feudal lord of Ferney, caricatured Quesnay's thesis in his famous satire: it was the approved method of hiding behind the poor little peasant when the privileges of the manorial lord were threatened. Nevertheless, the satire had fair game: Quesnay's disciples and epigoni, beginning with abbé Baudeau, and with the sole exception of Turgot, themselves worked hard to confuse this explosive conclusion and to drown it in confusion by transforming the feudal proprietors and the princes of the Church into honorary husbandmen. By this simple trick of prestidigitation, which destroyed the *Tableau's* very structure by confusing what it had so neatly separated (namely, those who furnished and those who collected the "net product") the whole "doctrine" became a laughable imposture and fairy tale. All that remained of it, under the unwarranted title of physiocracy, was a pale idealization of rural life in the style of the *bergeries de la Reine* at Versailles, a sentimental and futile idyll perched on the edge of the abyss.

From Quesnay's doctrine, which was the crown and culmination of the whole literature of "household" economy, many subterranean paths lead to the present. When, in 1863, Karl Marx worked on the draft of the *Process of the Circulation of Capital*, he began with an attempt to construct an "Economic Tableau of the Process of Reproduction" conceived wholly on the model of Quesnay's *Tableau*, which he hailed as "the most brilliant finding ever made by political economy." But Marx meted out to Quesnay the same treatment which he meted out to all his teachers: he turned him on his head, while proclaiming, as he did with Hegel, that he was setting him on his feet again.

In the Marxian transposition, the lords of the country and of the land have become capitalists; the "sterile class" —purged of capitalists who, in Quesnay, formed part of it —is thenceforth the only productive class, and the net product deriving from the gift of the earth has become the surplus value extorted from this class of proletarians. As for primary production, it simply has disappeared as a particular category, annexed on the one hand to "the industry of the goods of production" for raw materials and on the other to the "industry of the goods of consumption" for alimentary products, so that the economy is reduced to two industrial sectors and society to two classes, the exploiters and the exploited.

Marx genuinely tried to resume Quesnay's "brilliant" idea, that is, to represent the whole functioning of the socioeconomic regime in a single tableau simultaneously showing the production and circulation of a surplus value in a single social process. But he could not succeed in so doing and finally dropped the project because it was impossible to transpose the idea of a social product arising from the economic circuit and freely disposable—disposable for whom?—to his view of a purely dualist society reduced to the antagonism between the proletarian and the capitalist, who is expropriating the surplus value for himself. Curiously, Marx does not seem even to have perceived—or he neglected it as a "feudal" anachronism—the key role allotted in Quesnay's *Tableau* to this central group which, independently of its historically ephemeral outline, represented *Power*. By suppressing this third term, through a vigorous simplification which at once makes for the polemical force and the historical weakness of his analysis, and by considering power—or the State—merely as the police appendage of the capitalist class, Marx, just like his liberal antipodes, constructed his socioeconomic model in an historical vacuum without institutions and without a frame of reference.

Two hundred years after Quesnay and a hundred years after Marx, it is striking to observe that the old *Tableau économique* of the Physiocrat physician, because it includes both the pre-economic sources of riches and the supra-economic institutions, remains capable of adaptation to all societal transformations. It would be easy, for example, to transpose it to Soviet society, with its strictly hierarchical summit which disposes of the social product and determines its distribution between the "productive" sector (heavy industry) and the "sterile" sector (consumer goods), whereas the classic Marxist and liberal models were only instantaneous abstracts from a state of local affairs at the middle of the nineteenth century.

Marx the economist (who is not Marx the philosopher nor Marx the historian of his time) was the twin brother of Manchesterian liberalism and thought along the same conceptual lines, while allotting them an inverse sign. But his enthusiasm for Quesnay's *Tableau* is significant of a profound nostalgia for an order that was more hieratic than the bourgeois materialist order of his time. And it should not surprise us that this dialectic mind proclaimed itself "materialist" out of anti-materialism. The same nostalgia is expressed at the beginning of the *Communist Manifesto*, in which Marx so curiously compares the "feudal, patriarchal, and idyllic relationship," those personal bonds "betwixt man and man," which the bourgeoisie has destroyed, to the "cold spirit of calculation" and to the "unscrupulous freedom of trade" and "unfeeling bookkeeping" of the capitalist economy. Perhaps without being overly aware of it, he projected this hardly ironic image of an ideal *ancien régime* into his future Society, which he never defined. The Marxian model of capitalism, a horrifying image of a social world without any interior cohesion or values other than of a commercial kind, returns to its negation, which was the physiocratic model from which he had started out, and which Quesnay had himself conceived in opposition to the "commercial doctrines" of mercantilism.

As an image opposed to the concept of an exclusively economic society, Quesnay's *Tableau* has never ceased to trouble and fascinate economists, and Marx is the most important link—but not the only one—between physiocracy and communitarian or totalitarian ideologies. To be sure, after two centuries of theoretical discussion and social upheaval, the contributions of all doctrines have been infinitely mixed. But in the two ideologies which today seem to confront each other apparently without possibility of compromise—Marxism, in which Marx would have difficulty in recognizing himself, and liberalism, whose evolutions would surely surprise its liberal ancestors—we could find dim shadows of the two great concepts which confronted each other in the eighteenth century. There, too, the disagreement over the premises of economic thought—the theory of value—made any mutual comprehension of accommodation impossible: the "household" doctrine, whose entire thought started out from the material and tangible social product, as opposed to the "commercial" doctrine, for which economy begins through exchange and receives its scale of values through the mechanism of the market. And behind this doctrinal opposition we can glimpse a *de facto* opposition, almost as old as history, between that of the authoritarian "agricultural monarchies" with fertile soil and a subject population, and the hustling and bustling "commercial republics," with a poor soil and free men.

This correlation between economic structure and political regime was so evident for Quesnay that, according to him, even in the Turkish capital "money, industry, and mercantile trade and illicit trading" constitute a kind of republic which "in the midst of despotism" gains "considerable ability and independence in its intercourse and in the free state of its commercial wealth." Further, he distinguished in the England of his time, with singular perspicacity, "a commercial republic which dominates this agricultural kingdom." In the crises of the "agricultural kingdom" of France, and in the face of the rise of the "commercial republic," Mme de Pompadour's physician tried to conceive a grand synthesis. Historically, it failed, but it remains the last doctrine in which the State and society, culture, economics, and nature, theory and history still constituted a single entity.

CHAPTER SEVEN

Edgar Faure's "Turgot"

The collection of historical works published by Gallimard under the general title *Thirty Days That Made France* is, by its very conception, dedicated to a dramatic approach to history which views it as a parade of great and prophetic events. With fitting piety the first volume deals with the baptism of Clovis; but if we break down the concept of "thirty days" it hardly comes to two days for each of the centuries under consideration, an accumulation being produced by the well-known "acceleration of history" from 1789 on. And once we deduct all the republican "days," this does not even come to a half day per reign for the forty kings who, according to an equally amusing conception, made France. There must have been more do-nothing kings than we have thought. Obviously, it would be easy to substitute "thirty" other days that contributed no less to the making and unmaking of France, conceived as a garment embroidered by Penelope. But the choice of these different events, provided they are sufficiently different and well distributed, mattered little because it enabled each author freely to embroider on *his* day, which has already granted us the boon of several excellent monographs. After the baptism of Clovis, there are still three coronations and three other events that we can classify as religious (the extermination of the Albigensians, the attempted abduction of Pope Boniface VIII, and the Massacre of Saint Bartholomew), two different assassinations (those of Étienne Marcel and of Henri IV), a bankruptcy (John Law's) and, most classically, eight battles (the more or less expected ones), an armistice ("The Armistice"), and nine revolutions, insurrections, or *coups d'état* in Indian file, from the storming of the Bastille to the Liberation. This makes twenty-eight well-filled days, leaving two days available for less expected events: a ministerial crisis which did not take place—the "*Journée des Dupes*," chosen no doubt because of its name—and another which actually took place: the fall of Turgot.

There are, to be sure, more prestigious catastrophes than the dismissal of a Minister of Finance. But this *Disgrâce de Turgot* [1] assumes the value of an event because of the author who presents him to us: President Edgar Faure, politician, university professor, and historian, who thereby joins that great line of historiographer-statesmen produced by France from Guizot and Thiers to Herriot, indeed to General de Gaulle. We should perhaps lengthen the list: Necker, formerly, made a bid for the office of Minister of Finance by an *Éloge de Colbert*. But this *Turgot* is more valuable. By analyzing the lengthy paths and byways leading to the fall of a minister, from the great failures to the most obscure intrigues, Edgar Faure in this thick 500-page book (not counting appendices and relevant documents), which is marked by a vast and well-proven erudition, pro-

[1] Edgar Faure, *La Disgrâce de Turgot* (Paris: Editions Gallimard).

vides sustained reading pleasure by making us hear, at every turn, the footfall (or at least the winking eye) of the man of government practiced in handling crises and corridor intrigues, in making subtle distinctions and in understanding the morphology of political fauna; it is a dazzling presentation of charming anachronisms. Thus the invitation to Turgot to complete a rather lackluster ministerial council was "what we today would call a broadening of the majority"—let us say, from Ferney's point of view. After the registration of the edicts of reform imposed by *lit de justice*,[2] "the parliamentary crisis was over. The ministerial crisis was about to begin." Turgot succumbed to "the habitual error of statesmen of his temperament, which is to keep calm during the favorable period . . . and to become tough, conversely, when the first reversals . . . would suggest greater finesse." His friend Malesherbes belonged "to the category of those ministers who begin to speak of their departure very shortly after they entered office." And a parallel between Choiseul and Turgot occasioned this already famous passage, which is hardly applicable to the two people who provided the pretext for it, but which sets the reader of the fifth republic musing:

> We can distinguish two opposite types among superior statesmen . . . the providential or Machiavellian type, with a career offered up to the great blows of fate, a genius oriented toward the problems of power: war, diplomacy, national dominance. And the realistic and logical type, inclined to regular promotions, drawn by problems of economy and finance, by the dynamic issues of the life of

[2] In a *lit de justice* (as described) the Parliament was obliged to register (i.e., ratify) the royal edicts without remonstration. It was a solemn session, attended by the King enthroned and seated on a pile of cushions under a canopy.—Trans.

societies. History shows that these two types rarely meet. They never understand each other.

We clearly feel which of the two types appeals to Faure, as a kindred soul, and which perhaps made him go in search of an ancestor in Turgot: the intelligent technician of State, attached more to problems and solutions than to power, who succumbed to the pack of intriguers, fanatics, and imbeciles. We shall not go thoroughly into the parallel, inasmuch as Faure himself does not insist upon it; the reader who would look for an elaboration of this would not have his hunger appeased. Nowhere, throughout this account replete with immature confrontations, do these two types of statesmen come upon the scene. No providential or superior Machiavellian man emerges to trouble the recently inaugurated court of Louis XVI, swarming with mediocrities. Choiseul himself, barely apparent on the scene, is only a distant and nebulous focus for obscure intrigues. And as for Turgot, who is constantly at the center of the story, suffused in a halo of immense tenderness by Faure, his figure remains singularly unsubstantial.

Faure proposed to study elsewhere "the experimental and doctrinal bases of Turgot's economic policy"; hence there is no question here of his thought or of his intellectual parentage. This creates the impression that he evolved in a void and was rather short on ideas. Perhaps Faure should have proceeded conversely. For, without the halo worn by the bearers of new tidings, at the junction of the liberal school of Gournay and the economist school of Quesnay (the first of these two names is mentioned only once, incidentally, and the second, the possibility of error excepted, does not appear anywhere), it is all but impossible to understand the hope that was attached to Turgot's ministry, and the despair felt at his fall not by "the nation," but by that vanguard of opinion which dreamed, for the last time, of a reformist breakthrough of enlightened despotism. Along with Turgot, the paternalist reformer of an "agricultural kingdom," the whole elitist generation, which had grown up in the age of Louis XV, was to sink into a slough of resignation and soon be totally extinguished. After him, with Necker and the dizzy spells of "credit" and of "confidence," with the War of Independence in America and the "American ideas," with the swift erosion of the prestige of a young King who had looked good-hearted and paternal at twenty and who seemed only foolish, feeble and abulic at thirty, all that was to remain of the monarchy by divine right was a frame—still standing but already empty. And the locus of the whole intellectual movement was to be outside this frame of what was already an *ancien régime*. The historical importance of Turgot's experiment and failure by far surpasses his person and his acts. It is on the level of the great changes effected in the orientation of men's minds.

This dimension, therefore, is absent from Edgar Faure's study. And without it, Turgot appears only as a good, honest administrator, "more economist than financier." In addition, he had suffered from gout since his thirtieth year; he was as shy as a young girl, myopic, distant, misogynous, and although indubitably inspired by the noblest reasons—to put bluntly what Faure dwells on at length and indulgently—impulsive or blundering in action. These qualities constitute a personage, not a statesman.

What then did this bearer of hope propose, at the dawn of a reign that was new and still innocent? In his first interview with the King, on August 24, 1774, Turgot excused himself for the disjointed and confused way in which he expressed his ideas, and requested permission to formulate them in writing "because I am upset." Thereupon the "two shy men," the King and the minister, for want of the ability to express themselves, shook hands, in the belief that they had understood each other. Now, on the eve of his fall, "Turgot's principal project was not yet ready, indeed it was never to be ready at all, and for an even greater reason it was never to see the light of day." Along with Edgar Faure, we can find it "quite surprising that during twenty months, the Controller-General did not find it possible effectively to take the Council in hand with precise proposals," nor even to present them for study, to initiate consultations, or to put in writing at least a general sketch of the "grand design" attributed to him: namely, the fiscal reform which had become a matter of life and death for the *ancien régime* and which would indeed have been a bold enterprise of Revolution-from-above inasmuch as it signified a genuine constitutional change. Admittedly, Turgot never found "the right moment" to speak to the King about it, and always had a thousand good reasons to postpone this trial until a later time. The archives of the *ancien régime* are cluttered with these ever postponed projects of reform, eternally being shunted from one ministry to another, and of those good intentions that were always being held up. But, to be precise, the archives contain no evidence whatever of this "great project" of Turgot's. Some remarks make by Condorcet and Dupont indicate that he was thinking about it, and a memoir by Dupont (who was not yet "de Nemours," but in whom we must not see merely the "utilizable disciple") does not contain the plan itself but an exposition of doctrine—not necessarily reflecting that of Turgot himself. This is all, and it is very little. Instead of the great reform, or even a beginning of this reform, at the last breath of the regime was to come the bric-a-brac of the "string of reforms" of the Six Edicts, ranging from matters as important as the suppression of the *jurande* to those as trivial as the tallow trade, which were to be revoked before being applied. But the trial of strength was located elsewhere.

For Turgot did not shrink from this trial of strength. Indeed, he provoked it on a badly posed question, at the worst possible moment, with a doctrinaire's blindness, while, at the same time, neglecting to obtain the requisite data or to take the most elementary precautions. Turgot staked his career on the issue of freedom of trade in grains—or, more exactly, on the suppression pure and simple of the existing regulations of the market and of prices. And although he won the battle, thanks to the energy with which he fought it, he lost his reputation as a reformer. Trade in grains had been an object of passionate debate even in drawing rooms and worldly letters for twenty years; after Turgot, there was to be no further talk of what thenceforth appeared as a pseudo problem as outmoded as the style of Louis XV. The exposition of this decisive experiment and the troubles to which it gave rise are the bravura part of Edgar Faure's book and represents a great achievement of historical writing, solidly documented and lucid. The history of the problem and of the system of trade in cereals of monarchical France has not yet been written (we are made acutely aware of this by the worse than useless introduction to this book by Gérard Walter, director of the series). But we do know that for the common people, constantly on the edge of undernourishment, the "bread budget" normally absorbed more than half their purchasing power and that in years of scarcity reached or went beyond it. At news of the least trouble with harvests, the people lived in panic fear of famine, and the regime in panic fear of riots and peasant risings. The cumbersome system of surveillance, regulation, and public purchases, devised to insure the provisioning of the markets, responded to this twofold fear. But it also impeded agricultural development and burdened the State with the heavy deficits of the control offices, while giving rise to scandal, malpractice, and above all to the blackest suspicions; the fearful legend of the "famine plot," which was gradually taking shape as early as the end of the age of Louis XV, is revelatory of the superstitious terrors that haunted the populace in the face of the scourge of hunger.

Turgot's experiment in free trade was not the first; but it was distinguished by an arrogant and naïve doctrinal certainty, which casually brushed aside all warnings without arranging for any safety device, while knowing that the harvest was bad. It was smugly assumed that prices would go up and that this would be all to the good because the high price would produce an abundance of grains. Here Turgot forgot even the fundamental maxim of the master: "Scarcity and dearness equals misery. Abundance and dearness equals opulence." Now, free trade in grains, concentrated in the seaports, poorly organized, and poorly informed about market conditions in the country's interior, speculating gropingly in the dark—and in the hands to boot of those who were suspected of the worst crimes when they acted on behalf of and under the surveillance of the State—was in no way prepared to effect the miracle of the multiplication of the loaves. Not only the "people," but also a good part of the local administrations themselves, could see in the freedom accorded to prices, to hoarding, and to speculation, an abdication of State authority that was beyond imagination. Riots sporadically took the form of looting sprees, but also that of a seizure of stocks which were taxed and sold officially at a "just price," frequently even under the authority of magistrates and municipal officers who, whether from routine, fear, or an outraged sense of order, found it inconceivable that the State authority could take no interest in the people's subsistence.

These riots were inspired by misery; admittedly, the *ancien régime* had seen many other riots in its time. But was it a revolutionary event, as Edgar Faure asserts? Yes, but only in the sense that, in the face of the patent failure of the accustomed authority, another spontaneously tried to take its place, in the confusion and disorder: the Great Fear of 1789, in truth, was naught else but this.

In order to elucidate this crucial episode of the "war of cereals," Faure has had recourse to all the available documents, including important material unpublished in French until now (above all, a list of those arrested during the riots with the reasons for arrest, which somehow had made its way to the Shchedrin Library in Leningrad), and his sympathy for his hero does not induce him to parrot the unproved assertions of "Turgotins" from Dupont and Voltaire to the most recent authors. His greatest merit, perhaps, is to make short shrift (hopefully once and for all) of the legend of a seditious plot of "brigands" in the pay of aristocrats, monopolists, Neckerites, or other "evil-intentioned" persons. After the "famine plot," thanks to Edgar Faure, another myth of this mythomaniac eighteenth century has been relegated to the common grave of historical puzzles. It is true that Turgot himself saw in these hunger riots only an "odious machination" of doctrinal or political foes, and he assumed the triumph of his sound doctrine by police repression and "hangings to set an example." Faure sadly observes that the people did not understand Turgot. But did Turgot understand the people? When he crushed the riots with force, "it was not a success of the Minister of Finance, but of the Minister of the Interior." Turgot represented not only the incarnation of the *ancien régime*'s hesitant will to reform, but also its last leap of authority and energy.

Was it the last leap, or the last gasp, of an authority that had already abdicated? In a remarkable passage, and one quickly forgotten, Faure observes that the opportunity available to the new regime was lost at the very outset and irremediably, through its first gesture of shortsighted appeasement of "opinion." This gesture was the restoration of the parlements, which was an abdication and, simultaneously, a humiliating disavowal by the defunct regime and of its last grand gesture of royal authority: the judiciary reorganization carried out by Chancellor Maupeou which was not only an admirable judicial reform which suppressed the venality of the offices of justice and of justice itself; but which above all was an assertion of the King's sovereignty against the flabbergasting claims of sovereignty made by the courts of justice—by the parlements, in other words. Everything, including the name, was equivocal in this startling institution of "sovereign courts," constituted by an oligarchy of owners of judiciary offices who represented only their own acquired privileges and fanatical *esprit de corps*. They did not even bother to practice their craft of rendering justice. Rather, in solidarity with all the privileged and the creditors, armed with all the chicanery of legal delays and obstructions, they never shrank from recourse to demagoguery and to inciting uprisings among the populace in order to defend their "liberal" doctrine conceived as follows. Any attack on even the most decrepit and abusive privileges was despotism; the exemption of commoners, "born to be taxed and subjected to the *corvée*," from this forced labor (*la corvée*) or from the personal tax (*taille corporelle*) was branded as Oriental despotism. To suggest that the nobility or the ennobled upper bourgeoisie should share the burden of taxation was "the despotism of Constantinople, which protects the people against the great." In the face of this "liberalism" and of this interdiction of any reform and any innovation, incarnated in the *noblesse de robe* of the parlement, it was precisely this egalitarian and reformist "royal despotism" which had been the dream of the *philosophes* of the generation of Voltaire. Through "Maupeou's *coup d'état*," which reduced the members of the legal profession to their craft of judgeship, the last ministerial team of Louis XV had finally, *in extremis*, created the conditions of all other reform. "Thus," writes Faure, "Louis XVI had the good fortune to inherit a power free of any mortgages. Between his accession to the throne on May 11 and the Saint Bartholomew of the ministers, Louis XVI had seventy-four days to opt in favor of reform, to consolidate his throne and, perhaps, to save his kingdom. On the other hand, after Maupeou's departure, the chips would be down. It was to be too late!"

Indeed it was—all too late . . . on the very day of Turgot's appointment to the office of Controller-General, which coincided with the "Massacre of Saint Bartholomew of the ministers," that is, with the dismissal of the last great royal "*commis*" of the reign of Louis XV, delivered up like criminals to the hoots and jeers of the populace of Les Halles, pamphleteers, lawyerdom, the parliamentary *Fronde*, and the nobiliary reaction. At the same time as the royalist magistrates of the "Maupeou parlement," the memory of the defunct reign, and the very idea of "royal dictatorship," were disavowed and delivered up to vengeance—an act of supreme imprudence on the part of the inheritor of absolute power who believed that he could redeem himself by repudiating the inheritance. Could it be that the editors of this series may have been mistaken about the "day" and that the prophetic date would not be that of Turgot's removal, but the very one of his appointment? And could not Faure have been mistaken about the hero? The great servants of the King, the technicians of power, the administration, and finances, insensible to the swirls and eddies of opinion and demagoguery, deaf even to the clamors of their own friends, were the members of this shock triumvirate—Maupeou-Aiguillon-Terray—which Louis XV had bequeathed to his grandson.

To be sure, in order to properly stage the arrival of Turgot, the bearer of hope, Faure at the beginning of his book presents the "triumvirate" in the diabolic outlines left to us by the pamphleteer portraitists of the parliamentary faction, "painted with in somber hues, under a miserly light." But Maupeou, whose "complexion was yellow with bile," possessed of "the most repellant face on which it is possible to spit," was, nevertheless, the great parliamentarian who had the know-how to sweep the streets of seditious lawyers in robes and wigs, his colleagues, and whose work of reorganization of the judiciary, repudiated by Louis XVI, was to be resumed in its essential features by the Revolution. Aiguillon, "yellow of face . . . predisposed to espionage and aridity," after having put down the rebellion of the Parlement of Rennes, nevertheless, by overthrowing Choiseul, had rightly prevented an absurd war of prestige to which the latter had gratuitously made France liable. And the abbé Terray, the most decried of all France's ministers . . . To read the scattered remarks that Faure dedicates to this accursed person on the occasion of the successive confrontations of his administration with that of his successor, we can imagine the "Rehabilitation of Terray" that he might have written. Here is the impassive minister-technician, called to the administration of finances when the situation was positively desperate, who knew how to effect an amazing recovery on the very edge of the abyss by energetically hacking away all the dead wood and by bequeathing to his successor a solvent treasury while taking upon himself all the unpopularity which such a reorganization involved among the adversely affected financiers and rentiers. If Turgot, quite wrongly, believed that he could see the parlements return without danger because he had no new taxes to demand of them, and if he thought he could postpone fiscal reform until a more opportune moment (which was never to present itself), this was due in part no doubt to the fact that, thanks to Terray and to the peace safeguarded by the triumvirate, he never had any pressing financial concerns during his ministry. The crisis was behind him and did not erupt again until after his departure and the involvement in the American War of Independence.

It is necessary to glean in passing all the praises heaped on Terray by Faure, who is obviously fascinated by the latter's "mastery of technical data," by his "mind, as clear and cutting as steel, by his marvelous equipment for furnishing effective solutions, by his analysis of the social and psychological incidences of the tax," a "masterpiece of lucidity to which there would be nothing to object today," by the boldness of his conceptions, "which could be at their ease in all epochs and before all problems." As for his sense of equity in the distribution of burdens, and even his opposition to the wasteful expenditures of the court, "Turgot was not to put it better, nor, in the end, to do more." And, to crown everything, in the very area of Turgot's crucial experiment dealing with the cereal policy and provisioning, "only abbé Terray perceived the heart of the problem and tried to resolve it." Only he had undertaken, by way of a detailed inquiry, to assure himself of the material, technical, and statistical data without which any directed, planned, or liberal policy was but a throw of the dice. Turgot, preferring the throw of the dice, halted the inquiry and ignored the findings that had already been furnished. The infamous Terray, "the fraudulent bankrupt," "the organizer of famine"; here we have a character which a dispassionate analyzer of his administration would not run the risk of botching up. To be sure, Turgot was a more respectable subject, indeed too respectable; one does not govern so innocently.

But Louis XV, his court, its scandals, and its men—Maupeou, Terray, Aiguillon—were execrated by opinion. This was the verdict of the "public voice" which, today still, weighs upon history and which weighed initially upon the hesitant beginnings of the new regime: it was necessary to repudiate this entire heritage in order to rally public opinion around the King. Louis XVI knew nothing, and was never to know anything, about the craft of kingship. What he wanted, naïvely and intensely, was to be loved. This was why he called Turgot "the friend of the people"; why he restored the parlements. For a long time historians have been struck by this fact: this last reign of the *ancien régime* began with two simultaneous gestures, which were aimed in the same direction from the point of view of an indolent search for easy popularity but which, from any perspective of positive action, went in opposite directions. On the one side, Turgot and the promise of reforms; and on the other, the restoration of the parlements, which throughout the century had systematically sabotaged any reform and would show no delay in starting all over again, worse than ever. And the resuscitated "gravediggers" were to gain the upper hand over the shy innovator without difficulty. For in the absence of any national representation and of any articulated public opinion, "popularity" was made and unmade by cliques and *lobbies*. Among the latter the parliamentary lobby, a sacred phalanx of the privileged of all orders, was still by far the most powerful. Having disavowed the "royal dictatorship," that is, the absolute power, royalty no longer possessed a weapon against the only organized political force in the country, the oligarchy of the privileged retrenched behind their "sovereign courts"—at least as long as the King did not have recourse to national representation against this oligarchy. By avoiding the choice between these two fundamental options, by trying to escape from it, by groping in the dark for the support of that elusive phantom called "opinion," the whole reign of Louis XVI, from 1774 to 1789, was merely a long, precarious suspension. And the whole series of ministers, beginning with Turgot, suspended in the void, was only a circle of transition ministries. Thus began this "reign of opinion" which made governments the playthings of clans and pressure groups possessed of an organized publicity, the reign of hired pamphleteers and of blackmailers, while awaiting the reign of "confidence" manipulated by the bankers. The factions that had agitated in the seraglio of Louis XV now did so on the public square, but their cries did not produce so loud an echo only because the nation remained voiceless. This "public voice" still awaits its sociology, a serious study of the political groups and financial groups who, themselves in rapid evolution, confronted each other in the melee. As long as such a study is not made, the political history of this quarter of a century before the Revolution will remain an illegible jumble of malicious gossip, anonymous libels, and confused shouts and murmurs.

To the extent that Faure's book descends into this arena of "political intrigues," the level of the work is lowered along with its subject and sources, and the threads become a knot of confusion. What are the "pious party," this "party of Choiseul," this "Austrian party," this "Neckerite party," which suddenly intervene at the turn of a page? Were not all these parties really only manifestations of that amorphous and ghostly brawl of individual ambitions and courtly machinations which it suffices to highlight with a few wicked or piquant "portraits" of the protagonists, by gleaning from the abundant *epistolary*, memorialist, and journalistic gossip of the time? The *petite histoire* of the reign of Louis XVI is in general incoherent, but it was not incoherent to this point. In an often confused mediocre way, constantly obscured by group and clan solidarities, these clashes of personalities were no less linked to the great problems besetting the regime; and the choices of people were inseparable from the political options—or, from the beginning, from the refusal to opt. And therein lies their interest for historical research. Antagonistic conceptions concerning the royal power, the political and social order, the economic regime, over which schools, special interests, and payees had their confrontations; options in the sphere of international policy, heavily mortgaged by the secret diplomacy of Louis XV and by its equivocal personnel encrusting the embassies. A policy even more heavily mortgaged by the alliance with the Austrian "hereditary enemy," which had already been half-disavowed since the fall of Choiseul, a few months after it had been sealed by the marriage of the Dauphin, but which remained incarnated in the Queen herself as well as in the powerful political and financial party thrown back into opposition, and which to the end was to poison the reign of Louis XVI. Finally, the option involving all the rest, posed ceaselessly, between peace and the war of revenge against the other hereditary enemy, England—and the author of *La Disgrâce de Turgot* does not seem to suspect that this question also concerned the Minister of Finance, who had predicted that the first cannon shot would signify bankruptcy, nor that his fall was linked to the orientation of foreign policy embarked on the glorious and disastrous intervention in the American War of Independence. On the contrary, he expresses astonishment over why Turgot meddled in diplomatic affairs which, technically, were not in his province.

Edgar Faure indubitably has a highly developed sense for intrigues, and he dwells upon them at length, lovingly, with a host of picturesque details; but the necessary distance from which to judge them is missing. These fastidious and incoherent "intrigues" appear only by way of their tawdriest personal side, reduced to the dimensions of quarrels among confederates. And a generous dose of psychology is administered in order to explain the reasons for the confrontations, as a substitute for any analysis of attitudes, concepts, and special interests. Marc Bloch, in his *Apologie pour l'histoire*, has already remarked ironically on this habitual failing of historians. "Is it a question of assuring oneself whether a human act really took place? They [the historians] cannot bring enough scruples into this research. Do they move on to the reasons for this act? The least appearance satisfies them: based generally on one of those apothegms of banal psychology which are neither more nor less true than their opposites." The King's obscurely irresolute sympathies and antipathies, determined by anecdotes or by trifles, by the Queen's senseless infatuations and spites, alleged anonymous letters, the malicious gossip of the royal aunts or chambermaids, the hypothetical machinations of Rigoley d'Oigny, director of the "Black Cabinet" in which the King gratified his unhealthy curiosities—all beautiful explanations rendered through the medium of eddies and swirlings that remain beneath any real explanation. And as a crowning piece we have the interminable "*affaire*" of the comte de Guines which Faure sums up sarcastically in this amazing parable:

> This ambassador had committed grievous professional blunders. The government was advised of them. The King recalled him and replaced him, and since the Queen had preserved her friendship for him, he made him a duke. And for this reason . . . he disgraced his Minister of Finances . . . renounced the policy of reforms, and was lost with his kingdom.

As history this is, in fact, nonsense. Turgot assertedly had mastered the riot of the "war of cereals" without understanding it; he stood up to the obstructionism of the parlements after having approved their resurrection. Dedicated wholly to his Herculean labors, he was therefore—absurdly—to succumb to an act of spitefulness on the part of the Queen over a matter, furthermore, which had nothing at all to do with him: "The Queen, as difficult to disabuse of her humors as a mob, but more difficult to contain, became *the new riot* for "Turgot" (Faure's italics). This is a formula that we can judge as more or less witty, but which shows the direction in which the narrative eventually bogs down. The "first riot" yielded the excellent and impressive study on the war of the cereals; the "new riot" yields us a performance of a shadow-theater, without faces or substance. The Freudian analysis of the royal couple, of whom Faure paints the cruelest portrait ever made, is certainly worthy of exegesis. Finally, we would even be satisfied with this conclusion, at once profound and lapidary: "An unsatisfying husband presupposes an unsatisfied spouse." Observers had perceived this long before Freud, but they had not found therein the key to history. For the physical propensities of the King, and the gratifications of the Queen, were neither the only deficiencies, nor the gravest. On the other hand, it was not only from the conjugal point of view that the consummation of this dynastic alliance was delayed. In reality, "*l'affaire de Guines*" was linked to the fluctuations of French foreign policy. And here it assumes a very clear significance since, materially, the fall of Choiseul was its point of departure. Indeed, too materially, as it were, inasmuch as Guines, the Ambassador in London, not only had been Choiseul's agent, but had taken advantage of his knowledge of the "*secret diplomatique*" to speculate through the London Stock Exchange on the decline in prices which the conflict, desired by Choiseul, would necessarily entail. The fall of his patron caused his coup at the Stock Exchange to backfire and, in the end, it also blasted his career, despite his powerful protection. From there, from the greatly publicized quarrel between Guines and Aiguillon to the procedures of the "Maupeou parlement" and to the procedures in an opposite direction of the resurrected parlement, the "*affaire*" broadened into a trial of strength in which the parties lined up on both sides with a logic at least equal to that of any comparable "*affaire*" of our days. But since Faure has interested himself only in the mud which was slung at Turgot, the treads of the "intrigue," their beginnings, and their implications escape him. Consequently, we have a recital without head or tail that drags through the last third of the book. Oddly enough, that personage well-known to *la petite histoire*, who unleashed the "*affaire*"—the secretary of the Embassy—who denounced the Ambassador and became the key witness of his foes, and under whose name the records of the "*affaire*" are classified in the archives of the Ministry of Foreign Affairs, was called, simply, Tort. But Edgar Faure, just as oddly, from one end of the book to the other, persists in calling him Fort.[3]

We shall conclude our discussion of Faure's book by saying simply, without any intention of blaming the author, that after having elucidated the "war of the cereals," incidents of the street riots, the parliamentary trial of strength, the administrative acts, the Six Edicts, in short all that really matters in order to judge Turgot's administration of his office, he lacked the patience to plunge into the winding paths of high and low diplomacy of the family pacts, or into the immense farrago of memoirs and proceedings of the "*affaire Tort.*" And if he dwells at such length upon this "*affaire*" which he, nevertheless, judges ridiculous, but which was the incident over which Turgot fatally tripped, then this was due to the sacrifice that he had to make to the conception of the "Thirty Days That Made France." This demanded that the subject was to be neither the work, the life, nor the ideas, but *the disgrace* of Turgot—somewhat like the view of the affairs of State entertained by poor Marie-Antoinette, who, according to Faure, could see in them only "favors, disgraces, and expenditures." Let us be grateful that this disgrace was merely a pretext which has yielded a brilliant and solidly wrought study of the last attempt at a paternalistic reform of the *ancien régime.*

[3] On this startling "*affaire de Guines*" and its consequences, my *La Banque protestante en France, de la Révocation de l'Édit de Nantes à la Révolution,* Vol. II, pp. 412–417; on the "party of Choiseul" see several remarks, *ibid.,* pp. 658–659 and *passim.*

CHAPTER EIGHT

Diplomacy Set Off By Mirrors: Geneva Under the French Protectorate

In eighteenth-century Geneva—that tiny city and sovereign republic of around 20,000 inhabitants and several thousand active citizens—everyone knew one another and all events, whether they involved struggles for political power, conflicts between social classes, or clashes of interest and ambitions between groups and parties, meshed into a tight web of family, clan, and personal alliances. In such a restricted community, questions of high politics, prestige, social rank, big or even little money, or of a personal, familial, private, and public order, merged into each other, and the respective weight of each of these factors varied from one case to another. The worst mistake any historian could make would be to establish a uniform order of priority among these factors, according to his own view of history.

This familiar and familial aspect of political history was characteristic of all the urban or allied republics of the ancient Helvetic League. It belongs to the very essence of oligarchical regimes which were common to them, regimes of communal democracy narrowed down to a circle of a small number of old families who, powerful by virtue of their ancestral right, refused to let newcomers share in the administration of public affairs or enter into public posts. Indeed, since the seventeenth century, it had succeeded in barring such access even to the bourgeoisie. It was a State founded on a corporation of families who were co-proprietors of sovereignty, just as that very Bernese "restorer of the political services," K. L. von Haller, described it in his nostalgic doctrine, erecting it into a universal ideal during the Restoration, to which epoch he practically gave its name.

Geneva, city of refuge for the Huguenots, lying on the fringe of the ancient Confederation, nevertheless presented an anomaly in this set-up. Its "oligarchy of refugees" [1] had always lived on a founding myth which contradicted the simple and clear legitimacy of hereditary right alone, that of an elite of the faith constituted by the refugees. The constitutional history of Geneva, so irregular in the details of its sudden changes of fortune, can be read very clearly in its broad outlines as a continual conflict between the suc-

[1] This is hardly an exaggerated expression, despite the primary role played by a dozen families of Genevan origin before the Reformation, but which had been amalgamated with the others after two and a half centuries of intermarriage. It was symptomatic that although in all the other municipal oligarchies, more recently arrived families invented for themselves a legendary local ancestry, in Geneva one of the oldest families, that of the Butini, which "among the families of the magistracy was one of the rare families who can be considered as truly autochthonous," invented for itself descent from the Italian refugee. (A. Choisy, *Généalogies genevoises*, p. 1).

cessive waves of immigrants, whose stratification at every given moment was roughly reflected in the juridical classification of the population into citizens, burghers, natives, and inhabitants. The almost automatic process of integration to which this classification corresponded became corroded in the course of time and finally was blocked as much by the massive arrivals at the end of the seventeenth century as by the quite natural effort of the already established families to consolidate their own positions. They did this by opposing the political rise of the most recent immigrants or, at least, by allowing only a selective integration, inasmuch as the dike had never been without its *fissures*, and the new families who succeeded in Geneva always managed easily to transcend obstacles by allying themselves with older ones. There is no need here to enter into the ambiguities, transactions, and confusions of this conflict.[2]

The fact is that the Genevan oligarchy, owing to its very origins and its structure, could never acquire either that al-

[2] The use of such terms as "burgher" and "burghership of Geneva" is, by itself, an inexhaustible source of confusion. Since the precise and very particular meaning of these terms in the Genevan constitutional law of that time (according to which a "burgher" referred exclusively to a person coming from the outside who had newly and personally acquired the right of communal burghership—*bourgeoisie de Genève*—any son of a burgher born in Geneva being a "citizen") is wholly different from the current acceptance of the term "bourgeois" or "bourgeoisie" as designations for a social class. Further, the front line of the civic struggles of Geneva was not situated between the "burghership" and the "aristocracy" (nonexistent in law), but between families of the burghership represented in the Councils and perpetuating themselves therein through mutual co-optation ("oligarchy") and the others, also burghers and enjoying the status of citizens of the city, who had remained outside this circle. To complicate matters further, the group of nonburghers, "natives," or "inhabitants of Geneva" formed a maneuverable mass which, from the years 1734–1737, could ally itself either with the "oligarchy" against the "burghership," or conversely. Since we are not dealing here with constitutional law, I have used the usual terminology, which is convenient but equivocal, in order to avoid complications of particulars outside the scope of our subject.

most incontestable legitimacy or the paternalist good conscience which were the hallmarks of the oligarchies of Bern, Lucerne, or Zurich. And the fact that it could erect only incomplete and provisional barriers was precisely what made Geneva the constitutional laboratory of Europe.

This local juridical debate, which was rather colorless and amorphous during the first half of the eighteenth century, quickened with ideological passions, almost religious in fervor, beginning with the 1760's. Here still we come upon ambiguities: the democratic claim which Rousseau, and after him the Geneva *émigrés* of 1782 translated into philosophical terms of universal significance, in its vehemence actually masks a set of indignations of a specifically Genevan character, incapable of translation in any other context. It was not against traditions deemed outworn, but in the very name of traditions that the "burgher" and "*représentant*"[3] opposition rose against a *de facto* oligarchy which, by its style of living and conducting its affairs, as well as by its political attitude, seemed to that opposition to betray everything that expressed the law, spirit, and *raison d'être* of the Calvinist republic. Thus after a half century's delay, the cleavage, at once economic and spiritual, of Genevan society, which harked back to the first years of the century, was articulated and exactly defined. A kind of original sin marked the beginning of Genevan fortunes and misfortunes in the century of the Enlightenment: Genevan banking activity, which was to become the foundation of its oligarchy, launched its dazzling career in the service of the finances of Louis XIV, persecutor of Protestants, and

[3] The burgher party claiming the right of the General Council (or plenary assembly of burghers and citizens) to "make representations," i.e., to present remonstrances and propositions to the State Councils, which come near to revindicating the direct exercise of democratic power by the People's assembly.—Trans.

of the renegade Protestant who became his "Court Jew," Samuel Bernard. And it was in the shady affairs of the War of the Spanish Succession that it forged the chain of gold which thenceforth was to bind the most powerful families and finally the republic as a whole, to the French court. Beginning in 1704 to 1707—only twenty years after the revocation of the Edict of Nantes which filled the tiny republic with Huguenot refugees—the Genevan government had to lean on the resident Minister of France and on the menacing power of the Too Christian King for support against the agitation of the guild trades. The latter had been adversely affected by the financial policy of the big merchant bankers, who dominated the Councils and gladly sacrificed Genevan industry (oriented toward the empire and its allies) to the attractions of financial transactions in the service of Louis XIV. This was the great watershed which determined the shape of Genevan history in the eighteenth century.

To be sure, this history was neither simple nor rectilinear, and it can in no way be interpreted in the light of a conscious conflict between material interests and spiritual values; the problem was never posed in this way. But it did unfold against the backdrop of a great general movement, which swept the whole of Genevan society along with it throughout the eighteenth century. The evolution of commercial and banking affairs, which has been the point of departure of our study and whose data can easily be reckoned and dated, is most significant in this respect. At the beginning of the century, we can still observe an almost perfect equilibrium in Genevan commercial activities and capital investments between France, Germany, Italy, Holland, and England, although exhibiting a marked preference for the last. At first this was a slow evolution, which began to take shape from the last years of the reign of Louis XIV. But it was prodigiously accelerated at the approach of the advent of Necker's first ministry, which in the last twenty years of the *ancien régime* managed to tilt the whole Genevan patrimony toward investments in the Royal French Treasury, whose terms were all the more generous the more it became encumbered with debts.

Concurrently, after the magnificent rise of Genevan international trade in the middle of the century—with the opposition to it shared remarkably between ruling families established in banking and in finance or living on their incomes, and burgher families of more recent origin or outside the Councils, who dominated the major trade and export activities in printed calicos—the Neckerian epoch saw Geneva transform itself almost entirely into a rentier city, in which even simple artisans and retailers drew more revenue from the income from their French Treasury bonds than from their trades. It was a twofold evolution, the upshot of which was that the fortunes and income of all Geneva now depended upon the King's solvency, and all were engulfed in the disaster of the *assignats*, that is, the paper money issued by the French revolutionary government.

The evolution of minds, though not without its hesitations, followed that of patrimonies. Beginning with the great ferment of the Regency and of the "Mississippi Bubble," a movement converging from both sides of the frontier began to tear down the spiritual walls and even the social barriers between the enlightened upper society of France and Geneva, and to overwhelm confessional differences in a common philosophical deism. We have been able to follow—in the immediate wake of the several big speculators of "Le Mississippi,"[4] who at that time had gained

[4] The "*Compagnie d'Occident*," popularly called "*Compagnie du Mississipi*," the first chartered company formed in 1717 by the Scots ad-

entry into the burghership of Geneva by means of opportune family alliances,[5] to the scandal of the "popular party" —the introduction of Freemasonry in Geneva, on the one hand, and the first Genevan desertions toward worldly Catholicism on the other. The latter included those of the abbé Huber and of the two sons of the notary Étienne Beddevole, not forgetting the man who was to bring his torments of conscience to the tribunal of the human race: young Rousseau. The work and life of this Prodigal Son—beginning with his war cry against a worldly civilization which he charged with depraving naturally good and virtuous man—is not comprehensible outside this Genevan context. Nor can it be understood without taking into account the psychology of the lost sheep who was unable to find his way back to the sheepfold, but who for all that was to incarnate, even more violently, the revolt of the old, austere and democratic Genevan spirit against corrupting France and against the spirit of the age of Voltaire which

---

venturer and later French Controller General John Law. Originally designed to exploit the territory of Louisiana, the name remained attached to Law's whole enterprise, which finally monopolized all of French foreign trade, finance, and banking. Hence the name "*Mississipiens*" given to the low and high speculators who enriched themselves in this gigantic bubble, which burst and collapsed in 1720.—Trans.

[5] Essentially this was the entourage of the great "Mississippian" Jean Vasserot (d. 1724), a close friend of Law, who invested his profits in the manors of Dardagny, Vincy, and Vaux and acquired Genevan burghership with his whole family in 1722. His eldest son, David, had already received this civic status in 1716 "gratis, in consideration of his father-in-law" (the syndic Horace-Bénédict Turrettini, whose other "Mississippian" son-in-law, Claude Perrinet des Franches, was received as "burgher" on the same conditions in 1724); the youngest son, Jean, had married the daughter of the notary Beddevole, whose office had served as a real estate agency for speculators in search of investments abroad; of Vasserot's two daughters, one married the banker Jacob Huber (brother of the "abbé" and of the writer-mystic Marie Huber, the prophetess of a "natural religion"), the other a big businessman fallen on evil days, George Hamilton, founder of the first masonic lodge in Geneva. This was a compact group which, from the standpoint of old Genevans, in itself constituted a whole source of infection.

had likewise won over the Genevan aristocracy. The evolution that ended up by making of Geneva a satellite of the French court on all levels, financial, economic and finally political and diplomatic (at times under the paradoxical aspect of a Genevan hold on the French Treasury), went hand in hand with the progress of worldliness and philosophical emancipation in the milieu of the ruling families. Whereas the democratic claim of the "*représentants*," burghers, and serious-minded, affluent artisans led by their pastors—and it was a sign of the times that the oligarchy no longer furnished pastors—armed itself with a Calvinist or pseudo-Calvinist morality against the government of the sons of families considered as traitors to the fatherland and its traditions, groveling before a foreign, papist, and frivolous court. All of Rousseau issued from this complex of circumstances and through him, as through the *émigrés* of 1782, issued much of the civic and virtuous ideology of the Jacobins.

The touching and ridiculous "quarrel over the theater" that broke out periodically throughout the whole of the eighteenth century in Geneva assumes meaning only in this climate, better still, in this complex of betrayal, at the same time that it illustrates the deepest emotional sources of the political or social tensions. The French actors, symbolizing at once the foreign "corruption of morals" and hold over the city, made their entry into Geneva three times: in 1737, under the protection of the plenipotentiary "mediator" sent by the French court to arbitrate the constitutional quarrels that had erupted in Geneva; in 1765, under the diplomatic pressure of Choiseul, in response to Voltaire's advice; and finally in 1782, in the supply wagons of the occupation troops of the Marquis de Jaucourt. Twice after a few months' stay, when they had gone bankrupt or their show booth had been burned to the ground, they had to flee from the city to the hoots and jeers of the "popular party." Their final victory, in 1782, was greeted in these terms by the councillor Jacques de Chapeaurouge in a letter to Minister Perrinet des Franches:

> Oh, if I could hug the knees of M. Vergennes, our great and generous liberator. . . . Let them re-establish good order and security, let them forbid discussion of the hundred-year Code [the Constitution]. . . . What we need is a good theater throughout the year and the State should contribute to it as to the maintenance of its household . . .

Was this the old Roman adage reduced to circuses for the people? But "the people" rejected the circus. And as for bread, it had no fear of going without a sufficient supply. This suffices to particularize the Genevan revolutions which, more than others, merit the designation "bourgeois."

Diplomatic history wormed its way into this general development and fixed certain stages. And it bears the mark of several personalities and of a particular setting to the degree that it is not possible to understand it without accurately pinpointing these persons and this setting. Without claiming to reduce a complex action, modified at every moment by individual or collective attitudes, to a simple family cabal, we shall limit ourselves here to indicating the crucial role played by a tiny group of characters.

Isaac Thellusson was the one who truly opened the series of diplomatic representatives of Geneva in Paris and staked out the path later taken by his successors. In order to define his position with regard to Geneva, we must begin by marking the distance, or rather, the displacement; for, paradoxically, Thellusson represented at the court of Versailles a Geneva which no longer existed except in his memory. His family, which had come from the Lyonnais to Geneva with the refugees from the Massacre of Saint Bartholomew, had enjoyed honors and prosperity there in the first half of the seventeenth century. It had sealed its rank by the twofold matrimonial alliance of Isaac Thellusson's grandfather and granduncle with two daughters of the famous theologian Théodore Tronchin, who ranked as the third spiritual leader of Geneva.

But the sequel, in the second half of the seventeenth century, was the history of the decline of a family and of a Genevan industry: silk. At the end of the seventeenth century, one of the Thellussons, after a reputedly fraudulent bankruptcy, escaped to Holland where he earned a meager living as a clerk in the employment of the banker-speculator-adventurer Jean-Henri Huguetan. The other Thellusson established himself in Basel as the founder of a branch which flourished in a middling way for a time and then faded out. The third Thellusson, Isaac's father, an indolent merchant and possessor of a modest fortune, involved in shady dealings, was not in a position to permit his only son, a studious and serious child, to follow his vocation to the pastorate. At the age of fourteen, in 1704, the young Isaac Thellusson had to leave Geneva with a small bundle of provisions in order to look for a means of livelihood in the countinghouses of trade. When his father died one year later, the name of Thellusson seemed to have been extinguished for all time in Geneva. Isaac Thellusson was to make his way in the world not through his Genevan relations, but through the relatives of his mother, a Guiguer of the "Swiss Nation" of Lyon. There is no need to retrace his commercial career here. Basically, it was that—in no way exceptional—of the model bank clerk who knew how to make himself indispensable and who ended up by being adopted by his old bachelor employer whom he eventually succeeded in the countinghouse. A career which at many points resembled that of Jacques Necker fifty years later. The important Parisian banking house trading under the name of Tourton and Guiguer, which had originated with a Helvetico-Lyonese group with international ramifications, had nothing of a Genevan character about it at that time. The young Thellusson, who became its director in 1715 and the sole successor in 1724 at the death of old Jean-Claude Tourton, remained quite a stranger to his native city, to which he owed nothing of his career or his fortune. The son of a German-Swiss mother (he himself married a Dutch woman of Huguenot background), it was only when he was nearing forty that he once more set foot in Geneva, which he had left as a poor boy. And he showed no concern over the fact that his children, born far from Geneva, were excluded from Genevan citizenship and the Geneva magistracy for this reason.

True, there is also the leitmotif of the *Memoirs* which Isaac Thellusson composed later for the edification of his children. The "presentiment that I was destined to restore the house" which he supposedly received from his mother, the vocation to pull his name and his family out of this decline—for which it had pleased God to make him the instrument. This was the restrospective view of an old man. But if it was a question of the vocation to get back his rank in the aristocracy of his tiny native country, we can fix the exact date of this effort. Isaac Thellusson, in point of fact, resumed his relations with Geneva only at the beginning of 1724, when he had to lay claim to his own civic status as a Genevan and to the rights of naturalization. This was recognized with respect to Genevans in France by Henri IV, at the time of Thellusson's disappointing trial for the Tourton succession, which placed him in opposition to the French and Catholic natural heirs of his former employer, during the anti-Protestant reaction following the death of the Regent, Philip of Orléans. For the Republic of Geneva this interminable trial was seen as a grave matter of State in which what was at stake was the defense, in the person of Thellusson, of the ancient privileges of all Genevans in France. The trial renewed Thellusson's ties with the syndics and Councils of Geneva, who sent a solemn and costly deputation to Paris at his (Thellusson's) expense, and in vain. He also renewed his ties of ancient kinship with one of the most powerful and haughty families of the Geneva oligarchy, the Tronchins. It was a political alliance, which at first assumed the form of a business alliance. At the time of his first and brief sojourn in Geneva, at the beginning of 1728, Thellusson had proposed to the syndic Antoine Tronchin, the regnant head of the dynasty, to associate one of his sons, of his choice, with the Paris banking house; or rather to hand over to him the management of this wholly formed establishment, which did a business of 4 million a year. This is not the place to recount the history of this association, which was disappointing in many respects and soon racked by stormy disputes. The attempt at a Genevan seizure of this old Paris bank turned out badly and caused it to break up into three rival houses, one of which gained, along with the name, the old clientele of the Tourtons. Two years later, the Thellusson-Tronchin association itself was to suffer from the death of the syndic Antoine Tronchin, which left Thellusson face to face with his young associate François Tronchin. The latter was to earn the sobriquet Apollo Tronchin; he was a foppish amateur of art and the theater, friend of the *philosophes*, Voltaire's future Genevan apostle, and representative of a less austere generation of the Genevan aristocracy. Thellusson did not understand him and had some memorable, heated arguments with him, which give us an excellent portrait of Thellusson himself.[6]

But the political association thus formed was pregnant with consequences, and it produced its whole effect before the noisy break between Thellusson and his young associate "of frivolous tastes," whose example seemed to have had no influence at all on his dogmatic political opinions. Having lived his whole adult life far from Geneva, save for rare and hasty visits, up to his retirement in 1744, Isaac Thellusson seems never to have had another image of his tiny fatherland and of its ruling Councils save that which had been stamped upon him by his very humble and pious childhood of the austere Geneva of 1700, before the time of the profitable business dealings with the financiers of the Sun King. Being without close relations or living contacts, he was kept informed on events transpiring in his native city, outside of official missives, only by some of his friends in the intransigent oligarchy to whom he felt the vocation of belonging. As he portrays himself in his *Memoirs*, and as his letters and his court pleadings show him from life, Thellusson was haughty, harsh, greedy more for respectability than for

[6] "Instead of training yourself and advancing in your relations and acquaintances, you run off to concerts, you compose, you pursue the reputation of a musician; by dint of complaints and requests on my part you gave all this up. But was it to apply yourself to something solid? No, your taste, fixed on trivia, fastened onto a play. . . . I grow angry, you oppose me with your family's decision which, you say, wants the play to be performed. . . . What does it bring you? The reputation of a man who is not suitable for trade, who neglects his business in order to pursue frivolities. I ask your conscience: have you kept the vow you made to me, in May, 1736, not to write poetry any more?" (A note written by Thellusson for use as evidence in his trial against François Tronchin: A.E.G. *Fonds Galiffe IX, procès Thellusson-Tronchin,* 1740–1748.)

riches, rigid to the point of meanness, crushing underfoot the unworthy who did not bend to his authority. Armed with the awesome good conscience of the Just, he was at heart a Genevan of another age, practically a stranger in the eighteenth century which, even in Geneva, had become more amiable in disposition. Aspiring to direct Genevan policy from afar, he passed sharp judgments on it which never underwent the modification that direct knowledge of its affairs might have suggested. Nothing could ever make him doubt the sacred character of this Genevan aristo-democracy, the government of the best people whom God had raised above the common herd, just as God had raised him to become part of them by blessing his work and by repairing, through him, the damage inflicted on his family by an indolent father, who had been lacking in Grace. Such is the portrait of the first titular Minister of Geneva at the court of Versailles.

Before him the Republic of Geneva had been represented only by a kind of business agent, the very inconspicuous Daniel Martine, accredited at Versailles as the envoy of the landgrave of Hesse-Cassel. On grand occasions the republic had dispatched extraordinary ambassadorial delegations to Paris, like that of 1726 in connection with Thellusson's trial against the Tourton heirs. Daniel Martine had died in July, 1727, and since this important issue of Genevan privileges was still very much alive, it was natural that Thellusson, to whom this was a matter of primary concern, should assume the post as interim minister. At the beginning of 1728, at the moment of his brief Genevan sojourn and of his "family pact" with the syndic Tronchin, Thellusson was co-opted by the Council of Two Hundred. Two years later, the Small Council nominated him titular minister of the republic at Versailles, not only, as he says, so that his children born outside Geneva could be recognized as citizens of that city but also "for the purpose of being in Paris with greater distinction." It was an excellent choice from a superficial point of view and from that of Thellusson's high-level connections in Paris. It was the first time that a Genevan representative became a member of the diplomatic corps, and Thellusson did not hesitate in having the French court pay protocol honors to the republic. It was also an excellent choice from the point of view of the oligarchy of the Councils, whose ardent and intransigent defender Thellusson was to become later in Paris. In 1733, finally, he was in addition nominated, *in absentia*, to the Council of Sixty of Geneva, which was the political body in charge of diplomatic affairs. In the same year, still through an epistolary campaign that marvelously illustrates this mechanism of familial co-optation, he arranged for his slightly plebeian brother-in-law Jean-Jacques Des Gouttes to enter the Council of Two Hundred, although later he was bent upon destroying him as soon as the latter exhibited annoying leanings toward what was called the "popular party."

Thellusson was involved in partisan struggles from the moment he assumed his official duties as the Genevan *chargé d'affaires* in Paris. They began with the affair revolving around Captain Micheli du Crest, who had criticized the plans and the budget for the fortifications of Geneva. In 1728 he was expelled from the Council of Two Hundred, his "burghership" status annulled and his possessions confiscated. Micheli's appeal against this judgment to the General Council gave his name to the party sponsoring the claims of the communal burghership against the arbitrary powers of the restricted Councils. Now Micheli du Crest, who was an officer in the service of the King of France, lived in Paris and the majority of the Genevan colony in Paris was "*Micheliste*" in its sympathies. Thellusson counted 200 "seditious" persons among them, workers and clockmakers, tradesmen, and even several merchant bankers. He expended great energy against Micheli at the court of Versailles, having the officer's friends in Paris shadowed and placed under surveillance and then denouncing their activities to the Magnificent Council of Geneva. It was Thellusson who the "*Michelistes*" held primarily responsible for the scandalous sentence which was handed down in 1736, condemning Micheli to death for contumacy.

And there is also the well-known story of the troubles in Geneva fron 1734 to 1738, of which Thellusson gives an exaggerated and distorted account in a lengthy passage in his *Memoirs*, considering that his only source of information came from partisan reports. But if this highly personal version of the events has no informational value as to what really transpired in the city, it does constitute, with its ample relevant papers, a key document to Thellusson's own action as the Genevan minister in Paris. What follows below is merely a faithful, and insofar as possible textual, paraphrase of this document.

From the outset, Thellusson notes with pride that he had done everything to prove to the "seditious Genevans" that he was "one of the most zealous partisans of the Councils"; in his missives to the Council he increases his warnings, denunciations, and exhortations to firmness. After each retreat of the Councils before the demands of the communal burghership, he tenders his resignation in increasingly more violent terms: "Not having enough effrontery to represent the Genevans any longer," and "not desiring to have any part in the obsequies of the Republic," Thellusson remained at his post only after receiving urgent pleas from Geneva. Increasingly his activity took on the character of a duel between himself and the syndic Louis Lefort, who was in favor of negotiations with the "popular party" and for whom Thellusson successfully created all kinds of diplomatic difficulties at foreign courts. In April and May of 1737, he himself came to sit in Geneva with the Council of Sixty in order "to fortify the party," and he worked so well at this job that Lefort handed in his resignation. But on August 21, the "*Michelistes*" of the Lower City seized the townhall, which became the scene of the only serious skirmishes that ever took place in all those years. The representative of France, La Closure—who had been in office for almost forty years and who had practically become an old Genevan himself, and a very moderate supporter of the established oligarchy—intervened to enable the partisans of the aristocracy to retire from the city to their country homes; while the curtailed power remained in the hands of the burghership.

This was the moment when Thellusson, seeing that "the magistrates were under the yoke" and that "he could not wait for orders from a mutilated Council which was groaning under that cruellest inquisition," decided on his own authority to reverse the situation by a diplomatic action, by provoking French intervention. Once the action had been successfully carried out, he justified his conduct with the utmost frankness and pride in his report—dated June 7, 1738—to the syndics and the Small Council, in terms which at bottom could hardly be considered flattering to the timorous governors he had saved despite themselves:

> Although there was no one, I believe, in the Councils, who did not confess to himself . . . that Geneva was in the greatest danger that the city had ever known on account of its internal troubles, such a great cry was raised against my resolution to have recourse to the King [of France], and I found

> so little encouragement of my first successes, even on the part of the Council, that I was willing to continue to assume all responsibility by myself. . . . In all these negotiations, I requested nothing except *in my own and private name,* having constantly declared by word of mouth and in writing that the Small Council, far from having the freedom to order what I do, did not even have that of applauding it. I hope that My Lords will be grateful to me for a precaution which left them all authority to leave everything to me and to extricate themselves from the extreme fury of those who were our masters. The fear of being disavowed and noted as the author of an irreparable evil did not slacken my zeal.

After being assured of the support of the Protestant powers in Paris who were allied to France—Sweden and Prussia—Thellusson, on August 31, ten days after the seizure of power by the burghership, obtained an audience with Cardinal Fleury. He drew him "so vivid and moving a picture . . . of the horrors of our situation" that he convinced Fleury to offer—or rather, to impose—the mediation of the King of France between the Genevan parties, and to rush a plenipotentiary minister to the scene. The burghership of Geneva, which had just rejected offers of mediation from Bern and Zurich, was forced to bow before that from France.

In fact, once unleashed, the French intervention did not follow the course foreseen by Thellusson and by no means achieved the end that had been counted on: the pure and simple restoration of the oligarchy of the Councils. The communications of the French representative in Geneva did not correspond over well with the somber picture Thellusson had drawn of anarchy in Geneva. The mediator appointed by Fleury was not the one suggested by Thellusson, and negotiations were carried on without him, despite the promises that he would be included which, according to Thellusson, were made to him by the Secretary of State, Amelot, who conducted the whole proceeding. The comte de Lautrec, who took the trouble to inform himself of Genevan affairs on the spot, was impressed by the arguments and complaints of the burghership, which were faithfully and sympathetically reported in his missives to the cabinet at Versailles, all the more easily inasmuch as the supporters of the oligarchy preferred to remain outside the city. Finally, the syndics and councillors of Geneva themselves, disturbed at the meddling of their all-too-powerful neighbor in their internal affairs, hastened to make concessions in order to settle the matter as quickly as possible. Thellusson criticized them bitterly in his final report, demanding his release because of his past action. "If Your Lordships regret the aims I had in view, you can seek in Geneva itself for the reasons which engaged M. de Lautrec to prefer conciliation and to authorize its accomplishment."

The "Act of Mediation," ratified almost unanimously by the General Council of May 8, 1738, and guaranteed by the three protector States, France, Bern, and Zurich, was to assure the republic twenty years of untroubled stability, in the laborious and very equivocal balance that was struck between the regime of oligarchic co-optation of the limited Councils, now slightly broadened in composition, and the principle of the sovereignty of the General Council, though reduced to expressing its opinion through a mere "yea or nay." The distant consequences of Thellusson's diplomatic initiative were not all as felicitous. The Act of Mediation had established the right of the French court to inspect Geneva's internal affairs, and as the power guaranteeing the Constitutional Act of 1738, France was to be present with full rights in the domestic quarrels of the republic which the very ambiguities of the Act of Mediation could not but renew. Thus French intervention remained suspended above the political and constitutional debates of Geneva like a sword of Damocles, and its threat alone sufficed to falsify greatly the internal balance of forces and to delay the accession of new families to the Councils—which would otherwise probably have taken place quite naturally, without disturbances—until an explosion took place. Indeed, it was through the French protectorate in power, and finally in action, that a tight group of ruling families—and in this very group, the exceedingly intransigent "Negative party" [7]—believed they could maintain themselves indefinitely in place.

After Thellusson, the diplomatic representation of Geneva at the Versailles court became the key post in Genevan political life. And to alert the Versailles cabinet, to bring pressure to bear upon the minister's entourage, to raise the threat of intervention became the permanent and almost infallible means of the "Negative party" in order to hold off the burghership which was excluded from the Councils. This was a situation as dangerous as it was one-sided. We cannot say that Geneva was a piece of prime importance on the French political chessboard, nor that the post of French representative in Geneva (whose holder was practically the arbiter of Genevan quarrels) ranked very high in the French diplomatic hierarchy. It was often a siding or a fledgling diplomat's post to which little attention was given, and one that was poorly paid and paid with more delays than any other. Practically all the representatives of France in Geneva fell heavily into debt there,

[7] The "Negatives" flatly denied any right of the General Council to "represent" any remonstrances.—Trans.

which of course might have made them all the more attentive to the opinions of their Genevan creditors. In 1738, a group of Genevans had the excellent idea of themselves nominating, so to speak, the representative of France, by advancing to their candidate Gauffecourt, a great friend of the Tronchins, a sum with which to pay off the 30,000 *livres* in debts left behind by his predecessor La Closure. The project failed by a thin margin. The French representative who was most deeply mired in debts was Pierre-Michel Hennin, who was stationed in Geneva in the extremely critical years from 1765 to 1778, and who extricated himself from his financial difficulties by marrying a well-dowried Genevan heiress, despite her heretical religious views. And Hennin, who was as fanatical a "Negative" as though he himself were a member of the Genevan oligarchy, until the death of Vergennes was to remain the minister's right arm in all matters affecting Geneva.

In order correctly to render the climate of Franco-Genevan relations, it would be necessary to have recourse to anecdotal history. Thus Voltaire, who could be the most disagreeable of neighbors, knew how to put the representative as well as the ministerial bureaus of Versailles in the service of all the good or bad farces with which he pilloried the "*Parvulissime République*," and to inflate the least coachman's smutty joke into a grave diplomatic incident merely for the pleasure of writing a quatrain. But the grave fact was not that the Versailles cabinet, in normal times, has treated the affairs of Geneva with a certain degree of negligence by leaving them to subordinates or to amateurs. Rather, Versailles had got used to the cat-and-mouse game of keeping the Genevan government at its mercy as though it hung on the benevolence of the minister or even one of his assistants, and of making the local potentates who constantly implored French diplomacy dance to its tune, finding less interest in establishing or supporting a stable government than—as Vergennes wrote to Hennin in 1776—in "keeping the Republic in the state of isolation, weakness and contempt which its present Constitution has brought upon it."

The situation was even stranger from the Genevan side. The diplomatic representation of the republic at Versailles was the key post of its policy. Now, Geneva seems never to have had a minister who was really the spokesman of the Geneva government and who was under obligation to execute its orders. The republic had accredited ministers in Paris—or, over and over again, and at crucial moments, semi-official representatives who did not accept even the duties of this title—who deigned to concern themselves with the affairs of Geneva at the French court only as a form of benevolence, discharging this function as they pleased. Up to 1777, the ministers of Geneva in Paris had never received, as expressed in a letter of the Council to Necker, "any compensation for their services except the sensibility of our hearts and our gratitude." Horace-Benedict Perrinet des Franches, in 1777–1785, was to be the first Genevan diplomat to receive an annual pension of 1,200 *livres* by special favor, for he had refused to be a titular minister. This custom of honorific unpaid functions is quite in keeping with the traditions of aristocratic republics, and was not only a case of Genevan parsimony. But in such a situation, to have a benevolent representative in Paris practically and morally independent of the government, and who in consequence escaped the Council's surveillance and even more the burghership's impulses to exercise control, could mean many advantages for the party to which he belonged, or which maintained him. Isaac Thellusson had acted in Paris outside the Councils, officially and even in fact without their knowledge, while generously leaving them the authority to disavow him if the matter turned out badly—a theoretical authority at best because he had included Cardinal Fleury and the King of France in his game. But it was precisely because he did not wait upon the orders of the Councils that he was able, as he said, to save them despite themselves.

Admittedly, it was not always possible to have in Paris a minister-banker with Thellusson's connections and scope of activity. The Genevan banking activity in Paris underwent a marked eclipse in the middle of the eighteenth century as a result of the financial, economic, and political consolidation of the kingdom under the untroubled reign of Cardinal Fleury—that period of stability that historians have been able to call a monarchic restoration, after the veritable crisis of the regime of the Regency—which was to be torn apart anew only by the Seven Years' War and its consequences. It was necessary to wait for Necker's arrival to have once again a Genevan as court banker without the title and to find the court once again begging for piddling aid from day to day. But Necker was an exception in the gallery of diplomatic representatives of Geneva in Paris: not only was he not dependent upon the Genevan government (and he made this very clear to it) but he belonged to no Genevan party and was beholden to none. Moreover, he had not actually been chosen either by the Council or by the oligarchy, which at that time was at the nadir of its power after the Edict of Pacification of March, 1768. He had imposed himself, or had himself imposed by Choiseul, on a government in distress. He was more of a stranger in Geneva than any other, not being a Genevan in terms of family stock or cast of mind. Between the somewhat evaporated Lutheranism of a Pomeranian father and the masonic deism of the sons, Genevan Calvinism hardly had time to influence the Necker household, which formed a kind of Anglo-Germanic enclave in Geneva.

The banker Necker's tiny diplomatic post was for him only a first and modest stepladder by which to lift himself from his countingoffice into the arena of public affairs. We know with what disdainful indifference, from afar, he watched the Genevan disorders, which seemed to him parochial quarrels, avoiding as much as possible the multiple chores of his mission under the pretext that he had more important things to do, or even that he was suffering from migraines. For him Geneva was a reservoir of capital to drain in the direction of the Royal Treasury, and naught else. From his entry into the countinghouse of the Vernet Bank, Geneva scarcely saw its famous son again, even at the time of his fall from grace and his periods of exile from France. Almost totally un-Genevan in temperament in every way, he was even less a supporter of the oligarchy. In the whole line of ministers of Geneva in Paris, Necker was the only one who had any sympathies for the "*représentant*" burghership, but these were the sympathies he had held before becoming minister. Once he was entrusted with this diplomatic post, his only concern was that the Genevans should maintain their tranquility and not force him to importune Choiseul with their eternal quarrels.[8] But this impartial indifference was tantamount to a partisan stance. It was during the years of the Necker ministry that the oligarchical government, badly supported in Paris, little

[8] "I most truly believe that M. Choiseul loves him . . . he is content providing that our minister does not talk to him about Geneva; and . . . M. Necker, whom he, moreover, finds pleasing and who has the art of not annoying him with our affairs, is just what he needs." (Report of Philibert Cramer on his unfortunate mission to Paris in March, 1770.)

by little was emptied of its substance and resigned itself to the invasion of the corridors of power by the "*représentant*" leaders. After this period of neglect, their resurgence of the situation was to be all the more harsh.

Geneva's diplomatic representation in Paris presented a remarkable unity, save for the very particular "case" of Necker. If this representation began with Thellusson, it ended with Jean-Armand Tronchin, the nephew and heir of both Thellusson's former associate and the Farmer-General Jean-Robert Tronchin, a scion of this great family of the Genevan aristocracy. Through his career as a banker Farmer-General, as well as through that of his famous cousin, Dr. Théodore Tronchin, and of his sons, courtiers of the House of Orléans, Jean-Armand had integrated himself into the upper reaches of the French society of the *ancien régime* more solidly than any of his predecessors. Between these two ends of the same chain, from 1744 to 1785, and with the sole exception of the Necker interlude, the post of minister or *chargé d'affaires* of the Republic of Geneva in Paris was an appendage, so to speak, of the Genevan group in the administration of the *Manufacture Royale des Glaces de France* (the Royal Manufactory of Mirrors of France) [9] in the Faubourg Saint-Antoine in Paris. Their seat in the administration of the *Compagnie des Glaces*—the prestigious Royal Manufactory of upper-class luxury products whose clientele was the court, the nobility, and the upper office-holding bourgeoisie, ennobled by letters patent or by the nature of their functions—was the social mark of distinction, the visiting card of the Genevan ministers in Paris. Indeed, it was much more impressive than the credentials of their "*parvulissime*" diplomatic rank.

[9] Today called the *Société des Manufactures des Glaces et Produits Chimiques de Saint-Gobain.*—Trans.

Among its sixteen titular administrators of the *Compagnie des Glaces*, alongside lawyers, office-holders, and the remnants of the French Protestant nobility—the Ségurs and the Jaucourts—stood the duc Anne-Léon de Montmorency, "*premier baron chrétien, chef du Nom et des Armes.*" It was a marvelous strategic and social position in the Parisian world, matched to boot by one of the most fashionable and more frequented salons of the capital, that of Mme Geoffrin and of her daughter, the marquise de La Ferté-Imbault. Both were young widows who were greatly admired, but they were also—especially the mother—excellent business women with a flair for public relations. Now, in this opulent Royal Manufactory, the masters of the house (or almost so) were the members of another ruling family of the Genevan oligarchy, the Saladins.

This privileged position in one of the leading and most exclusive industries of the *ancien régime* was the choicest inheritance of the Genevan speculations made during the War of the Spanish Succession. We have been made privy to the particulars of its mode of operation and even to its State secrets, thanks to the voluminous records of contestations left behind as a result of the *coup de main*, in 1704, through which the Genevan provisioner of munitions Jacques Buisson, in association with the Protestant Parisian banker Étienne Demeuves, got their hands, at a cheap price, on the *Compagnie des Glaces* which was in great difficulties at that time. We cannot go into this matter here.[10]

[10] According to ancient custom, the social capital in the beginning was represented by a "social *livre*" divided into 20 *sols* or 240 *deniers* (in other words, the share of the capital of each associate was so many *sols* or *deniers* per *livre*). With the successive reorganizations and the free shares offered to highly placed protectors, the capital was finally divided into 24 "social *sols*," and the statutes granted a deliberative vote to the owners of a sixteenth, at least, of the capital of the undertaking, or 18 social *deniers*. It was this part that we call "a share." These parts,

Thanks to Demueve's relatives and alliances the shares of Saint-Gobain were acquired by these Protestant or crypto-Protestant families, noble by birth or office, which we have already named—the Ségurs, Jaucourts, the Boucharts de Champigny, the Huets d'Ambrun de Montalet, and others. They were absenteeist shareholder lords who gladly left matters to their Genevan friends, or who could not sit in the administration because their shares, like those of other groups, were parcelled out in tiny lots. Among the sixteen seats in the administration prescribed by law, only about ten were ever occupied. At best only six or so titular officials regularly attended the meetings of the board of directors, which were held twice and, soon, thrice weekly. This circumstance enabled an assiduous minority of shareholders to direct the manufactory. The capital shares owned by Jacques Buisson, amounting to 4 *sols 6 deniers* out of 24, or 3 shares out of 16, had also been cut into rather thin slices through successions, and especially as a result of lawsuits between his heirs and creditors, in the forefront of whom were his former associates, the Saladins, with whose money, but without their knowledge, Buisson had managed to pull off his brilliant coup.

Without going into the complications of these divisions of shares, we shall state that in the middle of the century roughly two out of the three shares belonged to the de-

or shares, were strictly registered and the company, by its statutes of 1703, had reserved to itself the right to approve transfers, that of the purchase of shares by a member of the administrative board before they were offered for sale to the public (which, according to the insinuations of the opposition members, enabled the "Geoffrin clan" to speculate on the shares of the enterprise by monopolizing their sale) and to refuse a deliberative vote to purchasers unacceptable to it (arts. 13 and 22). On the history of the Genevans associated with the *Manufacture Royale des Glaces,* see *La Banque protestante en France,* especially Vol. I, pp. 143–147, and Vol. II, pp. 292–295 and 736–746, with the references to all the sources cited.

ceased Jacques Buisson (the possession of two shares entitled the owner to two seats in the administration) remained in the hands of the Saladin family. The third and last had been forcibly ceded in 1740 by Buisson's heirs to a composite group of creditors, which was dominated by the families of Boissier and Sellon, allied through marriage, who were newcomers to Geneva and whose rise into the ruling oligarchy, from the first generation on, had been meteoric. It is noteworthy to recall that in 1772 one share in the Saint-Gobain Manufactory was worth around 400,000 *livres*, and almost double that amount on the eve of the Revolution, which explains the crumbling of these shares by minute fractionings.

Despite this fragmentation of shares, however, the Genevans throughout the eighteenth century always managed to keep three active administrators in the *Compagnie de Saint-Gobain*—each one of whom represented a whole share—by combining all these fractions of shares through fictitious transfers under the name of three titular proprietors. The documents of transfer, duly notarized and made known to the company, were always accompanied by counter letters, likewise notarized, which specified that the transaction was void and had been made in order to enable the transferee to become a member of the board of directors. Thus, from 1740 to 1790, all the infinitely parcelled out parts of Buisson's last share, through all the partitions and changes of ownership, nevertheless still remained represented by a sole fictitious owner, Jean-François Sellon, the minister of Geneva in Paris whom we shall meet again. This practice, in principle illegal, no doubt presupposed a tacit benevolence on the part of the majority of the administration officials of Saint-Gobain because the administration in charge always possessed the statutory authority to blackball an undesirable intruder, even the legitimate owner of a whole share. Indeed, it had often exercised this authority since the beginning of the century; for example, against a financier as powerful as Antoine Crozat. There was a desire to keep things in the family, as it were, among people who knew each other, and in this the administration was remarkably successful. Now the part of the capital which belonged to the Genevans, modest for all that, would not have sufficed for this strategy of exclusion: it succeeded thanks only to a constant alliance of the Genevan administrators with the cashier, later director, and veritable manager of the undertaking, François Geoffrin, and his family.

We know through anecdotal and literary history that François Geoffrin, the elderly, unobtrusive husband of a young society woman thirty-five years his junior, was interested only in his manufactory of mirrors and had spent his life buying up all the fractions of Saint-Gobain shares that were up for sale. This he did by exercising his right, as prescribed by the company, to buy them before they were put up for sale to the general public, so that he left his young widow a considerable and highly maneuverable block of shares which enabled her, through opportune transfers (fictitious or not), to bring into the board of directors anyone who suited her convenience and, more often, to remove from that body anyone she found inconvenient. Now, Geoffrin was a protégé of the brothers Saladin, who occupied seats in the administration of the Royal Manufactory and who had kept him on despite the criticism raised against his nepotism. And this alliance was continued with his widow on an even more intimate basis after Geoffrin's death in 1749. Mme Geoffrin was a very authoritarian administrator, with the air of a mistress of the house; and the continuing alliance with the Saladins also included her daughter, the Marquise de La Ferté-Imbault, already a well-to-do widow at the age of twenty-two. Innumerable documents relating to the correspondence and inner administration of the company, as well as the letters preserved in the archives at Crans and in the sequestered papers of Perrinet des Franches in Paris, attest this concerted strategy, and also the very affectionate personal relations with these ladies, "our beautiful neighbors," who lived on the rue Saint-Honoré. In 1757, Mme Geoffrin's daughter could write justifiably, if not without simplification, to the brother of Mme de Pompadour, Intendant of the King's Buildings and by virtue of this title the official protector of the company, expressing her grave disquiet over "the plan of Messieurs Trudaine and Gournay for freedom" which threatened its monopoly: "My father [M. Geoffrin], the grandfather of M. de Saint-Vincent [a Pocquelin] and the father of M. Saladin had governed this manufactory for fifty years as honest people. . . ."

All this is still only a tale of business deals and inheritances, but it is not without political significance in the ambiance of the *ancien régime:* a very close-knit circle of Genevan families, animated by the Saladins, which gave the *Manufacture Royale des Glaces* a strategic position, at once economic and social, in Paris. The salon run by the Ladies Geoffrin formed a supplement, just as the Tronchins had on their part, since 1762, with their position as Farmers-General, with Mme d'Épinay and her salon behind them, with which was connected in turn the literary and philosophical *Correspondence* of Baron Friedrich Melchior Grimm with the great of Europe, not to mention the collection of offices of the House of Orléans and Dr. Tronchin's upper-class clientele. All the members of this world, moreover, met each other at the same receptions, dinners, feasts, and confabulations. In this connection, I have always deplored the fact that the historians of these literary and philosophical salons where opinion, court intrigues, and, at times, high-level policy were undoubtedly fashioned, have interested themselves only in the trivia of worldly gossip and apparently have never tried to find out who maintained these costly "public relations" agencies, except where it was very obvious, as in the case of the salon Necker.

But to return to the diplomatic representation of Geneva in Paris; its history is easily read after what has just been said. Upon Isaac Thellusson's retirement in 1744, which had been announced long in advance, at a point when a large number of delicate questions relating to the regulation of frontiers and rights of passage were pending between Geneva and France, and when the irritation aroused at the court by the recrudescence of Protestant assemblies in Languedoc was equally vented, by instinct, upon the tiny but quite judicious Calvinist republic, the Genevan government exerted itself mightily to find a minister in Paris who carried the same weight and enjoyed the same broad scope of connections and activity as Thellusson. The man best qualified for this mission, in principle, wholly available and already in place, was Jean-Louis Saladin d'Onex (1701–1784), the former minister of King George II, Elector of Hanover, in Paris. He had remained there since 1734 despite the Franco-English rupture, by taking up residence with his two uncles who were administrators of the *Compagnie des Glaces.* At once a great diplomat and man of society, enjoying excellent relations with the court of ministers, Jean-Louis Saladin had already played a role since the Act of Mediation of 1738; we shall mention, as a point of information, that he was likewise the first Genevan to enter into the administration of the Indies Company, the other major masterpiece of the French royal economy, which he had defended in a difficult court case in Holland. For as long as he could, Saladin refused the mission offered to him by the Genevan government, one without prestige but highly burdensome because of the multiplicity of Franco-Genevan affairs, often petty in character. He alleged a fragile health, the pressure of other business, and his desire to leave Paris once and for all. In the end he accepted, on condition that he would take care only of Geneva's diplomatic affairs, *per interim,* without credentials or an official title.

We know that he acquitted himself of his office extremely well and that Geneva could only congratulate itself on his services. But in March, 1748, he requested his definitive release from duty which the Council could not refuse, although it let the matter drag on for another whole year. The first successor to be solicited for the post was his young cousin Antoine Saladin, the future Lord of Crans, but he bluntly refused the job. Thereupon, at the suggestion of the cousins Saladin, the Genevan government had recourse to their colleague in the administration of Saint-Gobain Jean-François Sellon (1707–1790), despite the objections raised in Geneva against the regency of his burgher status, being the son of a Frenchman. The transfer of powers took place in the family, so to speak, in April, 1749. From then on, a tradition had been created.

When Sellon, in May, 1762, in turn demanded his release, and Saladin refused the post as always, an administrator of Saint-Gobain was no longer available. But after many equivocations, an elegant solution was found by appointing Jean-Pierre Crommelin (1716–1768), honorary professor of civil history at the Academy of Geneva, to the post in Paris, with the title, not of minister, but simply of *chargé d'affaires*. The professor was a highly cultivated man, reputed to be an excellent jurist and diplomat, but practically penniless. Antoine Saladin remedied this inconvenient state of affairs by transferring to him (by lending to him for the duration of his mission) together with Mme Geoffrin a share of the *Compagnie des Glaces*, and by quickly appointing him as an administrator of the company.

This first experience with a straw man did not turn out too happily and it threatened the Saladin-Geoffrin reign in the kingdom of rue Saint-Antoine, by providing an opposition group among the French shareholders with excellent grounds for attack. Poor Professor Crommelin, who really found it very difficult to maintain his rank, did not content himself with supplementing the emoluments received as administrator of the King's mirror factory with all sorts of vouchers, for "candles," "New Year's gifts," etc. He ended up by dipping indiscreetly into the company's coffers in order to meet his obligations in connection with some unfortunate speculations, replacing the monies withdrawn only by some worthless papers. The cat was let out of the bag at his sudden death in July, 1768. And despite the efforts of Saladin and Sellon to hush up the scandal by offering to make reparations—since Crommelin's sister and only heir could not or would not make any restitution—the upshot was a boisterous revolt on the part of several old shareholders against what they called the usurpation of the administration by fictitious shareholders who, as we read in the memoirs of one of the protesters, "have arrogated to themselves the authority of a sultan's divan." There were disputes of an equally vexatious character in that the rebels threatened to divulge the profits of the company, which was already under strong attack at that time, from the general assault on monopolies.

As early as 1772 Mme Geoffrin and her daughter implored Antoine Saladin, who at that time had retired to Crans, to return immediately to Paris to put in order the affairs of the company in which, they said, "frightful scenes are taking place." The dispute came to a head in 1774 when the board of directors, under the baton of Mme Geoffrin, simply struck off its lists the leader of the opposition, Courtin de Saint-Vincent, the representative of one of the founding families of the manufactory, who replied by publishing his memoirs and by inciting to revolt the big absenteeist shareholders, with the Montmorencys in the lead. It was necessary to mobilize Maurepas, Necker, Trudaine, and even Vergennes to meet the revolt head-on, and the storm subsided only ten years later, in 1777.[11]

Crommelin's misfortunes had been the first pretext for the attack, but the latter, directed against the whole system of administration, chose as its principal target the new

[11] See National Archives, Paris, Vol. 161, the sequestered papers of H. B. Perrinet, portfolios 14–17, particularly the letters and memorials of A. Saladin to Mmes Geoffrin from March 14 to April 19, 1770, setting forth the whole affair. Crommelin, ill, had come to die in the Genevan "countryside" of the former Procurator General Jean-Robert Tronchin, *la Boissière*, from July 16 to 18, 1768; a bachelor, without Genevan relatives, he left as his sole heiress his sister Elizabeth, likewise unmarried. Tronchin defended her so vehemently—producing, according to Saladin, "a grand memorial to prove that a cat was not a cat nor Rolet a knave"—that he caused the failure of all attempts at an amicable arrangement, and it became necessary to hush up the matter in order to avoid legal proceedings. Archives of the Château de Crans (Vaud), Saladin papers, A. Saladin's personal journal "of the affairs of the Company relating to M. de Saint-Cinvent," reporting the details of the meetings and proceedings from March to August, 1774; a printed copy of the *Mémoire* of Saint-Vincent against Perrinet des Franches, Jaucourt, and other "usurpers" (1777). Rolet was the name of an eighteenth-century attorney noted for his avarice and knaveries, whom Boileau immortalized in a verse: "*J'appelle un chat un chat et Rolet un fripon.*"—Trans.

straw-man administrator who had come to replace Crommelin, Horace-Bénédict Perrinet des Franches, to whom Saladin and Mmes Geoffrin had just loaned the share wrested from the hands of Crommelin's heirs. Perrinet himself, in a disorganized defense, touchingly described how he entered into the administration of the Royal Manufactory of Mirrors: "Arriving in Paris by chance in 1768 for personal matters, two respectable ladies invited me to remain there and to acquire an interest in the *Compagnie des Glaces,* which the death of an associate had enabled them to make available. . . ." The very same record of Perrinet's sequestered papers contains the documents of the fictitious transfers of parts of the share, at a fictitious price, with the customary notification of the transfer made to the company and the counter letters attesting that these parts of the share remained the property of Saladin, and that a sixth part belonged to the respectable ladies Geoffrin.[12]

Perrinet—the son of the "Mississippian" who had been received into the burghership of Geneva in 1724 "in consideration of his father-in-law," under conditions that caused a scandal at that time because these ultras of the Genevan oligarchy were not all Genevans of the old stock—had in fact left Geneva for Paris in 1768. He had done so partly

[12] The same sources: the authentic duplicates of the transfer documents and the counter letters (certified on February 1, 1769) are found in Perrinet's sequestered papers (Paris) and in the *Archives d'État de Genève,* Min. Ch. G. Flournois, Vol. XXIX, p. 493 (initial share and deposit, January 27, 1779). In the counter letters for Saladin, Perrinet declares that "nevertheless the truth is that the said transfer is not serious and it was made only in order to facilitate the entry and acquisition of the deliberative vote in the Company of the said Sr. Perrinet Desfranches"; the counter letter for the Ladies Geoffrin specifies that they lent him the value of 3 *deniers* (40,000 *livres*) at 4 per cent, having in view the completion of his deliberative vote, so that he could "watch over, for the said ladies, the management and direction of the Manufactory" and that in case of Perrinet's death, or in the event that he left Paris, these *deniers* would again become the property of the Ladies Geoffrin.

because of his opposition to the Edict of Conciliation of that year, which, in his view, had made too many concessions to the burghership. But chiefly he had left out of personal disappointment because his ambitions to rise in the magistracy of the republic had been thwarted and also, no doubt, to attempt to re-establish his business affairs, which had dropped to a very low point. Was he from this moment on intended to relieve Crommelin, not only at the Royal Manufactory of Mirrors, but also in the post of Minister of Geneva in Paris? Probably, but the moment was not favorable to the ultras, and the Council let Necker have his way. Perrinet had to content himself with an official mission from Their Excellencies of Bern—let us not forget that all these rural lords of the district of Vaud (Saladin de Crans, Perrinet de Bossey et de Bogis, Vasserot de Vincy, and others) were equally subjects of Bern. He gave proof of the indisputable diplomatic talents during the course of the lengthy negotiations preliminary to the last Franco-Swiss alliance in 1777, drafting memorials that were greatly appreciated by Vergennes. It was only in September, 1777, one year after the retirement of Necker, who was summoned to higher destinies, that Perrinet was to become the Genevan *chargé d'affaires* in Paris, a choice that was almost imposed by Vergennes, just as Necker had been by Choiseul. The appointment was made with bad grace on both sides, the Genevan government in the face of the mistrust of the *représentants* nominating him only in an interim capacity. But Perrinet was frank enough to refuse the official title of minister or that of *chargé d'affaires*, expressly declaring that "this would leave him greater freedom to express his sentiment" and to act as he pleased.[13] At the end of the eighth year of this mission, the

[13] *Archives d'État de Genève*, Registres du Conseil (Minute Books of the Council), 278, pp. 276–316 (June–July, 1777), the reports of J. de

Magnificent Council of Geneva was to have great difficulty in ridding itself of this interim minister, titleless, living on a grand scale but crushed by debts, supported by quasi-public loans contracted on his wife's fortune which was separate from his own (he pledged to pay them after her death), up to his neck in shady deals, discredited even in the eyes of Vergennes who demanded his dismissal. Yet Perrinet clung desperately to his function by means that virtually bordered on blackmail. The archives of the Council of Geneva contain few documents more startling than these missives in which the Council in contorted, flattering circumlocutions implores this diplomat to take his leave.

This behind-the-scenes view of diplomacy, or rather of the Genevan diplomats in Paris, in no way prejudges the qualities and integrity of the majority of these *chargés d'affaires*, needless to say. The fact of placing at the disposal of the representatives of the republic the prestige and even the retributions of a seat in the most beautiful Royal Manufactory of the French capital was a gesture of patriotism which became problematic only with the progress of the internal dissensions in Geneva. Jean-Louis Saladin was

Chapeaurouge on a mission to Versailles. He cannot find enough words to describe the position of trust which Perrinet enjoys with Vergennes —the only way of imposing him upon the "*représentants*" and the moderates. "One . . . must have read and heard all that has come to my attention to understand the kind of connection that he has the good fortune to have with M. de Vergennes; I had no idea of it. . . ." Perrinet himself had introduced Chapeaurouge to Vergennes "as his friend, as an old citizen[!] attached to the true principles of a prudent government and at all times devoted to France, and finally as a magistrate of a Republic full of admiration for the talents and the virtues of this minister and desirous himself of expressing it to him." Such was the tone from there on. Compare a letter of Perrinet's to Marc Cramer, a Genevan banker in London, dated April 22, 1781: "My principles respecting our Government, which we share in common, fortified my desire to work to the advantage of our Republic, but they could not permit me to be dependent upon a Council that was so different from what it was formerly," Perrinet Papers, Arch. Nat., Vol. 161/32.

the best advocate that Geneva could have had at Versailles; the long administration of Jean-François Sellon, during a period of domestic peace, did not seem to have occasioned any objection. And although the unfortunate Professor Crommelin had dedicated himself body and soul to the ruling oligarchy (his public obsequies, in 1768, were boycotted by the "*représentant*" party) his activity was ineffectual. The second French mediation, in 1766, was rejected by the General Council, and up to Choiseul's disgrace in 1770 it was a ceaseless war of pinpricks between France and Geneva, culminating in the economic blockade and in the establishment of "Port Choiseul" at Versoix. At that time, moreover, in this sphere as in the more important ones of French policy, the turmoil of interferences of all sorts of official, officious, "secret" agents or simply amateurs was such that their efforts conflicted with and nullified each other, and it is very difficult to discern the role of this or that person in the confusion. Doubtless Necker's indifference and "neutralism" toward Geneva's internal quarrels had a calming, sedative effect.

With Perrinet des Franches on the other hand, a fanatical agent of the aristocracy appeared once more to complete (for the Genevan side) the teamwork between Vergennes and his resident minister, and later his assistant, Hennin. Perrinet pushed with all his might for French partisan intervention in the internal conflicts of his native city. In the crisis which came to a head in Geneva, Perrinet acted openly not as the representative of the Republic of Geneva and of its government, but as the exclusive agent of the intransigent "Negative party" now actually forming a "constitutionary" countergovernment under the direction of his patron Antoine Saladin de Crans. On the eve of the convulsions of 1781–1782, the oligarchic party, having completely lost support in its own city, clung on only through the diplomatic chain which encompassed the tiny republic; but this chain was firmly held. The history of this great complicated and cynical maneuver was brilliantly analyzed fifty years ago by Hippolyte Aubert,[14] on the very basis of the correspondence between Perrinet and Saladin. Perrinet was the dynamo behind the maneuver and—aided in his task by Jacob Tronchin, the brother of the former Procurator General and correspondent of the "*constitutionnaires*" in Paris—was the mainspring in relations with Vergennes; but direction was taken over by Saladin de Crans himself at crucial moments. The upshot of Perrinet's systematic intensification (to the point of paroxysm) of the internal tension, and of his discarding of the conciliatory influence of the co-guarantors Zurich and Bern through a series of reversals in policy, was the occupation by troops under the command of marquis de Jaucourt. The spirit of these events is summed up in a quotation from a correspondence of Perrinet's, the banker Marc Cramer, who carried out a parallel mission to London, in October, 1781: "I know very well that I would a thousand times prefer to be

[14] For the activity of the "*comité des Constitutionnaires*," a virtual parallel government which grouped the intransigent "Negatives" around Saladin de Crans, the key document is Saladin's "*Journal Politique*" in 22 volumes, preserved in the Crans château, which reports in minute detail on the gatherings and secret meetings (often held at the *hôtel* of the French resident), the proceedings (demands for intervention addressed to the powers as early as November 9, 1780), and the great council of war held in Paris in September-October, 1781. It also contains, among others, the original of one of Vergennes's letters which shows that Vergennes tried to brake developments up to the last moment. "We feel here that the re-establishment of the internal order of the Republic and of a good government cannot be only the work of the parties who divide it and requires a conciliator." (Autograph letter from Versailles, March 20, 1782; *Journal Politique*, 3rd series, Vol. VII, no. 10 bis. H. Aubert, "Les Troubles de Genève en 1781 et 1782," in *Bulletin de la Société d'Histoire et d'Archéologie de Genève*, Vol. III, pp. 418–441, has reproduced some extracts from this journal.)

a subject of the King of France rather than of Messieurs du Roveray, Clavière, Vieusseux, and such people," and in this other almost biblical remark of Marc-Conrad Fabri's: "All our eyes are turned in the direction of Versailles as though it were toward the sun from which we await light and life." There is no need to recapitulate the political and diplomatic narrative of this crisis here. But the knowledge of the material organization and of the "social seat" of Geneva's diplomatic mission in Paris can, it seems to us, contribute to clarifying its activity and efficacy.

This government by co-optation within a closed group of closely allied families—some of the main pillars of which are clearly distinguishable in this history of the representation of Geneva in Paris—managed to keep itself in power beyond the middle of the eighteenth century, wresting it again in 1782, not so much by its own forces within the republic as by action from the outside; the most solid foundations of its power were situated outside Genevan territory, in which its leaders hardly ever resided. Indeed, it disposed of more means of wielding influence and of orchestrating opinion in Paris and at the Versailles court than in Geneva itself. Above all, an even more restricted group of families had succeeded in making Genevan diplomacy a kind of familial fief which enabled it to manipulate that dangerous instrument forged in the time of Thellusson: the appeal for French intervention. Thus the oligarchic regime ended up by being identified with the French protectorate. The jangled nerves and seeming incoherence of Geneva's internal troubles now become more comprehensible; the issues were constantly being confused and falsified from the outside.

But as the eighteenth century neared its close, the traditional ministerial policy of the *raison d'État*, of which Vergennes was the last example, no longer moved without unforeseen counterblows in a world already entering the age of ideologies. The tiny Republic of Geneva, so ridiculously impotent on the material level, but strengthened by an ancient and inexhaustible mine of Protestant intransigence, suddenly awakened and transformed into political radicalism, became a singularly powerful center of ideological agitation. Nothing better illustrates how far the moribund French monarchy had set itself against itself than its rushing to the aid of the rebels in America (through a ministerial calculation that was indifferent to the problem of the contagions inherent in ideas) by which it unleashed, indeed legitimized, a deep wave of revolutionary and republican enthusiasm, while at the same time launching an armed intervention against the Genevan revolution. Such a contradiction could have been exhibited and overcome without difficulty at the time of the Too Christian King, who, while persecuting his own heretics, allied himself with heretics beyond his realm and with the Great Turk against the empire and the Pope. But this was no longer possible at the end of the eighteenth century, and it was grist to the mill for the Genevan exiles, who gained the sympathies of the whole "American party" of France.

From this an almost grotesque consequence ensued which, however, is outside the scope of our subject: since Geneva's internal conflicts were settled not in Geneva but in the French capital, all the Genevan parties ended up by transporting their quarrels to the Parisian scene. Beginning in 1782, with Clavière and his following, the Geneva opposition in turn began its grand maneuvers in Paris, not in the discreet atmosphere of ministerial antechambers as the "aristocrats" could do, but on the public squares. In order to set foot again in Geneva, in order to "shake off the yoke," as the exiles said, they had to begin, paradoxically, by overthrowing French policy, if not the monarchy. Étienne Dumont has reported Clavière's macabre sally, uttered in 1793, that he had been forced to sign Louis XVI's death warrant because, ten years earlier, Louis XVI had ordered him to be exiled from Geneva. The French *ancien régime*, which had supported its counterpart in Geneva, was to drag it down with it into the abyss. By a tragic concatenation, the series of upheavals which culminated in the annexation of 1798 was a replica of the occupation of 1782 and a distant consequence of the Act of Mediation of 1738.

CHAPTER NINE

Rousseau the Genevan

As he himself took great pains to explain in his *Dialogues*, for the sake of all authors of histories of literature, the whole of Jean-Jacques Rousseau's work is devoted exclusively to the development of a single theme: Nature has made man happy and good, but society depraves him and renders him miserable. From the contradiction inherent in this simple thesis springs the passionate, plaintive, and accusatory tension that marks his work and all the unreasonableness of his "eloquence of the heart," transforming his least tenable sophisms into evidence of sentimentality. It is the eternal myth of Paradise Lost; the transposition, slightly distorted by Rousseau's secularized religiosity, of the theological mystery of the appearance of evil in a Creation which was wholly good, on the sixth day, having issued from the hands of God. Hence for Rousseau, the blessed state of nature was the state before all law and before all knowledge of good or evil; the man of nature was happy and good because he was ignorant of any morality and followed only his brute instincts. As in the Book of Genesis, the Fall is identified with the act of knowledge itself. And as in Paul's Epistle to the Romans, sin appeared in the world only with law or, in Rousseau's terms, with civil society, which defined its essence precisely through the establishment of laws. Only "this passage from the state of nature to the civil state," he says in the *Social Contract*, transformed man from a dim-witted beast, subject exclusively to his physical appetites, into a being capable of reason and of distinguishing between the just and the unjust. As a result of this transition from the state of nature to the state of society, "his ideas are extended, his sentiments exalted and his whole mind is enlarged and refined." In short, he is transformed "from a dull and stupid animal to an intelligent being and a man." It is the paradox of Paradise Lost, translated from metaphysics into a sociological thesis: man became man only through the Fall.

But what constitutes Rousseau's "modernity," what separates him radically from any tradition of the moralists, is that he sees the origin of evil not in the soul of man but in society, namely, in others. As an inscription on his work, and indeed on his life, we could imagine the celebrated Sartrean maxim, "Hell is other people." The originality of this philosophy of society against the grain already resides in the promises which Rousseau announces incidentally, as it were, without developing them, as self-evident. His man of nature, good and happy as he may be, is in no way a social animal but solitary and wild; far from seeking the company of his fellows, he avoids and flees from it. Even the fusion of the sexes is only a transient physical need which does not establish any associations. "This blind propensity, deprived of any feeling of the heart," says the *Discourse on Inequality*, "produces only a purely animal act; once the need is satisfied, the two sexes no longer recognize each other, and even the child is nothing to the mother as soon as he can do without her." Only irresistible external necessities—the nature of which Rousseau hardly makes explicit—were able to force men, against their nature, to enter into an association with each other and to domesticate themselves in order to survive. Thus, in order to be complete, his fundamental thesis could be formulated as follows: Man would be good, ignorant, and happy if he were permitted to be alone and far from his fellows. This is the sociology of a hermit, the interpretation of which always leads us to Rousseau himself. A motherless youth, passed on from hand to hand, soon thrown into exile and errantry, uprooted and incapable of adapting himself to a stable life in any society, but nevertheless obsessed by a nostalgia for other people, a fatherland, a community, Rousseau was incapable of finding a human communion according to his heart's desire anywhere, except in his reveries or in the tender imagination of remembrances. There were philosophers and critics of society before Rousseau; but his work, which is at heart an anti-sociology, marks the entry on stage of the solitary accuser, who raises the torments of his frustrated private and sentimental life to the rank of outrages committed against the human race and who makes a badly wrought society responsible for all his personal misfortunes, failures, failings, and even his vices. For it is society which bears the fault of his faults, it is society which has depraved and perverted him, whereas he was naturally good and pure.

Man is good by nature, but the society of men does not permit him to be good. This seems contradictory both as a theory of history and of the social process, but it becomes flawless logic as an accusation of this single man, this "loner" against the society which rejects him. *Man* in the singular is Jean-Jacques Rousseau, who *feels* that he is good *in himself;* men in the plural, society, are the others, who, incomprehensible and incapable of understanding him, prevent him from being himself. The great theme is roughly sketched at the time of that "illumination" that swept over him on the road to Vincennes, which inspired the paradox on the corrupting effect of civilization, the sciences, and the arts. And it is significant that this act of cognizance, which was the beginning of his glory and his career as a writer, retrospectively was to appear to him as his Fall, "the origin of his misfortunes," and the expulsion from Paradise. By becoming a man of letters, even if only to condemn literature, civilization, and society, Rousseau thenceforth was to be allied with what he condemned. He was to be the very image of the literary man whom he claimed to despise. No longer would he be able to stop writing just to prove to the world that he was not a writer, nor to stop filling the world with the din of his name by his very effort to return to a state of blessed solitude. It was necessary that the world should know that he wanted to remain alone and ignored, and that the world should admire this exemplary resolve. It was a conflict, often exhibiting whimsical features, between an inexhaustible need for communication and an unsociability that amounted to a fear of self-giving, a fear of betraying a role he could sustain only on the stage of his hermitage, to which his visitors came as pilgrims, or in the chiaroscuro of his confidences, in which he mixed his tears with those of the "consoling sex."

This cleavage aroused the tremendous tumultuous tension of several creative years in which Rousseau—an irritable and vociferous suitor—hesitated on the threshold of the Paris republic of letters, banging on the door so that someone should come to hold him back. Piling blow upon blow, in 1761–1762, he threw three works at the public which overturned the modes of thought and feeling of his epoch: *La Nouvelle Héloïse*, or *The Letters of Two Lovers Living in a Tiny Village at the Foot of the Alps*, which opened the dikes to the torrential tears of sensitive and misunderstood hearts; *Émile*, those reveries of a solitary pedagogue inventing the perfect education, not as discipline and compulsion, but as the art of a gardener who surrounds with his protection the harmonious flowering of the natural goodness of the adolescent; and finally the *Social Contract*, amazing fragment of a social doctrine which abolished the conflict between the individual and society in the unanimity of the general will. The connecting thread of these works, written almost simultaneously, is the search for reconciliation with the world (even at the price of painfully elaborated stratagems) in the sublime union of souls of a marriage *à trois*, in an ideal education without family or social setting, in an ideal republic of unanimous citizens.

The reconciliation took place only in the imaginary world of solitary monologue, from which he was awakened by an external catastrophe: the temporal and spiritual authorities, the republic of letters and, worse still, the Republic of Geneva itself responded by condemnation, proscription, and by heaping ignominy upon him. In the growing solitude produced by real persecutions and in the delirium of imaginary persecutions, the original theme was developed to its pathological conclusion. In the *Confessions*, the *Dialogues*, and throughout the hallucinatory passages of the *Rêveries d'un promeneur solitaire*, the antithesis between man, viewed as naturally good, and society, which is intrinsically corrupted, was reduced to pure egocentrism: the charge sheet drawn up by this solitary, Jean-Jacques Rousseau, the best, the most tender, the most innocent, the most loving, and the most unhappy man whoever lived (for now, having replaced "man" by the Self, Rousseau knew only the superlative of his absolute singularity) against the sinister conspiracy society had woven against him, which the whole of mankind had ended up by joining. All the excesses of self-deification and self-abasement are included without contradiction in the same rigorous demonstration. For that which in the life of the purest of men appeared as bad, perverse, and contrary to nature, that precisely was the inexpiable fault of others. *Ecce homo*, behold what a man I was in the purity of my heart, and behold what you have made of me! Yet there was a flaw in this demonstration: nothing had wounded Rousseau as much as Diderot's trenchant declaration, "Only the wicked man is alone." This whole unmeasured and tangled portrait of himself which Rousseau was never to cease to remake over and over again like Penelope's garment was but a painful effort to resolve this mystery of iniquity: How could it be that he, intrinsically so good, was nevertheless so unhappy? In the radical isolation of his solipsism, this problem was no more than a fight with his own shadow, for what is it to be good or bad in total isolation from one's fellows?

There are two ways of approaching this work, and all emphases and judgments change according to which one we choose. The first is to accept his thought, without any mental reservations, as the proclamation of a new equalitarian society and a newer and truer image of man. This is the main road that has been taken by generations of admirers of Jean-Jacques. And the parting of the ways between the political radicalism of liberty, equality, and fraternity and the romantic radicalism of feeling merely separated two equally legitimate successions of this sower of revolt against the civilization of a skeptical and aristocratic elite. Hence what is disconcerting in the confession of his last years is but the moving and saddening testimony of a martyr to truth whose corrupted epoch crucified alive. The other road, which Rousseau's egocentrism makes practically inevitable for the reader today, leads us to start out precisely from this final point, seeing it as the history of a long physical, moral, and mental illness, and to discover in it the first specifically clinical document of world literature. As such it has never ceased to interest doctors, psychiatrists, psychoanalysts, and exegetics of the alienation of modern man. Since Freudian psychoanalysis has deprived us of all candor in the rationalizations of the consciousness, it has in fact become difficult for us to appreciate Rousseau's philosophical theses as a critique of society and civilization, as the effort of a mind thrusting toward truth, and not as the reasoned ravings of a sick sensibility. It has become too simple, apparently, to dismantle the mechanisms of psychological compensation which made of this masochist visionary the apostle of natural man, simple and spontaneous; of this wandering uprooted individual the founder of an ideal city of brotherly souls; and of this unnatural father the prophet of an education which grants the child all his rights.

Yet neither his work nor its historical significance is lessened thereby. It is precisely the extreme deviation of the movement of the pendulum between his personal misery and the vision of redemption which gives the measure of his thought and of his genius. No doubt what haunted his dream was the lost, or always unknown, paradise of a coddled childhood, of maternal warmth, of an affectionate home which he had never known. But what he drew from this was the idea of a new childhood of the world, of a new education of man, of a fervent communion of republican citizens. Rousseau was both, the mentally sick and the prophet, and other ages have always known that the prophet is an unbalanced person: a well-balanced mind would never have filled his work with such explosive passion. Even if we read his writings as the history of an alienation, they would not have acted on generations present and those to come, as they have, if this alienation had been only his own, and if he had not touched the heart of his age. An age in which the traditional social order had manifestly ceased to be a tissue of humanly transparent, familiar bonds forming the natural setting (coherent and accepted without question) of the life of men and was sliding instead toward an anonymous administrative order, encompassing, without binding, a mass of administered individuals. From this ensued Rousseau's insistent question concerning the elements that could possibly constitute a community of men, a political and social body which would be something else besides a multitude of individuals forced to co-exist. Before trying to find out how a people can be governed, he says, we must examine that which henceforth is no longer evident: "The act through which a people is a people." It was a radical questioning of what—in political theories in general—appeared as given, *a priori*. Rousseau was the seismograph whose flayed sensibility registered all the precursory signs of the imminent disintegration. It would be an endless task to list the motifs and even the slogans of modern disquietude which appear for the first time in recognizable terms in Rousseau's work, from alienation to depersonalization, and from the uprootedness of socialized man to the formerly fashionable antitheses between soul and intellect, between the organic and the ready-made, between culture and civilization, between people and mass. We shall deal only with two extreme points of departure here.

In the age of the Enlightenment, dominated by the ideas

of emancipation of the individual, toleration, liberal order, progress, and of the perfectibility of man through civilization, which is the domestication of nature and of the instincts by reason, Rousseau marked the fateful moment at which the movement of ideas tottered and reversed itself. With him, the proud individualism which proclaims the autonomy of the person against all conventions and all temporal and spiritual authority seemed to reach its climax in an absolute subjectivism—a subjectivism that, in the name of its interior truth, repudiated all the standards of morality, propriety, and of reason itself, erecting its own irrationality as last judge of good and evil. But this paroxysm—far from being the flowering of the sovereign and self-possessed personality—was no more than the pathetic anxiety and lamentation over one's self which has made of Rousseau the ancestor of an inundating literature of obsessional exhibitionism. And at the same time it was the mortal leap of this morbid individualism toward redemption in an integral collectivity. In the polarity between social servitudes and individual freedom, political philosophy, from Locke and Montesquieu to Voltaire, had sought the balanced position of a political and juridical order which protected the individual in his private life, in his convictions, and in his conscience against the arbitrariness of power.

Rousseau, who had posed the antithesis between man and society as absolute, could not admit such a compromise between order and freedom; only the totalitarian integration of his *Social Contract* can wipe out the opposition between individual and society, by suppressing the individual through the constitutional act demanding "the total alienation of each associate with all his rights to the whole community." His integral, egalitarian, and closed democracy did not recognize the differentiation of organs, nor the separation of powers, nor the autonomy of groups or of particular communities, nor the guarantee of individual rights, nor toleration, nor, at bottom, private life. The totally collectivized individual is no more than a particle in a sovereign whole. His will, his interests, and his faith are identified with the general will, with the public interest, and civic religion —for "instead of as many separate persons as there are contracting partners, this act of association produces a moral and collective body," a "common self" which causes the individual self to disappear. Freedom, thenceforth, is that of the sovereign collective, which abolishes all others and which no law will be able to restrict, because its will at every moment is the law of all. And whoever refuses to obey it "shall be compelled to it by the whole body, which means nothing else than that he will be forced to be free." When the French Revolution had used up all the political doctrines of the liberal school, all that remained to it were Rousseau and the *Social Contract* as justifications of the Terror in the name of freedom, of the extermination of any local, corporative, or spiritual autonomy and of all particular communities in the name of indivisible sovereignty, of the tyranny of virtue and the installation of the cult of the State. And the spirit of Rousseau still hovers over the current successors of the Jacobin People's commissars.

By the same movement of thought, this vagabond without a homeland who, nevertheless, was so little a citizen of the world, finally effected the break with the cosmopolitan spirit of the eighteenth century. The idea that a civilization without frontiers destroys the primitive and closed communities that are the source of all virtues had already appeared in his first *Discourse on the Sciences and the Arts.* "National hatreds will be extinguished, but so will love of the fatherland." And in this last work of political doctrine, the *Considerations on the Government of Poland*, he lamented that: "Today there are no longer Frenchmen, Germans, Spaniards, even Englishmen, no matter what may be said about it; there are only Europeans. All have the same manners, the same passions, and same customs, because none of them receive national form through a particular institution . . . provided they find money to steal and women to corrupt they are everywhere in their own country." In this essay, published in 1772, in which he posed the question of the means of saving Poland (at that time on the eve of the first partition), Rousseau gave this haughty response: "Make of the Poles a nation so unassimilable that her neighbors might be able to swallow her, but never digest her." For Rousseau it was self-evident that nations, like societies, are in no sense gifts of nature; that the national sentiment is not born spontaneously from a pre-existent organism. On the contrary, the nation must be forged from the raw material of amorphous population, by inculcating in it the national sense—by legislation, militarization, education, the cult of the fatherland; in short, by the national ideology, stamped on souls from the cradle:

> You will give their souls a national physiognomy which will distinguish them from other peoples, which will prevent them from mixing, liking, allying themselves with others . . . begin always by giving the Poles a great opinion of themselves . . . by giving them a natural repugnance to mixing with the foreigner. . . . A child upon opening his eyes must see the fatherland, and until the day he dies he must see nothing else . . .

The nation also must become a total, monolithic and closed collectivity in which the individual is absorbed body and soul, in a state of permanent exaltation and "patriotic drunkenness."

The *Considerations* are a startling anticipation of all the proper recipes for cultivating nationalist fanaticism, through an exclusively patriotic education and historiography, through the mysticism of the armed nation, civic festivals, parades, monuments to the dead, the cult of the hero, flags, symbols, and rites. The national State of the nineteenth century faithfully put into practice most of these recipes, and the memory of the last deliriums of these organized collective frenzies is still fresh.

Would Rousseau, therefore, be the ancestor of all the totalitarian ideologies of modern Europe—he who so many times expressed his horror of all sedition and all disorder and who, in his *Letters from the Mountain*, warned his Genevan fellow citizens: "The blood of one single man is more precious than the freedom of the human race"? Let us simply say that this great, sick man had a sharp sense for everything in the society of his time which was secretly sick and morbid, and that he instinctively felt what enlightened and progressive minds could not or would not see: that modern societies once cut off from the soil and from bonds consecrated by custom, by piously venerated ancestral rites and authority, if they were not to fall to pieces, would need other practices more effectual than those of reason and utility, and other frameworks besides constitutional and administrative ones in order to reconstitute a moral and emotional unity for themselves. He was intuitively aware of the problem of the new principle of legitimacy, which elevated a popular will to sovereignty without asking whether such a will existed elsewhere than in theory. And he was the first to announce, as a visionary, the advent of those secular religions which, since the French Revolution, have served as integrating ideologies for mass societies.

These forecasts are quite striking. But Rousseau would have seen in all such interpretations sinister misunderstandings. In the *Dialogues*—those Kafkaesque protocols of the imaginary trial he conducts against himself because the world refused him justice—he complains that by interpreting the *Social Contract* as a universal constitutional model, "the great nations have taken for themselves what had for its object only the small republics"; "he had worked for his fatherland and for similar small constituted states"; or, as he says in his *Letters from the Mountain*, the *Social Contract* is nothing else than "the history of the government of Geneva." In fact many pages of the *Contract* insist upon a condition for the exercise of popular sovereignty: namely, a very small city whose entire population can at any moment gather together as a deliberative body, as in Geneva and in the tiny Alpine republics. That the *Discourse on Inequality*, which denounces property as the source of all human ills, is dedicated to the republic of wealthy citizens that was Geneva, and that the *Social Contract* begins with the praise of the Genevan constitution, should be enough, moreover, to demonstrate that only the hyperbolic eloquence of Rousseau could raise to the level of the abstract and the absolute that which in his intimate vision was concrete and limited, namely, the image of the tiny city still close to natural simplicity, the Geneva which stirred his memories, if not the Geneva of reality.

This is another movement of the pendulum characteristic of his thought, this time swinging back in the opposite direction from the doctrinal message of universal significance to the humble nostalgia of the tiny fatherland which was at the base of his inspiration. For what in the *Social Contract*, disassociated from his model, appears as the revolutionary utopia of a collective and totalitarian despotism is merely the principle of the free commune, administering itself. The general will of the assembled people, the physical and moral identity of the government and the governed, was the burghership of Geneva gathered in general council in the Church of St. Peter, or the assembly of the citizens of the valley-cantons of the Swiss mountains—the last organisms of simple, almost unicellular, structure subsisting among the European states. The idea of applying their forms of government to the great territorial States must have appeared absurd to the citizen of Geneva himself. "No French author that I know," he says in a note on the *Contract*, "has understood the true meaning of the word citizen." And in his *Considerations on the Government of Poland*, he exclaims:

> The grandeur of nations, the size of States: the first and principal source of the misfortunes of the human race. . . . Almost all the small States, whether republics and monarchies, prosper only because they are small. . . . All the great peoples, crushed by their own masses, groan, either like you in anarchy or under the subaltern oppressors which a necessary gradation forces the kings to give them. . . . The first reform which you will need will be that of your size. Begin by contracting your frontiers, if you wish to reform your government. Perhaps your neighbors are thinking of rendering you this service. . . .

In place of this imminent dismemberment, on which he invites the Poles to congratulate themselves in advance, he counsels them to constitute themselves into a federation of autonomous palatinates, as the only means of combining the advantages of a big State with the vigor and civic cohesion of the tiny republics (and here we must regret that Rousseau never wrote that treatise on "Confederations" which was to form the sequel to the *Social Contract* and which would really have brought to Europe a "wholly new matter"). Needless to say, nobody appreciated such counsel. Rousseau, at heart, had the right feelings about his obsession with the great conspiracy which was to distort his message and his personality; but he himself was part of the conspiracy. By transposing his atavistic ideal of the small, primitive, and fervently united community to the dimensions of the great powers and of the continents, the Europe of the great nations forged the terrorist ideologies of national unity and plebiscitary despotism. And Rousseau carried in triumph to the Pantheon, where he presides in effigy over all the revolutionary tribunes, has eclipsed even in his own country the humble citizen of Geneva who, fundamentally, should have been only the State ideologue of the Swiss Confederation.

Now Rousseau was a citizen of Geneva to the marrow of his bones, in all his instincts and in all his passions, precisely because he was the Prodigal Son who never found his way back to the fold, but who, in compensation, embodied with the most passionate intensity the revolt of the old Genevan against the temptations and corruptions of the century of which he had become a victim. In order to define himself and to assert his singularity against the whole Parisian world of letters, he discovered and labelled himself Genevan. He made himself a Genevan who was more Genevan than was natural, to the point where he annoyed his compatriots themselves: but a Genevan he was, nevertheless. Neither the apostasies nor the apparent confessional indifference could hide the almost frenzied Protestantism of this soul ceaselessly obsessed with the need to plumb its own depths and to justify itself. It was the old Calvinist intransigence in its entirety which came through in his constant moral passion, in his cries of indignation, and in his confused and vehement demand for justice and truth—the eloquent political and moral radicalism of which was to imbue successions of generations thereafter—even if it came through in the new language, accessible to the men of his century, of a sentimental religiosity without Church or dogma. Indeed, we could say that, through Rousseau's work, two centuries after the revolutionary impetus given by the Genevan reformers themselves, the Puritan Calvinist democracy shook the world for the second time.

But Geneva, at that time, was no longer in Geneva. The tiny republic which Jean-Jacques had deserted—following in the footsteps of many other deserters for the attractions of the papist world—was no longer the austere and fervent community living in the fear of God, whose ideal image he had carried away with him. The Republic of Calvin had been delivered up helplessly to the temptations and corruptions of the new Parisian Babylon, ever since an oligarchy of Genevan merchant bankers had engaged in the career of being the provenders of war supplies and the court Jews of Louis XIV, at the very moment when the latter was persecuting and hunting down their co-religionists in France. These enriched oligarchs entrenched in the Councils, in order to protect their trade and their power against the hostility of the common Genevan burghership, had ended up by transforming Geneva into a protectorate of the court of Versailles, which had been promoted to the status of mediator and guarantor of their usurpation.

In 1720, when Rousseau was eight years old, Geneva was no longer the asylum and the Zion of Huguenot refugees who saved their faith by sacrificing their earthly possessions. It had become instead a haven for the speculators of "Le Mississippi," who saved their dubiously acquired fortunes and brought with them the cosmopolitanism of the

Regency, the customs of the *Palais-Royal*, the taste for play and masonic philosophy. Chains of gold and silver thenceforth bound the oligarchs of Geneva to the court of France. And it would require a singular lack of sense of their respective proportions and weights to believe, as some historians have done, that these chains bound Versailles to Geneva, rather than Geneva to Versailles. The Republic of Geneva, in all it had preserved of local patriotism and the old republican and Calvinist spirit since the beginning of the eighteenth century, through those internal struggles ever renascent and culminating each time in French intervention solicited by the oligarchs in power, had lived in the secret obsession of being betrayed by its own ruling families and of being sold out to the enemy of its faith, customs, and ancient Calvinian constitutions.

Without being aware of this at first, Rousseau personified the revolt of the Puritan and democratic atavism of the citizen of Geneva against his own fall and that of his tiny fatherland, equally victims of the world's seductions. And his stubbornness in engulfing himself deeper in the well of his unhappiness was a desperate search for atonement. All that had set him at loggerheads with his Parisian friends and protectors was born of this Genevan atavism: the war cry against the whole dazzling, skeptical, and frivolous French civilization of the Enlightenment, his revolt against the cosmopolitan spirit of this enlightened society which had seduced and mislead him; his hostility against Voltaire, this personification of Evil, installed at the gates of the tiny republic in order "to smarten up the Genevans"; even his war against the establishment of a theater in Geneva, a quarrel that is bound to strike us as extremely ridiculous if we do not see it in its historical context.

French actors were able to force their entry into the city of Calvin three times during the eighteenth century, under the pressure of the resident ministers of France, to the joy of the worldly oligarchs and to the indignation of the good people of Geneva: in 1737, under the imperious protection of the plenipotentiary sent by the court of France to arbitrate Geneva's constitutional disputes, in the name of the King; in 1765, during the renascent troubles following the proscription of *Émile* and of the *Social Contract* by the will of Choiseul—on the advice of Voltaire—conspiring to break the "sectarian turbulence" of this center of agitation. And on both these two occasions, after either several weeks or several months, after bankruptcy or after their stage booth had been set afire, the actors had to flee the city under the hoots and jeers of the "patriot party." And, finally, for the third time, when they came to Geneva in the wagons of the occupation troops under the command of the marquis de Jaucourt, in 1782. This time the troupe of actors was able to establish itself permanently, a living symbol of the corruption imposed by the foreign seizure finally victorious, forcibly introducing a worldly and frivolous cult which Geneva for so long had stubbornly rejected.

All that distinguishes Rousseau in the movement of ideas of his time assumes its meaning from these emotive sources, up to this nightmare of the universal conspiracy which would crush the true citizen, the true citizens of Geneva—and which was no mere hallucination. Rousseau, under all these disguises of his reasoning and distraught mind, was the incarnation of the revolt of Genevan atavism against the spirit of the age, and his posthumous triumphs were its violent and unmeasured revenge. The insurrection of the Genevan burghership against the French tutelage, and against its own oligarchy imposed by this tutelage, and Vergennes's military intervention in 1782 which crushed this burgher revolution, had an eminent role in the preparation for the French Revolution. It also affected the American Revolution, which Vergennes, at the same moment, decided to support according to a logic of ministerial policy which had already become anachronistic, but against all logic on the level of ideas, at a time when ideas had become political forces. Now "American ideas" and "Genevan ideas" were merged in the movement of minds which swept the monarch toward its fall, and the crushed commune of Geneva already represented the victorious ideology incarnate. It was the leaders of the Geneva democratic party, forced to flee from their invaded city, who in their turn invaded France by bringing there—along with their constitutional doctrines and their experience of political debate deepened and fully ripened in their internal quarrels—the message of the *Social Contract.* A message which nobody, or practically nobody, had read or taken seriously in France before 1789, but which every militant Genevan knew by heart. Mirabeau's "brain trust," composed of Genevan *émigré* lawyers, pastors, and politicians—Dumont, Reybaz, Du Roveray, Clavière—formed an editorial committee and an ideological factory from which poured forth the great speeches of the people's tribune (i.e., Mirabeau's), including the text of the *Declaration of the Rights of Man.* And through the medium of the later virtuous republican eloquence of Robespierre and Saint-Just (wholly nourished on Rousseau), the moral radicalism of the proscribed citizen of Geneva, and even a great distant breath emanating from the Church of the Desert, all imposed upon a France rapidly disintegrating in the debacle of the ancient order their fanatical demand for the establishment of a reign of justice, equality, and fraternity. Rousseau's triumph in France, and over France, in a strange way was the vengeance of the republic of Calvin over its corruptors.

CHAPTER TEN

From the "Protestant Plot" to the "Golden Mean"

The revocation of the Edict of Nantes crowning the "armed and booted conversion"—this grand gesture by the Too Christian King, which was not only arbitrary but gratuitous and useless, accomplished what the religious wars of the preceding century had begun: the establishment of a Protestant society of French stock cast outside the laws of the kingdom and, as far as its most active elements were concerned, outside French nationality. It was a society which was truly international. The fragments scattered, but never completely separated inside and outside France, were all in different degree strange to the royal society which was legal France. The human substratum of the international "Huguenot circuits" was formed of Huguenots from the outside, who were solidly implanted and who had often risen very high in the countries in which they had found refuge; refugees or sons of refugees who had returned to

France under the protection of an acquired foreign nationality, and families who had remained in France and who were still linked to those outside through bonds of ancestry and intermarriage. The social situation thus created survived religious intolerance. And this social factor, which is more evident, more tangible, more easily accessible to historical research than are the equivocal kinships of mentalities or spiritual affinities, was at the very center of my work on *La Banque protéstante en France.* For our present purposes it will suffice to summarize the multiple aspects of this social fact: the importance of the dispersion for the establishment of international webs of trade and banking; the separation from the soil and the transition to movable wealth imposed by emigration—and even by that interior emigration which pushed many ancient provincial landowning families, such as the Perrinets or the Girardots, toward Paris or toward the ports—so symbolic of a minority elite's painfully acquired mobility; the formation of familial dynasties sometimes as supra-national as those of the royal and princely houses, and which, thanks to legal discrimination, were not reabsorbed by the career of offices and ennoblements. And finally, a special case explicable only in this general context, the formation of that Genevan "State of Israel," asylum and beehive, point of passage and home port, a crucible in which new amalgams were constantly being formed, a political, social and intellectual laboratory whose enormous influence was totally disproportionate to the exiguity of a tiny city without a hinterland.

No doubt, this society of Huguenot origin was not at all homogeneous; it too had its aristocracy, its bourgeoisie and proletariat, its antagonistic clans, and its diverse amalgamations with Protestant societies beyond its borders. Even if we do not include the external contributions of

Swiss Protestantism and of Alsatian Lutheranism, there was neither spiritual communion nor real solidarity among the poor and fervent folk who were natives of Cévennes, the parvenu Huguenots who had come from England and Holland, the affluent bourgeois of Paris, of the north and the trade centers, the "old" Genevans and the newcomers. There was a very complex interior sociology to this world born of French Protestantism, so much of whose agitations were reflected in the miniscule mirror of Genevan society, with its perpetual troubles, and with the constantly renewed thrust from the south of France which shook the "established" out of their torpor, up to the time of the civil war that broke out in Geneva and was so bizarrely entangled with the French Revolution through the Genevan emigration. At the top of the scale, throughout the eighteenth century, stood the re-entry of the newly rich into the royal society of France, into the economic administrations, into the offices, and into the *noblesse de robe:* the Cottins, Protestants of the interior, but also, for a time, the Saladins, through the India Company; the Perrinets, Protestants of France, but also the Tronchins, citizens of Geneva, through the Farmers-General. And we have seen how at the twilight of the monarchy an entire upper-class Protestant society, Genevan as well as French, was established in the *Manufacture Royale des Glaces* as in an hereditary fief, equally well integrated into the *ancien régime* and as fanatically attached to its maintenance as the most intransigent courtier could be. Nevertheless, this still constituted a small handful of people, and these individual crossovers did not invalidate the demarcation line. Even for the newly rich, no doubt, there remained a shadow barrier which it was impossible to cross without breaking all their attachments: the burden represented by their descent, setting, kinships, and by that final criterion of social discrimination, marriage.

The opposition was distinct, formal, and indubitable in the sphere of finances, where money was professionally handled, which was a reflection—abstract, precise, and summary—of the social structures; namely, the opposition between the governmental financial administration (*la Finance*) and the banking system (*la Banque*) which has been analyzed many times. The former was the financial service of the King and, by extension, of the princely houses and higher social reaches of the royal society; the latter the financial service of international trade. Obviously, *la Finance* was bound body and soul to the established regime, whereas *la Banque* was alien to it and, in the words of the Physiocrats, alien to the constituted nation. One arrived at *la Finance* through the acquisition of an office which marked one's solemn entry into the royal society and which had been the most prestigious means of upward mobility for the entire bourgeoisie of the *ancien régime*. But this entry in principle was not to be purchased without proofs of adherence to the Catholic faith. The *Banque*, on the other hand, was a free profession and open to all, and it had remained outside every corporation or guild organization of society. Anyone so desiring could set himself up as a banker as long as he had a domicile; the banker, acting only through correspondence, having neither tools, nor warehouse, nor merchandise, nor any operational expenses, escaped all the ordinances decreed for the administration of the *natural* economy. By the same token, they escaped that requirement of religious conformity which, even though tacitly turned aside or ignored, remained no less irksome in the exercise of any trade or profession organized according to the law.[1] It was even normal for the man to whom one

[1] The distinction between trading and banking—international trade on the one hand, and centralization of the payment operations neces-

addressed oneself to pay or deposit a sum abroad to be a foreigner himself, for it was through his connections with other countries that he could assure these services. Herein lies the explanation, alongside so many other explanatory reasons, of the attraction exercised by the *Banque* on French Protestants, as elsewhere, over other minorities disadvantaged by law. In the international banking structure they found the equivalent of this social elevator which the Catholic bourgeoisie had found in the administrative set-up of the royal financial system, which was closed off to them.

But the opposition was not only juridical and social; it involved the whole technique of the craft. The mere fact of operating "within" or "outside" the established regime was in keeping with all the differences of laws and mentalities of two separate worlds. The government financial administration handled the hard cash or currency, the tangible wealth of the country; its realm was bound, as much as to the "feudal" regime, to the regime of the metallic money of the agricultural kingdom, the only currency that was legal and accepted in all classes of nontrading society. And when the financiers were obliged to issue paper currency, this was viewed as an action contrary to nature and the sure harbinger of calamities to come. The *Banque*, on the other

sitated by this trade on the other—was slow in being exactly defined, as we know, and it was still very dimly perceived even beyond the middle of the eighteenth century. Toward the end of the *ancien régime*, however, the notion of the "merchant banker" was no more than a relic from earlier times, in some dictionaries of arts and trades, a point of confusion. The banker did not trade in goods but in letters of exchange and if, profiting from the commercial connections resulting therefrom, he speculated in goods it was only through a go-between, through orders of purchases and sales executed on his account by merchants residing elsewhere, or more often by joint accounts, and by financing these operations through the convenient instrument of credit by acceptance. But these goods were not bought or sold by him and never entered his warehouses. These operations, conducted through correspondence, did not require membership in a craft guild, any more than did the purchase and sale of letters of exchange.

hand, operated through the cabal of compensations "from place to place," which required "neither roads nor rivers" to transport sums at a distance. As Rivarol said: "It merely moves signs around," notes, letters of exchange, the transference of accounts between private individuals—all the scriptural money which had been slowly elaborated by international trade since the Late Middle Ages. This alone responded to its needs of international regulations, and this alone, again despite all the prohibitions, enabled it to carry out those current operations of intermediary credit that were indispensable to its functioning. By forcing things slightly, we can say that in the France of the eighteenth century, *la Finance* was Catholic in spirit as well as in fact, whereas *la Banque* was Protestant. This is tantamount to asserting, in unwarranted religious terms, that the former was integrated into the economic organization of the *ancien régime* as it was constituted, and that the latter was not. Or that the former corresponded to the "noble" pursuits and callings reserved to the privileged subjects of the kingdom, and the other to low, menial employments reserved for people without quality. The great Catholic bankers themselves confirmed the rule: the Lecouteulxs, the Magons, the Labordes were much closer to *la Finance* than to *la Banque*, in the ordinary sense. These great merchant dynasties, invested with offices and public charges, had developed their banking activity on the basis of the trade in *piastres*, of the importation of the metal currency drawn from Spain and America, and thereby, from services connected with the Royal Mint and the Royal Treasury. Laborde and Magon had been bankers to the court, an official function whose most outrageous privilege was precisely the "sur-purchase of monies" granted to those provenders of specie currency. The Lecouteulxs and, above all, the Magons, had organized the monopoly of the importation of *piastres* through the Bank of Saint-Charles at the time of Calonne. The separation was even further accentuated in the eighteenth century. Paradoxically, it was under Louis XIV, exterminator of unbelievers, that Protestants and "new converts" were able to invade the preserves of the financial administration and the Royal Mint. And it was under Louis XV, the misunderstood restorer of the agricultural monarchy, that they were completely ousted from those privileged sectors of the economy. The orientation toward banking, moreover, was in accord with religious affinities: the trade in *piastres*, the trade with Spain and the Spanish Empire, was dominated by the Catholic "*Finance*," while relations with England and the countries of the North were assumed preferably by the Protestant *Banque*. And it was England's commercial and financial rise which we have discerned behind the sudden rise of Protestant bankers in the period of decline of the age of Louis XV. We know very well that the Protestant bankers did not shy from handling metal money and from speculating in *piastres*, and that the financiers and importers of *piastres* availed themselves abundantly of letters of exchange. But although they made use of such techniques and poached on one another's preserves, the fact remains that the former operated "within the regime" and the latter outside it.

This opposition, which was of no interest either to theology or to public opinion, was perceived clearly by professionals. Necker's appearance on the scene marked a point of departure from the *ancien régime*, not because he was a Protestant or Genevan, but because he was a banker. The Farmer-General Augeard, secretary "*des commandements de la Reine*," pamphleteer against Necker, was very explicit on this point:

> For a long time a rivalry has existed between the bankers and the financiers. Up to the present time, the latter had the upper hand; but you [Necker] reign, and your bankers have the best of it. All our predecessors, since Sully, had preferred Companies of financiers to Companies of bankers, because they were pursuaded that the latter *have two fatherlands, one where they find money at bargain prices, and another where they sell it very dear.* These great ministers knew that the bankers are so independent of the government that, on the contrary, they make the government dependent upon them when it has dealings with them.

By having recourse, through the intermediacy of bankers, to international credit, the government deprived itself of all means of authority:

> The government perforce must pay without being able to retreat, otherwise, inasmuch as the bills payable have passed through the banks of Geneva, London, and Holland, the government would be reduced to declare itself bankrupt, not only with respect to its subjects who are accustomed thereto [!], but with respect to Europe, which subsequently would no longer wish to deal with a perfidious and dishonored administration . . .

whereas financiers subject in person and possessions to the governments they served "fear for their situation, their jobs, and entrepreneurs fear for their undertakings, farmers for their leases, title holders for their offices," exhibiting great caution as to the extent and fidelity of their resources.

> Your bankers are sheltered against everything; they have nothing to fear, they have had your bills payable, they took care to rid themselves of them, they are no longer their holders. . . . A gentleman of quality, Monsieur comte de Laura-

> gais, last year declared in print that never had a minister had a more preponderant credit than yours, precisely because you were not minister, and you did not enter the Council. He was right; through the game of your bank, you are the most dangerous Cosmopolite. . . .[2]

This was a polemic *pro domo*, out to demonstrate that an arbitrary government cannot do without its domestic financiers, subject to arbitrariness, enriched but always "hangable" at discretion, and that the government faced ruin by contracting commitments which it had to respect. This corresponded to the ancient "system of confusion," previously described by Colbert:

> It was necessary to permit business people [*gens d'affaires*] to earn great profits, in order to establish a large credit among them, and so that a means could be found to draw eight or ten million from them in a few days . . . and after all if they made huge profits, a means could always be found to levy taxes on them so that they could be made to return a part thereof.[3]

Curiously, by usurping Turgot's name and by invoking Sully, Augeard cloaked himself in the authority of the Physiocrats and borrowed their vocabulary, and he was not entirely wrong. His fundamental thesis, which sticks out from

[2] Letter from M. Turgot to M. Necker, in the *Collection complète de tous les ouvrages pour et contre M. Necker* (Utrecht, 1781), Vol. I, pp. 13–14. The sentence italicized in the text was extracted by Augeard from the "Lettres sur l'Emprunt et l'Impôt" by the Genevan lawyer, Théodore Rilliet.

[3] The "*gens d'affaires*" of whom Colbert spoke, like the "entrepreneurs" mentioned by Augeard, were the financiers, "entrepreneurs" of "the extraordinary affairs of the State." The predominance of "*la Finance*" pervaded the whole economic vocabulary of the *ancien régime*, whose terminology if transposed carelessly to the modern age is an inexhaustible source of confusion.

his confused polemics, was very clear: the King, the first proprietor of France, cannot have recourse to credit like a merchant. He cannot pledge his territorial real estate as if it were his personal effects—the republic, by realizing the value of its landed property in *assignats*, or paper currency, was to experience this catastrophic experiment—and the King is lost if he delivers himself into the hands of "cosmopolitan" bankers, independent of his authority. This was a perfectly tenable thesis, but one that precisely brought to light the weakness of the regime: if the *Banque* was suspect, the financial administration had fallen into irremediable disrepute. At the very time of this polemic, around 1780, a silent revolution was being carried out in the most formalist and conservative world of red tape that ever existed. In notarized documents the abridged formula written on the margin of treasury bonds and redemptions which had read "due from the King" and "full receipt to the King" was replaced by a formula reading "due from the State" and "full receipt to the State." Thus changes of mentality were produced long before the visible upheavals: the corporeal debtor, Louis, King of France, had given way to the impersonal debtor, the *res publica.* The ideological debate over Physiocracy had come full circle. Augeard's polemic was no more than the rearguard action of a formidable special-interest group, powerful enough to have Necker dismissed after it had brought about Turgot's fall, and which was so thoroughly built into the regime as to be carried along in its fall. Nevertheless, it was unable to arouse an echo in public opinion. The only partisans of the administration of finances were its beneficiaries. More than any other institution of the *ancien régime*, it was a ponderous and inadaptable monster from another age. After the great slaughter of the financiers under the Terror, the former *Fi-*

nance was the only one of all these institutions that no post-revolutionary regime was ever to think of reviving, even if it is true that its spirit did not die with the office.

In all these polemics between ideologies and economic interests, no allusion was ever made to the "Protestant fact." It must have appeared awkward and inconvenient at the end of this enlightened regime to awaken memories of intolerance or discrimination which proper society had decided to ignore. At most, we find a discreet insinuation in the listing made by another pamphlet, issued in the same period, of the "foreign" administrators of the *Caisse d'Escompte* (Bank of Discount). "Messieurs Germany, Girardot, Haller, Rilliet, Deodati, Cottin . . ." For what these bankers had in common was not the fact that they were foreigners—neither the Girardots nor the Cottins had ever emigrated—but that they were Protestants.[4] But let us confess it, the slip is easily explained: they were certainly all members of the same family. At any rate, no one in the world able to express himself and hold a pen entertained the idea of looking for a confessional war behind the clash of ideas and clans.

It was only after the collapse of the *ancien régime* that survivors, nostalgics, and penitents also, like Rivarol, discovered, tardily, the "social necessity" of a sacred authority. Unable to admit the inconceivable liquefaction of the monarchy from within, they began to expose the infernal machinations of a sinister conspiracy mounted by an "Anti-France," protean in its numberless faces. This was

[4] *Sur l'administration de M. Necker, par un citoyen français,* another pamphlet whose probable author was likewise Augeard. In it we find, in a particularly concise form, the thesis that the absolute monarchy and public credit were mutually exclusive, an idea which had been current and generally accepted since the beginning of the eighteenth century. "It is impossible to ally credit with absolute power."

exactly parallel to the fantastic fiction of the international philosophico-masonic conspiracy mounted in the trial of Cagliostro, the intuition of a vast philosophico-Protestant conjuration evoked, without conclusion, at the secret Consistory as early as June, 1793; and finally, in a twofold version, Jacobin in the revolutionary Tribunal, and royalist in the salons of the emigration, to the multiple and incomprehensible "plot from abroad." From "The Real Authors of the Revolution of France in 1789" by Sourdat, published in Neuchâtel in 1797, to the "Hidden Authors of the French Revolution" by Pouget de Saint-André, which dates from 1929, the chain was unbroken, and the list of the accused, who are always anonymous entities, is prolonged with the monotony of curses hurled into the air: the Protestants, the *philosophes*, Freemasons, the Jews, foreigners, bankers, agents of Pitt. . . . All this forms quite a crowd of persons without even designating anyone in particular.[5]

Is this a literature of maniacs and mythomanes, such as is found in the refuse bins of all countries, on the lines of the *Protocols of the Elders of Zion?* To be sure, after being at work for a century and a half, this witchhunt has yet to

[5] The chapter titles of Pouget de Saint-André's work suffice to sum this up: *The Freemasons, The Israelites, The Protestants, The Swiss, The Foreign Invasion, Austria, The English Agents, Where Did the Money Come from?*, etc. The excellent study by Roger Priouret, *La Franc-maçonnerie sous les lys* (Paris, 1956), analyzes, in the Freemasons, a process exactly similar to that which has influenced some Protestant writers. Accused after the event of being the authors or inspirers of the Revolution, the Masons, or rather the speakers at the masonic banquets of the nineteenth century, could not resist the temptation to claim proudly this honor they so little deserved. From this time on, all the accusers and glorifiers of Masonry had to do was to quote each other, the "confession of the adversary" exempting them from any other proof. As regards the Jews, who had no part whatsoever in this matter, we have noted in passing the tendency of some historians to scent a Jew under any unfamiliar name, the biblical first names of Protestants lending themselves marvelously to this hunt.

produce the shadow of a definition of an index or of a presumption worthy of examination, and the fantastic assertions it draws from its own nightmares by their very nature escape all serious discussion. But the persistence of these fictional constructions, which ridicule does not kill and which have a good chance of surviving all historiographical criticism, is not explainable without a grain of psychological evidence diluted in a porridge of confusions and forgeries. By taking the risk of distorting into a positive demonstrable fact what can scarcely be distinguished as a state of mind, diffused in a community as amorphous as French Protestantism at the end of a century of legal nonexistence, let us try to extract the kernel of truth in this intuitive "evidence."

We must start out from the state of deliquescence of French Protestantism in the period of decline of the age of Louis XV. There was no longer either a Protestant party or an organized Church, or a spiritual community. The renewal of the first half of the eighteenth century, the recovery of stubborn resisters after the great persecutions, had waned in the tepidness of equivocal toleration. After the series of national synods convoked in the desert amid the worst perils, from 1715 to 1748, the second half of the century was not to see a single one, thanks to the effective sabotage on the part of the bourgoisies of Paris, the North, and the West, who were getting along very nicely without ecclesiastical organization, pastors, or public worship. They would gather together at their ease, without noise or "scandalous songs," either in the bosom of their own families or in a selected small circle, to read an edifying passage from Scripture, or for common prayer. It is difficult to exaggerate the theological fluidity and the lack of existence, as a Church, of this vague familial religiosity. There was neither a credo, nor discipline, nor cult, nor symbol, which are the mainstays of a community of the faithful. For many, Rousseau, or the highly edifying masonic meeting, or a wholly personal spirituality, perfectly satisfied the need for fellowship and communion. This was the milieu to which belonged all the men who had houses of their own, bankers, merchants, and manufacturers, who were not a phalanx of the Calvinist faith. But in the South itself, which was more fervent, more alive, and more communitarian, the neglect of things theological was extreme: a handful of pastors, numbering around forty at the zenith of the "revival" in the middle of the century, and pastors who had been trained hastily without a solid theological instruction, also fashioned their own personal religiosity. Paul Rabaut himself, the organizer and soul of French Protestantism after Antoine Court, did not know Calvin's *Institutes of the Christian Religion* after twenty years in the ministry, and was concerned above all with "simplifying religion," with stripping it of its doctrinal "accessories" in order to render it conformable "to the taste of the *philosophes*" and "accessible to the people." [6]

The very vagueness of the concept of the Church in Protestantism, aggravated to the point of nonexistence of either institution or discipline, because of its legal situation in France, enabled the Protestant to stray from his faith without his being aware of it. If the Catholic could not leave his Church without a deliberate rupture, the Protestant slid outside of his without perceiving it, believing always that he believed, and crossed the threshold without

[6] Rabaut's comment, in 1755, when he received a copy of the *Institutes of Christian Religion,* was merely a literary appreciation on the theme of the preferability of the ancients to the moderns, then in vogue: "I am reading this excellent work with very great interest. Our ancient theologians, in my opinion, are preferable to the modern." That was all!

knowing that he was outside. And he could go very far in the nebulous region between theism and deism, between revealed religion and "natural" religion, between positive Christianity and a philosophy of Christian inspiration without breaking his ties. But, also because of the fact that he did not break them, he was never to go as far as the philosophers in an open rupture with the Catholic Church: as far certainly as Rousseau, and with some difficulty as far as Voltaire, but never as far as Holbach and the materialist philosophy of the eighteenth century. This difference in behavior—the violent break for the Catholic who lost his faith and the imperceptible sliding away for the Protestant who did not know that he had lost it—characterized many of the fine shadings of attitudes in the spiritual wave of the eighteenth century in which Rousseau, and Necker even, assume almost the appearance of believers holding aloft the banner of faith in the face of a society that sneered at religion.

It is no less a fact that these men called themselves and believed themselves to be Protestants, and assumed the disabilities, or at least the inconveniences, attached to this status. How then are we to define their Protestantism? At first sight by a wholly negative attribute: that of their not being Catholics. "Partisan spirit," "pride," was what Catholic priests in contact with French Protestants said of them. "Few among them are attached [to their religion] with a genuine zeal," said one of these priests around 1740; "most of them are not even instructed in it. It seems that all they have inherited from their ancestors is this venomous hatred of the Church and of its ministers which has always characterized Protestants." [7]

[7] *Mémoire au sujet des religionnaires du Bas-Languedoc et des Cévennes*, presented to the court by the abbé de Saint-Maximin, doctor of

It was the pride of the descendants of a persecuted minority which glorified its martyrs; the pride of resisters or sons of resisters, active or passive, who had emigrated or remained in the country without an abjuration of a faith sprung from the heart, who had not bowed their conscience before the tyranny of the Throne and the Altar. This word "resist," which in the 1760's the wives of Protestants condemned to the galleys for having taken part in Protestant assemblies engraved on the walls of their cells in the Constance Tower at Aigues-Mortes; this defiant battle cry was at the heart of French Protestantism. At least they knew what they were rejecting: the subjugation of conscience, imposed dogma, the papacy, clericalism, the idolatry of images and relics, the paganism of pomp and ceremony, the whole apparatus of the embodied Church, all authority save that of Scripture interpreted according to reason, all intermediaries between personal conscience and God alone, who was not the merciful God of the "Papists," but the righteous God of Israel and who, imperceptibly, began to resemble the Supreme Being of philosophy. And they had firmly retained the whole anti-dogmatic and anticlerical content of the faith which their fathers had professed, gently disposed toward the spirit of the age: free examination, critical reason, the sovereignty of individual conscience, the contempt for rites and superstition, this spirit of rationality felt as a moral requirement. In the last analysis, therefore, it was the pride of having been right. Why should they have denied what all philosophy and all enlightened society had just confirmed, this whole century of the Enlightenment tardily catching up with the truths

---

the Sorbonne, provost and grand vicar of Alais; cited in Burdett C. Poland, *French Protestantism and the French Revolution* (Princeton, N.J.: Princeton University Press, 1957).

which their martyred fathers had defended, alone against all? Although it was they themselves who were going toward the spirit of the age, they saw the spirit of the age come toward them. Their indifference even to their oppressed Church and to the legislation of the Protestant cult is explicable by a state of mind which asked: What was the importance of having a Church of their own if the whole century was about to celebrate their principles? And why narrow this religiosity without dogma, which was on the eve of its triumph, into the tight frame of a religious minority?

They were fully at home in the "spirit of the age," and without those troubles of conscience of Catholics on the loose, without any apparent conflict between philosophy and faith. In all this, for them it was not a question of an option between conflicting loyalties, neither of a religious nor, even less, of a political character. For them, religion was a matter of personal conscience; and for the rest, the King of France was the King of France, nobody questioned it. His subjects never had occasion to take political options, or envisage any, before 1788. Neither communication nor conflict was possible between the royal government and the nation since the former had renounced rule over souls. As for what we could call the "options" of religious policy, obscurely stirring in the semi-secrecy of this shadow of a Church in the second half of the century, we know about the opposition of the "Messieurs of Paris" and of the bourgeois Protestants of Normandy, of La Rochelle, and of Bordeaux to the attempts of the South to keep alive the Calvinian ecclesiastical democracy. And there was the passive but effective sabotage practiced against the convocation of synods, the intrigues against the "agent general" of the Churches of the South, Court de Gébelin, and the tiny cabal mounted under the leadership of the chaplain of the Dutch Embassy, Armand, in order to organize, with the blessing of the Versailles cabinet, a semblance of a tolerated Protestant Church, properly subordinated, discreet, docile and purged, in which honest folk could meet in their element. This was a pale reflection of the struggles in Geneva which, on a closed field, on a political and social level already arrayed against each other the two internal tendencies of Calvinism, namely, the oligarchic and the democratic. But what in the tiny republic clashed harshly in the tight Genevan enclosure, in France was a clash of two separate worlds which never met, and these vague stirrings scarcely troubled the general euphoria. On the eve of the Revolution, in the last enchanting hours of unquestioned monarchy in which all audacities of mind were still permitted without drawing inferences from them, Protestants without distinction, affluent bourgeois, enlightened pastors, or little people proud to belong to an elite free of superstitions, could all feel themselves in harmony with a France touched by the Enlightenment.

The sociological facts fitted the spiritual facts. Let us not say that the Protestants were all strangers to the regime, outside of the offices and the privileged orders. But the very fact that some managed to arrive at such positions remained an abnormal event. One wholly natural consequence of the religious discriminations and of the almost complete desertion of the nobility (which had obtained for more than a century) was that French Protestantism, taken as a whole, belonged to the Third Estate and even to the liberal elite of the Third Estate and shared its ideas, for which 1789 marked the hour of triumph. But as the abbé Siéyès had proclaimed, the Third Estate was "the whole nation," and it was so in fact, since the abdication of the *an-*

cien régime in August, 1789. From that moment on, all the struggles of the Revolution were no longer to take place between the old and new regimes, but within the very depths of this sundered nation in which liberalism, almost in advance, was the first to be vanquished. In these struggles there was no longer to be a party or even a faction in which Protestants were gathered together, even less a Protestant party; but individuals and groups scattered through all the contending parties. We are still dealing here with a fact of religious sociology and even geography which explains why the bulk of the Protestant representation to the revolutionary assemblies came from the South: 11 deputies —6 of whom were from Nîmes—out of the 15 at the Constituent Assembly, 20 out of the 22 at the Convention, 4 of the remaining 12 being Lutherans from Alsace. As for the deputy of Paris, Jean-Paul Marat, it would be difficult to consider him representative of the Protestant spirit. If the attitudes and the votes of these men were opposed at every turning-point in the drama and were often nullified among themselves, the most coherent and brilliant group quite naturally belonged to the liberal Girondin faction, and was exterminated along with it. A century away in time, under other signs and in the name of another ideology, the "Parisian Monster" once again pounced on the South in the form of conventional armies, as it had pounced upon it before in the form of the dragoons of Louis XIV—and as it had done so many times since the Crusade against the Albigensians. Since de Tocqueville, a particular highly significant aspect of this paradox has frequently been discovered, namely, that the Jacobin Revolution merely accomplished on all levels, ferociously and to the finish, the profound organizing tendencies of the collapsing monarchy, as shown in the nationalization of the Church as well as in the political and administrative centralization of the nation.

On the political level French Protestantism, or what was most authentic about it, was annihilated by the Jacobin Revolution. On the religious level it simply became nonexistent. What we have said of its neglect of theological concerns and of its ecclesiastical decrepitude explains this phenomenon sufficiently. Without a Church worthy of this name, virtually without public worship, without pastors, and without dogma, it had been armed for individual resistance to the clericalism of the *ancien régime*, and all its "ideology" was aimed at this sole enemy against which the spirit of the age had been so powerful an ally. Once the enemy was no more, the resistance fell into the void. And the wave which had swept along this Church without dogma cast it into nothingness. The triumphant anti-clericalism and the violent de-Christianization, the "civic religion" of the Goddess Reason or of the "Supreme Being," were shattered against the centuries-old walls of the Roman Catholic Church incarnated in its discipline, its hierarchy, its priests, and its faithful, retrieved from the debris of the Church of the royal State. But the Protestant temple was swept away. This Calvinist Church, which had been nourished by the cult of its martyrs from the Massacre of Saint Bartholomew to those condemned to the galleys by the Sun King and up to the trials of Rochette and Calas, had neither resisters nor martyrs in the face of the Terror. Or rather, those it did have were political, not religious, resisters. As a Church it was liquidated, leaving only individuals carried away by the spirit of the age, or isolatedly and gropingly seeking to redefine their spirituality. Once the storm abated, the consul and the empire were again to raise up the Temple, but not the faith: it was a fleshless, administrative, "prefectorial" Church, the bare shell of a spiritual void from which, very, very slowly and timidly a new faith and a new community were to be born.

The legend of the Protestant plot, retrospectively, was born around this empty temple. In order to grasp its meaning, we must seek outside. The Protestant minority as such was absent from the tragic conflict between revolutionary France and the Catholic Church which for so long marked French history. It was not the handful of votes (which for that matter were always split) of the one or two dozen Protestant deputies that decided the great symbolic acts which consummated the break—the secularization, the civil constitution, the regicide. And the insoluble conflict between the temporal and spiritual authorities, the National Church and the Universal Church, an institutional problem peculiar to Catholicism, did not concern them. It was this problem, and not that of the form of the State, which made of the Revolution a religious war marked by wounds that were to be difficult to heal for a long time, and which split the France of Catholic stock into two spiritually irreconcilable families. Neither Thermidor nor Napoleon, nor the Restoration was able to weld the sundered unity and to reestablish peace in the minds and hearts of divided French Catholics. As early as the day after Thermidor, men of order and sobered revolutionaries began a joint search for a neutral conciliatory, arbitrational, or mediatory third party —such a party as would be able to terminate the Revolution without negating its achievements or threatening the interests of its beneficiaries, to stabilize the regime, as Lafayette said, "at a tolerable point between Jacobinism and counterrevolution," and to bring back the faithful followers of the dead King and of the dispossessed Church while leaving intact in place the regicides, the defrocked priests, the sheltered and repentant terrorists. A monarchical restoration which would not be that of the brothers of the guillotined King, a religious restoration which would not be that of the refractory clergy, a restoration of order which would not be that of the *ancien régime*.

It is the subtle, tortuous, and subterranean search for a mediator who was least compromised on both sides, or equally compromised on one side and the other, which explains so many of the meanderings of French political policy since the Revolution. As early as 1796, the entourage of Talleyrand, an apostate bishop, and of Siéyès, a defrocked abbé—the two most brilliant minds engaged in the search for a third solution for the problems without issue—nursed the seed of the brilliant and preposterous idea of giving France, in order to reconcile the country with herself and with themselves, a Protestant and if possible a Prussian monarchy, outside and above the battle. This project was never realized, and its place was taken by the Orléanist project, of identical inspiration. In default of the ideal "Prussian" solution of a prince alien to the country and to its Church who, therefore, would not be compromised by either side, the country would have a prince of royal blood, but the son of a Jacobin regicide, sufficiently compromised on one side and the other. But the memories that the name of Orléans revived were still too close. Finally, there was the last solution of replacement, the simplest and the least satisfactory. Instead of a crowned but illegitimate King, a glorious military man, an apolitical technician of authority. All this was mixed in the murky dealings which paved the way for the *coup d'état* of 18 Brumaire in which the name of the candidate was left blank up to the last moment. Eventually, almost by accident, General Bonaparte was the only available candidate. But at a distance of thirty years, after the debacle of the empire and of the abortive Restoration, it was the Orléanist project which triumphed. Moreover, this was to be an almost Protestant reign, not only in the Academy and the university, the salons and the banking, but in the government. François Guizot, "that shy man with a Genevan accent," was to be minister from as the advent of Louis-Philippe and soon irremovable Prime Minister, flanked by Gasparin and Pelet de la Lozère, old Protestant members of the Convention, and including even a princess who was a Protestant heiress, and a duc de Broglie, admittedly Catholic and of the *ancien régime*, but the son-in-law of Mme de Staël-Necker.[8]

Inasmuch as it existed, and in a form created by a none too clement history, the tiny Protestant minority perforce had to try to find a place on the complicated chessboard of postrevolutionary France, and its natural bent plus stray liberal impulses drew it toward the "center-left." The legend of a Protestant plot, absurd and particularly ridiculous when it is transported to the context of the *ancien régime*, in the nineteenth century twines itself around the most ambiguous reality of French politics, a reality marked by constantly changing aspects and compromises but which found its clearest expression in Orléanism. *Tertium datur:* to be sure, it was not a Protestant party, nor the triumph of an

[8] Albert Vandal, *L'Avènement de Bonaparte* (Paris, 1902–1903), cites an unpublished memorial by Mme de Staël proposing to establish Protestantism as a State religion in France. It reached the point where Napoleon declared: "The opportunity to establish the Protestant religion in France was missed, and it was not my fault." We come upon this singularly tenacious idea again in Edgar Quinet, Charles Renouvier, Ernest Renan. Indeed, France in the nineteenth century, especially from 1830 on, was to see very active Protestant evangelical movements. Favored by public instruction, intellectual emancipation, and militant anticlericalism, these registered veritable mass conversions (if rarely lasting) toward the middle of the century, which appear more like a prolongation of the Enlightenment than a popular revival of the spirit of the Reformation.

occult Protestant power. It was the very mixed party of the golden mean, of the anti-clerical conservatives and of former revolutionaries who had gained entry into the armorial of the nobilities of the empire and of the Restoration, the party whose heart and interests were divided between the two great family enemies, and which appealed to the reputed neutral arbitrator or technician to reconcile the irreconcilable. There is nothing surprising in the fact that it was doubly execrated and that the legend of a plot was perpetuated in two conflicting traditions, legitimist and Jacobin, which on this point succeeded in coming together. But such is at times the role of a minority, religious or otherwise, which is self-sufficient only to a small extent. Persecuted, tolerated or privileged, discarded or pushed forward, scapegoat or designated arbitrator, it does not choose this role but it can accept it with pride and escape it only by imploring pity or by excusing itself. In general, French Protestants have accepted their exposed and unusual role proudly, without excusing themselves and without asking for pity.

No doubt the legends were not invented out of whole cloth; Orléanism too had roots that went far back into the eighteenth century, from the intrigues of the Regency to the disorganized and sinister maneuvers of Philippe-Égalité. But in a completely different context; at that time it was but one of the dissolvent elements within the regime. As for the "Orléanist spirit," it was strikingly related to that of the parliamentary *Fronde* of the age of the Enlightenment, this irremovable oligarchy of acquirers of offices which constituted another dissolvent force, often flirting with the House of Orléans. And the temptation to have recourse to the neutral arbitrator or to the technician was also present in the last reign of moribund absolutism, which had lost its will, its ideology, and even the reality of power when a King, goodheartedly bourgeois and abulic, lost among the rival factions of his teeming court, himself appealed to an honest technician alien to the regime: Jacques Necker, that baron Louis[9] in reverse, astray under the Most Christian King.

[9] Baron Joseph-Dominique Louis (1755–1837), Minister of Finance under the Restoration and again under Louis-Philippe. He was a former *abbé defroqué* belonging to Talleyrand's retinue, very representative of the new bourgeois oligarchy issued from the Revolution, and his name became almost a synonym for the financial orthodoxy of the "*Enrichissez-vous*" era.—Trans.

Index

Index

Index

Index

Index

Index

Index